THE COUI

THE COUP

1953, THE CIA, AND THE ROOTS OF MODERN

U.S.-IRANIAN RELATIONS

Ervand Abrahamian

THE NEW PRESS

NEW YORK
LONDON

First published in the United States by The New Press, New York, 2013
This paperback edition published by The New Press, 2015
Distributed by Two Rivers Distribution

ISBN 978-1-62097-086-7 (pbk.)

LIBRARY OF CONGRESS CATALOGING-IN-PUBLICATION DATA

Abrahamian, Ervand, 1940–
The coup : 1953, the CIA, and the roots of modern U.S.-Iranian relations / Ervand Abrahamian.
pages   cm
Summary: "A history of the CIA's 1953 coup in Iran and its aftermath"—Provided by publisher.
Includes bibliographical references and index.
ISBN 978-1-59558-826-5 (hardcover : alkaline paper)
ISBN 978-1-59558-862-3 (e-book)
1. Iran—History—Coup d'état, 1953. 2. United States. Central
Intelligence Agency—History—20th century. 3. Iran—Politics and
government—1941–1979. 4. Iran—Foreign relations—United States. 5. United States—
Foreign relations—Iran. 6. Iran—Foreign relations—Great Britain. 7. Great Britain—
Foreign relations—Iran. 8. Petroleum industry and trade—Political aspects—Iran—
History—20th century. 9. Petroleum industry and trade—Political
aspects—United States—History—20th century. I. Title.
DS318.6.A26 2013
955.05'3—dc23   2012031402

The New Press publishes books that promote and enrich public discussion
and understanding of the issues vital to our democracy and to a more equitable world.
These books are made possible by the enthusiasm of our readers; the support of
a committed group of donors, large and small; the collaboration of our many partners
in the independent media and the not-for-profit sector; booksellers, who often hand-sell
New Press books; librarians; and above all by our authors.

www.thenewpress.com

Composition by dix!
This book was set in Walbaum MT

Printed in the United States of America

To Emma and Rafi

CONTENTS

PREFACE

I would like to thank the History Department at Baruch College for giving me the opportunity over the last ten years to write this book; the Research Committee at the City University of New York and my union, the Professional Staff Congress, for travel grants to Britain; and the Center for Persian Studies at the University of Maryland for inviting me to present some of my findings at their Biennial Ehsan Yarshater Lecture Series. I would also like to thank librarians at the British Petroleum archives at Warwick University for their assistance, and Dr. Hamid Ahmadi and Dr. Habib Ladjevardi for providing me with easy access to their oral history projects in Berlin and Cambridge (Massachusetts). Thanks also go to André Schiffrin for encouraging me to complete this book, to Sarah Fan for production editing, and to Rachelle Mandik for copyediting.

The vexing problem of transliteration needs some explanation. To ease the problem, I have modified the elaborate system developed both by the Library of Congress and the *International Journal of Middle East Studies*. I have dispensed with diacritical marks and adopted spelling used by the mainstream media—for example, Tehran instead of Tcheran, Mashed instead of Mashhad, Hussein instead of Husayn. I have also spelled the name of the central figure as Mossadeq rather than Mossadegh as used at the time by the *New York Times*, Moussadek by the London *Times*, or Musaddiq by the Foreign Office and the State Department.

CHRONOLOGY

1901	D'Arcy Concession
1908	Oil struck at Masjed-e Suleiman
1909	Formation of Anglo-Persian Oil Company (APOC)
1912	British Navy converts to oil
	Abadan refinery opened
1914	British government buys majority shares in APOC
1932	Oil concession canceled
1933	New concession signed
1935	APOC renamed Anglo-Iranian Oil Company (AIOC)
1943	Standard Vacuum negotiates for concession
1944	Shell, Sinclair, and Standard Vacuum negotiate
	Soviets seek oil concession
1946	Soviet Oil Agreement with Qavam
1947	Majles rejects Soviet Agreement
	Negotiations start on Supplementary Agreement to 1933 concession
July 1949	Premier signs Supplementary Agreement
August 1949	Fifteenth Majles ends without approving Supplementary Agreement

xi

October 1949	Mossadeq and nineteen others sit in at the palace gardens
	Formation of National Front
January 1950	Sixteenth Majles opens
June 1950	Majles Committee vetoes Supplementary Agreement
	General Razmara named prime minister
November 1950	Razmara renegotiates Supplementary Agreement
March 1951	Razmara assassinated
	Oil workers strike
April 1951	Mossadeq named prime minister
	Majles passes Oil Nationalization Law
May 1951	Shah ratifies Oil Nationalization Law
June 1951	Britain submits case to Hague
	NIOC takes over industry
	HMS *Mauritius* anchors off Abadan
	Britain stops tankers
July 1951	Harriman mission
August 1951	Stokes mission
October 1951	Mossadeq at the UN
	Churchill elected prime minister
	All AIOC personnel leave
November 1951	Point IV offered to Iran
	Mossadeq receives vote of confidence
December 1951	Clashes between Tudeh and Toilers Party
January 1952	International Bank mission
	British consulates closed
	British Bank closes

	Newspapers announce plot on Mossadeq's life
	Voting for seventeenth Majles starts
February 1952	Foreign Minister Fatemi wounded by Fedayan-e Islam
March 1952	International Bank mission fails
April 1952	Seventeenth Majles opens
May 1952	Mossadeq at Hague
June 1952	British impound tanker *Rose Mary*
July 13, 1952	Mossadeq seeks special powers for six months
July 16, 1952	Mossadeq resigns
July 20, 1952 (30 Tir)	Mass uprising
July 22, 1952	Mossadeq renamed prime minister
August 7, 1952	Ayatollah Kashani elected Majles president
October 1952	Break in Iran-UK diplomatic relations
	Britain asks all citizens to leave
	Majles reduces Senate term to two years
December 1952	New International Bank mission
February 1953	Fighting in Bakhtiyari regions
	Arrest warrant for General Zahedi
February 28, 1953	Pro-Shah riot outside Mossadeq's home
	Mossadeq takes shelter in Majles
March 1953	Mossadeq's ninety-minute address to the nation
April 1953	General Afshartous murdered
	Zahedi takes sanctuary in Majles
July 8, 1953	Eisenhower announces no aid
July 14, 1953	National Front deputies resign from Majles

August 3, 1953	Referendum to dissolve Majles
August 15, 1953	Failed coup
	Shah flies to Baghdad
August 19, 1953	Coup
August 21, 1953	Shah returns
October 1953	United States grants Iran $45 million
	AIOC renamed British Petroleum (BP)
November 1953	Mossadeq's trial starts
December 1953	Vice-President Nixon in Tehran
	Three students killed
	Mossadeq sentenced to three years' imprisonment
September 1954	Consortium Oil Agreement

LEADING
PERSONALITIES

Akhavi, Ali-Akbar (1903–83)—Mossadeq's last minister of economy. A French-educated lawyer, he had retired from the high court rather than rule in favor of Reza Shah in land disputes. He remained a staunch Mossadeq supporter even though his brother, Col. Hassan Akhavi, helped organize the 1953 coup.

Ala, Hussein (Mu'en al-Vezareh) (1884–1964)—prime minister preceding Mossadeq. From a wealthy aristocratic household and married into the Qajar family, he had been educated in England and spent much of his career in the diplomatic service serving as ambassador to both the UK and the United States. He was described by the British as "nationalistic despite his Westminster School tie." The Fedayan-e Islam tried to assassinate him in 1955.

Amidi-Nouri, Abul-Hassan (1893–1979)—editor of the muckraking paper *Dad* (Justice). From a wealthy landed family in Mazandaran, he was trained to be a trial lawyer but turned to journalism. A founding member of the National Front, he soon broke with Mossadeq, participated in the 1953 coup, and became a member of the new ruling elite. He was executed immediately after the 1979 revolution.

Amir-Alai, Shams al-Din (1900–93)—a Mossadeq adviser. Son of a landed aristocrat, he had graduated from the French Lycée in Tehran and studied political science in France. Much of his career was spent in the ministries of justice, finance, and interior. After the 1953 coup, he was briefly imprisoned and then permitted to leave for France, where he obtained a doctorate in political science.

Azad, Abdul-Qader (1893–1987)—editor of the muckraking paper *Azad* (Freedom). A veteran politician who had spent ten years in and out of Reza Shah's prisons, he was a founding member of the National Front but soon became a vocal critic of Mossadeq.

Azar, Dr. Mehdi (1901–94)—Mossadeq's last minister of education. He had been born into a prominent clerical family in Tabriz and was sent to France to study medicine. He was a professor of medicine when invited to head the Ministry of Education. He was often attacked by royalist and clerical deputies for having an elder brother living in exile in the Soviet Union. After the coup, he remained prominent in the National Front and consequently found himself in and out of prison.

Baqai, Muzaffar (1912–87)—maverick politician who first vociferously championed Mossadeq and then equally vociferously opposed him. From a prominent family in Kerman, he was educated in France, taught philosophy at Tehran University, and represented his hometown in the fifteenth through seventeenth Majles. He headed the Toilers Party.

Fatemi, Sayyed Hussein (1917–54)—Mossadeq's right-hand man. Son of a religious dignitary in Nain, he studied at an English missionary school in Isfahan before going to Paris to study journalism. His newspaper, *Bakhtar-e Emruz* (Today's West), was the main organ of the National Front. Deemed the most anti-shah of the National Front leaders, he was executed after the coup.

Haerizadeh, Sayyed Abul-Hassan (1894–1987)—an early Mossadeq supporter who soon turned against him. He was a retired judge and veteran Majles deputy. The British embassy described him as an "extreme neutralist" who was "quarrelsome and usually at logger-heads with his colleagues."

Hajazi, Gen. Abdul-Hussein (1907–90)—former governor of Khuzestan. The British considered him friendly toward the Anglo-Iranian Oil Company. A close adviser to the shah during the Mossadeq period, he put his name forward as a prospective leader for the 1953 coup.

Haqshenas, Jahanger (1910–91)—one of Mossadeq's trusted advisers on technical matters pertaining to the petroleum industry. A European-trained engineer, he taught at Tehran University and helped found the Iran Party. After the coup he lived in exile in Britain.

Hassebi, Kazem (1906–90)—another Mossadeq adviser on the oil industry. He came from a modest merchant family and had studied in Europe—first civil engineering in Paris, then petroleum engineering in Britain and Czechoslovakia. He was a founding member of the Engineers Association, Iran Party, and the National Front. After the coup, he was kept under house imprisonment for two years.

Imami, Sayyed Hassan (1912–97)—brief president of the seventeenth Majles. A staunch royalist, the shah appointed him to be Tehran's Imam Jum'eh (Friday Prayer Leader).

He had studied theology at Najaf and law in Switzerland. From an aristocratic family, he was related to Mossadeq but deemed him a traitor to his class.

Imami, Jamal al-Din (1893–1968)—a leading Mossadeq opponent. Son of the Imam Jum'eh of Khoi, he was elected to the Majles first from Khoi and then from Tehran. He became a vocal critic of Mossadeq in the latter stages of the sixteenth Majles. After the 1953 coup, he was rewarded with the ambassadorship to Rome.

Kashani, Ayatollah Sayyed Abul-Qassem (1888–1961)—the most prominent cleric supporting oil nationalization. Son of a senior cleric, he had studied in Najaf, participated in the 1920 revolt against the British in Iraq, and subsequently found shelter in Reza Shah's Iran. During World War II, he was interned by the British on suspicion of having ties with Nazi Germany. During the oil crisis, the British deemed him a "bitter enemy" but one who could be bought off. He played an important role in undermining Mossadeq.

Kazemi, Sayyed Baqer Khan (Muazeb al-Dawleh) (1892–1976)—diplomat who served Mossadeq as foreign minister. From an old landed family, he had studied in the United States and spent much of his life in the diplomatic corps. He was forced into early retirement after the 1953 coup.

Lutfi, Abdul-Ali (1879–1956)—Mossadeq's minister of justice. Born and raised in Najaf, he had moved to Iran in the 1920s and helped reform the legal system in the 1930s. A meticulous respecter of constitutional laws, he opposed military courts trying civilians. This brought him into conflict with the shah. He died in a prison hospital in 1956.

Maleki, Khalel (1901–69)—prominent Marxist intellectual. He had studied chemistry in Germany in the early 1930s; was imprisoned in 1937 for "propagating Marxism"; joined the Tudeh Party in 1941; headed a group of intellectuals who left the party in protest of Soviet policies in northern Iran; helped establish the Toilers Party; and left the latter when it began to oppose Mossadeq. He is reputed to have said to Mossadeq, "We will follow you even unto the very gates of hell."

Makki, Hussein (1911–99)—an orator. He made his mark in the Majles denouncing the oil company and initially acting as Mossadeq's spokesman. He served on the parliamentary commission sent to Abadan to take over the AIOC. He broke with Mossadeq in 1952 and later reinvented himself as a historian of modern Iran.

Matin-Daftari, Ahmad (1895–1971)—Mossadeq's main adviser on international law. Educated in France, Switzerland, and Germany, he taught law at Tehran University and during Reza Shah's reign attained a number of high posts, including that of prime minister. He favored a neutralist foreign policy and was briefly interned by the British during World War II. He was Mossadeq's nephew as well as son-in-law. His estranged brother, Gen. Muhammad Daftari, played a leading role in the coup.

Moazemi, Abdullah (1909–71)—a Mossadeq supporter in the fourteenth Majles through the seventeenth. From a titled, landed family, he studied law in France and taught at Tehran University. He was elected president of the seventeenth Majles. After the 1953 coup he was briefly imprisoned. His brother, Sheifullah Moazemi, was an electrical engineer who served Mossadeq as his minister of post and telegraph.

Nariman, Sayyed Mahmud (1893–1961)—Mossadeq's main adviser on financial matters. The son of a bank manager, he had studied economics in Switzerland and Britain. He had a long career in the civil service before becoming mayor of Tehran. After the 1953 coup, he was in and out of prison.

Navab-Safavi, Sayyed Mojtaba (Lowhi) (1924–56)—founder of the Fedayan-e Islam. A young and low-ranking cleric, he created one of the first truly fundamentalist organizations in the Muslim world. Claiming descent from the Safavid dynasty, he changed his family name from Lowhi. He was responsible for a series of high-profile assassinations, including that of Ahmad Kasravi, the historian; Hezher, the court minister; and Razmara, the prime minister. He was executed in 1956 after a failed attempt on the prime minister.

Qavam, Ahmad (Qavam al-Saltaneh) (1875–1955)—reputed to be Iran's paramount eminence grise. Prominent in politics since the 1905 revolution, he had presided over at least seven cabinets—many of them before Reza Shah. From an aristocratic family, he was related to the former dynasty and to Mossadeq. After World War II, he was bestowed the title "Highness" for persuading the Soviets to evacuate northern Iran. But three years later, when he opposed the shah increasing royal constitutional powers, he lost the title. In July 1952, the United States and the UK saw him as their last civilian hope against Mossadeq. The British embassy deemed him "intriguing, ambitious, and fond of money but of great experience and competence."

Razavi, Sayyed Ahmad (1906–71)—a Mossadeq supporter in the Majles. From a prominent landed family, he graduated from the French Lycée in Tehran and studied mineral engineering in France. He was a founding member of both

the Engineers Association and the Iran Party. He represented his hometown, Kerman, in the fifteenth and seventeenth Majles. After the 1953 coup he was sentenced to life
imprisonment but was soon released and permitted to go into
exile.

Razmara, Gen. Hajji Ali (1900–51)—premier assassinated
by the Fedayan-e Islam in 1951 for opposing oil nationalization. From a long line of military officers, he attended
St. Cyr; fought in the tribal campaigns of the 1930s; headed
the military academy, where he oversaw the publication of
the official *Geography of Iran*; and became chief of staff in
1943 and again in 1946. He was related by marriage to some
of the oldest aristocratic families.

Sadiqi, Ghulam-Hussein (1903–92)—Mossadeq's minister
of communications. He was highly respected in the intellectual community. He had studied sociology at the Sorbonne
and introduced the discipline into Tehran University. Although a longtime member of the National Front, the shah
in the early stages of the 1979 revolution offered him the
premiership—which he declined.

Saleh, Allayar (1894–1981)—Mossadeq's ambassador in
Washington. Son of a titled landowner, he studied at the
American school in Tehran, where he campaigned actively
against the 1919 Anglo-Iranian Agreement. A career civil
servant, he served in a number of cabinets between 1941 and
1953. He also represented Kashan in the sixteenth and seventeenth Majles. After the 1953 coup, he resigned from his
Washington ambassadorship.

Sanjabi, Karem (1904–96)—Mossadeq's last minister of education. From a prominent Kurdish family in Kermanshah, he

studied law in France and served as dean of the law school. He represented his hometown in the seventeenth Majles. He was briefly imprisoned after the 1953 coup. He succeeded Mossadeq as the leader of the National Front.

Shayegan, Sayyed Ali (1904–81)—one of Mossadeq's legal advisers. From a respected Shiraz family, he had studied at Lyon University and taught law at Tehran University. He served as dean of the law faculty (1945); education minister (1946 and 1953); Majles deputy (1949–53); member of the oil commission (1951) and of the delegations to the Hague and the United Nations (1951–53). After the 1953 coup, he was arrested, sentenced to life imprisonment, released after two years, and permitted to leave for the United States. Those who knew him would be surprised to discover the Foreign Office categorized him as a "leftist," "fanatical," "extremist," and "unbalanced."

Taheri, Sheikh Hadi (1888–1957)—one of the leading pro-British deputies. A wealthy landlord-businessman in Yazd, he represented his hometown from 1926 until 1953. He was considered an expert on parliamentary procedures and on the foibles of his Majles colleagues. The British embassy admitted somewhat embarrassingly that he was "regarded as their mouthpiece."

Zahedi, Gen. Fazlullah (1890–1963)—nominal head of the 1953 coup. A member of the Tsarist-trained Cossack Brigade that had carried out the 1921 coup, he was promoted to the rank of general by Reza Shah. He was incarcerated by the British in 1942 on suspicion of being part of the German fifth column. The British deemed him less a professional officer than a politician-businessman who had made a great deal of money while governor of Khuzestan. After the 1953 coup he was named premier but retained the post for only twenty months before being exiled to Switzerland.

Zirakzadeh, Ahmad (1905–93)—staunch Mossadeq supporter. Son of a cleric from the Bakhtiyari region who had perished in the 1919 pandemic, he was raised by relatives in Tehran and won a government scholarship to study mechanical engineering in Paris. He was a founding member of the Engineers Association and the Iran Party. After the 1953 coup, he hid for more than two years; spent five months in prison; and then raised money from friends to open a garage.

THE COUP

INTRODUCTION

For the last three decades the United States and Iran have been locked in a deadly embrace—so much so that they have been dubbed "bitter" even "eternal" enemies. The former tends to depict the latter as a cross between the Third Reich and Stalinist Russia—an "evil" force scheming to export revolution throughout the Middle East, dreaming of rebuilding the old expansive Iranian empires, and harboring "nuclear ambitions" with long-range missiles capable of delivering weapons of mass destruction as far afield as Israel, Europe, and even North America. It also bears a deep grudge for the humiliating 1979–80 hostage crisis when students invaded its embassy in Tehran, seized fifty-five diplomats, and held them hostage for 444 days with the taunting slogan "The U.S. Can't Do a Damn Thing." The latter, in turn, depicts the former as a warmongering colonial-imperial power—in its own language, a "world-devouring arrogant Satan"—determined to dominate the whole region and bring about "regime change" either by restoring the old order or, if that proves impossible, by dismembering the country into small ethnic enclaves. The two have found themselves locked inside an iron cage.

Much of this hostility is rooted in the 1953 coup in which the Central Intelligence Agency (CIA) overthrew the highly popular government of Muhammad Mossadeq and thus laid the groundwork for the establishment of the autocratic rule of Muhammad Reza Shah Pahlavi. The 1953 coup, in turn, is rooted in the 1951–53 oil crisis between Iran and Britain. In April 1951, the Iranian parliament had elected Mossadeq premier with the clear mandate to nationalize the British-owned Anglo-Iranian Oil Company. This sparked the famous international crisis known as the Anglo-Iranian oil dispute. It began with Iran taking over the oil installations. It escalated with heated debates in the Hague and the UN, with an economic embargo, with secret plans for an invasion, and with a break in diplomatic relations. The United States tried to cool down the crisis by presenting itself as an "honest broker" with a series of so-called compromise solutions. The crisis, however, did not end until August 1953, when the CIA, together with the British Secret Intelligence Service (SIS), better known as MI6, organized a group of tank officers to overthrow Mossadeq. These twenty-eight months form a defining fault line not only for Iranian history but also in the country's relations with both Britain and the United States. It is often said that major wars and revolutions carve in public memory clear defining moments separating "before" from "after." The same can also be said of 1953 with regard to the public memory and political culture of Iran.

Much has been written on the 1953 coup. Much has also been written on the 1951–53 oil crisis. One could well ask, So why yet another book on the same topics? The aim of the present book is to challenge on two separate grounds the conventional wisdom established by previous works. First, it questions the conventional notion that the British negotiated in good faith, the United States made serious attempts to act as an honest broker, and Mossadeq failed to reach a compromise because of his intransigence—traced invariably to his presumed "psychological makeup" and Shi'i "martyrdom complex." Even authors sympathetic to Mossadeq claim he should have, and could have, reached a fair and just compromise if only he had been less intransigent. For example, William Roger Louis—author of some of the most thorough works on the decline of the British Empire in general and on the Anglo-Iranian crisis in particular—argues that Britain accepted the principle of nationalization but decided together with America to overthrow Mossadeq because of his "irrational behavior."[1] The present book counterargues that compromise was unattainable simply because at the very core of the dispute lay the blunt question of who would control the oil industry—its exploration, production, extraction, and exportation? Would control be in the hands of Iran or the Anglo-Iranian Oil Company—or, possibly, a consortium of large oil companies known at the time as the Seven Sisters? For Iran, nationalization meant sovereign control. For the oil companies, Iranian nationalization meant loss of Western control—something deemed unacceptable in the early 1950s. Pseudonationalization—nationalization in form but not substance, in theory but not in practice—although heralded far and wide as a "fair compromise" by both the British and the Americans was in reality at best a meaningless oxymoron and at worst a deceptive smokescreen. In the years 1951 through 1953 neither the British nor the Americans were in any way willing to accept real oil nationalization.

Second, this book questions the conventional wisdom that places the coup squarely and solidly within the context of the Cold War—within the conflict between East and West, between the Soviet Union and the United States, between the Communist Bloc and the so-called Free World. Mark Gasiorowski—the author of the most meticulous works on the coup—expresses the view of many who have written on the subject when he argues that the coup had little to do with oil but much to do with geopolitics, fear of communism, and the Soviet threat. He writes: "At first the US decided to stay

out of the fray. It encouraged Britain to accept nationalization, tried to broker a settlement of the dispute and dissuade
the British from invading Iran. It maintained this neutral
position until the end of the Truman administration in January 1953, though by then many US officials thought Mosaddeq's refusal to settle the oil dispute was creating political
instability that put Iran in danger of falling behind the Iron
Curtain." [2]

This book, by contrast, will try to locate the coup firmly
inside the conflict between imperialism and nationalism, between First and Third Worlds, between North and South, between developed industrial economies and underdeveloped
countries dependent on exporting raw materials. Since the issue at stake was oil, the book argues the United States had as
much invested in the crisis as did Britain. The United States,
thus, participated in the coup not so much because of the
danger of communism as the repercussions that oil nationalization could have on such faraway places as Indonesia and
South America, not to mention the rest of the Persian Gulf.
Control over oil production did eventually pass from Western companies to local states in the early 1970s, but such a
loss was deemed unacceptable in the early 1950s. Some may
remain nostalgic for the "good old days" when production of
oil and therefore its price was safe in the hands of the major
companies—and thus free from such "irresponsible cartels"
as OPEC (Organization of Petroleum Exporting Countries).
They would love to save so-called rentier states from the
"curse of oil." Such nostalgia, however far-fetched now, was
part and parcel of reality until just before the emergence of
campaigns to nationalize oil. And this campaign in the Middle East was spearheaded by Mossadeq.

This book will argue that although the United States and
the UK used the language of the Cold War—the dominant
discourse of the time—to justify the coup, their main concern

was not so much about communism as about the dangerous repercussions that oil nationalization could have throughout the world. It was precisely because of this that many Iranians admired—and continue to admire—Mossadeq. They see him as a national idol, equating him with Gandhi in India, Nasser in Egypt, Sukarno in Indonesia, Tito in Yugoslavia, Nkrumah in Ghana, and Lumumba in the Congo. In the age of anticolonial nationalism after World War II, Mossadeq, together with Gandhi and Nasser, appeared as trailblazers in the Third World. They remain so to the present day.

The 1951–53 crisis can be pieced together from a number of diverse sources—some of them opened up in recent years, especially after the 1979 revolution. The Anglo-Iranian Oil Company, later named British Petroleum, has donated its extensive archives to the University of Warwick in England. These archives contain a wealth of information not only on the company's negotiating positions but also on the internal working of the industry—particularly its labor relations. The British government, at times observing its thirty-year rule, has declassified some of its files, including those of the Cabinet, Foreign Office, consulates, and the Ministry of Fuel and Power. They are available in London at the British National Archives, formerly known as the Public Record Office. Of course, the MI6 files remain closed.

The U.S. State Department, after dragging its feet for more than three decades, eventually in 1989 released some useful materials in its annual volumes entitled *Foreign Relations of the United States*—better known as the FRUS series.[3] The Iran volumes, however, continue to have large unexplained gaps. It is difficult to believe that days, sometimes weeks, passed without any correspondence whatsoever going back and forth between Tehran and Washington—especially when these days coincided with major crises in Iran. The American Historical Association has complained that the State Department has failed to observe its own declassification rule and has found various excuses for delaying the release of documents on Iran—as well as on Guatemala and the Congo.[4]

The CIA, for its part, after years of arguing it did not have the financial resources to abide by the 1995 Presidential Executive Order to "automatically declassify" after twenty-five years, unexpectedly turned around and argued that the same files had been inadvertently shredded in the early 1960s because of "a culture of destruction."[5] It now argues that about 1,000 pages "remain locked in agency vaults" but they have to be held in "abeyance for the time being."[6] It explains their publications would break trust with the British, since the latter still officially claim they had absolutely no role in the 1953 coup. Hopefully, future historians will see them before they, too, are inadvertently turned over to the shredders.

One important CIA study, however, known as the Wilber document, was leaked to the *New York Times* in 2000—at a time when the U.S. administration was trying to initiate a détente with Iran by offering an olive branch in the form of an implicit apology for the 1953 coup. The document appeared first in summary form in the print edition of the newspaper; then in an expurgated eighty-page form on the newspaper's website; then in a less expurgated 169-page form—with many names redacted—on another website cryptically named Cryptome; and finally in a longer form on the same website with some of the names spelled out.[7] The only section left secret was an annex listing the journalists and politicians in the pay of MI6 and the CIA during the coup.

Commissioned by the CIA's Historical Division and entitled the "Overthrow of Premier Mossadeq of Iran," the document was authored by Dr. Donald Wilber, an archeologist turned spy and the agency's chief Persian-speaking operative. It was intended both as an autopsy on 1953 and as a handbook for future coups elsewhere. The preface forthrightly offers "recommendations applicable to parallel operations." Although the author provides a fair outline of the coup, he most probably practiced a considerable amount self-censorship, well aware that the document might circulate not just within the CIA but also in the Pentagon, State Department, White House, and even the Senate Foreign Relations Committee.

This Wilbur document has attained the status of an authoritative text—even a definitive history—in Iran as well as in the West. The *New York Times* presented it as "the secret history" disclosing "pivotal information" and the "inner workings of the coup."[8] The *Guardian* billed it as the "very first detailed US account of the episode to be published."[9] Similarly, the National Security Archive—a nongovernmental organization in Washington committed to the mission of declassifying official documents—hailed it as "extremely important." It called it an "after-action report from agency cable traffic and interviews with agents on the ground in Iran."[10]

The document, however, contains deafening silences. Although commissioned by the CIA, it is not clear whether the agency ever published it. The Web version contains innumerable typos—indicating it was a prepublication draft. The late author probably left his own draft copy with trusted friends with instructions to leak it at some appropriate time. Wilber had retired from the agency with bad feelings. He felt he had not been given his due for his role in the coup. He also felt slighted because the agency had redacted his own memoirs to the point of absurdity but had permitted Kermit Roosevelt to publish *his* version of events in *Countercoup.* Published just as the Iranian Revolution was unfolding and written in the genre of a Hardy Boys adventure story,

Roosevelt's *Countercoup* immediately gained the status of a valuable and readable eyewitness account. Wilber died eager to set the record straight.

The available government materials have been supplemented in recent years by a flood of interviews, biographies, memoirs, reminiscences, personal histories, and private documents. They have appeared in scattered newspapers, journals, magazines, edited works, and private publications—both inside and outside Iran. Most informative have been memoirs published posthumously by Mossadeq's close advisers. What is more, oral-history projects, both inside and outside the country, provide valuable new information. Foremost among these are the Iranian Oral History Project at Harvard University and the Iranian Left History Project in Berlin. The former, supervised by Dr. Habib Ladjevardi, interviewed 132 prominent figures from the Pahlavi regime—most of whom can be described as members of the old elite.[11] The latter, carried out by Dr. Hamid Ahmadi, videotaped 126 dissidents living inside and outside Iran—some had been Army officers and members of the communist party during the 1953 coup.[12] These interviews, together with memoirs published after the 1979 revolution, provide useful countervoices to the royalist ones heard after the 1953 coup. Until the unlikely day when MI6 and the CIA permit daylight to disturb their buried archives, we historians have no choice but to settle for these varied and scattered sources to put together any coherent picture of the 1953 coup.

1

Oil Nationalization

Never had so few lost so much so stupidly in so short a time.
—Dean Acheson on the AIOC

Origins

The history of oil in Iran begins with the famous—or, rather, notorious—D'Arcy Concession. In 1901, William Knox D'Arcy, a British gold speculator turned oil entrepreneur from Australia, bought from the shah the exclusive sixty-year rights to explore, extract, refine, and export all petroleum products across the whole length and breadth of the country—with the exception of the provinces bordering Russia. In return, he gave £50,000 in cash to the shah, issued £20,000 in shares to other prominent figures, and promised the government royalties totaling 16 percent of net annual profits. He seemed to be following King Leopold's famous dictum that "treaties must be as brief as possible, and the natives must grant us everything in a couple of articles."[1] A company chairman later ranked D'Arcy among the greatest imperial heroes of all time—along with Cecil Rhodes, Benjamin Disraeli, and Winston Churchill.[2]

Oil was struck in 1908 at Masjed-e Suleiman in the southwestern province of Arabestan—later renamed Khuzestan. D'Arcy soon sold his rights to the Burmah Oil Company, which had little success in Burma but had been encouraged by the First Lord Admiral, John Fisher, to take an active interest in Iran. Fisher, known as the "oil maniac," was determined to convert the British Navy from coal to petroleum.[3] A year later Burmah became the Anglo-Persian Oil Company (APOC). Meanwhile, the British government persuaded Sheikh Kha'zal, chief of the main Arab-speaking tribe in the southwest, to lease to the company his island of Abadan for the construction of an oil refinery. Abadan, although desolate, was strategically situated at the northern tip of the Persian Gulf on the estuary of the Tigris and Euphrates Rivers. The British government also obtained dominant say in the oil company—52.5 percent voting rights and two ex-officio directors with one chosen directly by the admiralty. These two directors had the right to veto resolutions passed by the board of directors.[4] The government also privately reserved the right to change the board of directors if necessary.[5] Churchill, the succeeding First Lord Admiral who completed the process of converting the Navy from coal to oil, told members of Parliament that the government needed to have guaranteed control over oil resources but assured them that the state would not actually interfere in the financial running of the private company. He later boasted: "This brought us a prize from fairyland far beyond our brightest dreams."[6]

Once World War I broke out, the British government dispatched troops first to southwest Iran and then across the border into southern Mesopotamia to protect the oil installations from the Ottoman armies as well as from local tribes allied to the Central Powers.[7] Similarly, in World War II, Britain invaded Iran and Iraq primarily to secure this vital industry. Christopher Hill, the great historian, in his lectures on historiography, would warn students not to believe everything they read in government documents. As an example he would give the 1941 British explanation for invading Iran. There, he would remark, you will find no mention of oil. But, he would add, the main reason was oil. How did he know? He knew because he, as a Foreign Office hand, had drafted that same declaration. Churchill, in his history of World War II, later admitted that the 1941 invasion had been necessitated by German activities in Iran as well as in Iraq that were directed at the oil industry in Abadan.[8]

By the time World War II ended, the Anglo-Iranian Oil Company—which had changed its name in 1935 to conform to the government decree substituting Iran for Persia—was vital to the British Empire in more ways than one. With six new oil fields near Masjed-e Suleiman—at Agha Jari, Gach Seran, Naft-e Sefid, Lali, Qasr-e Shirin, and Haft Kel—the largest outside Texas, the AIOC produced more than 357,000 barrels a day. It ranked among the other so-called Seven Sisters dominating the world market—the others being Royal Dutch Shell, Gulf Oil, Texas (later named Texaco), Standard Oil of New York (known as Socony and later Mobil), Standard Oil of New Jersey (later Exxon), and Standard Oil of California (later Chevron), as well as the often overlooked Compagnie Française des Pétroles.

The AIOC provided steady sums to the British Treasury—more than £24 million a year in taxes and £92 million in foreign exchange. These were substantial sums, especially in the years of post–World War II austerity. The Ministry of Fuel and Power calculated that the Abadan refinery alone gave the sterling area more than $347 million a year.[9] The company regularly gave its shareholders—mostly British citizens—dividends as high as 30 percent. Its Iran operations contributed as much as 75 percent of the company's overall profits—much of which went not only to shareholders in Britain but also to other oil ventures throughout the world. AIOC owned 50 percent of Kuwait Oil, 23 percent of Iraqi Petroleum, 23 percent of Qatar Petroleum, 34 percent of Anglo-Egyptian Oil, and 55 percent of Consolidated Refineries Ltd.

in Israel.[10] It built refineries in Britain, France, and Australia, as well as carrying out extensive oil explorations as far afield as Trinidad, Nigeria, Sicily, and Papua. Its oil reserves in Iran were estimated to be the third largest in the world. Its production in Iran was the largest in the Middle East and the fourth largest in the world—after that of the United States, USSR, and Venezuela. Its exports of crude were the second largest in the world—after those of Venezuela. Its Abadan refinery was the very largest in the world, covering three square miles and producing 24 million tons a year. It also built a much smaller refinery in Kermanshah to take care of Iranian needs. The Abadan refinery met 85 percent of the fuel needs of the Royal Navy and the Royal Air Force in Asia. The company docked as many as two hundred tankers a month at Abadan, and owned more than three hundred ocean-going tankers throughout the world. Refined oil was exported directly from Abadan; crude oil was piped some 150 miles from the main fields directly to the new port of Bandar Mashur. Not surprisingly, company scientists, geologists, engineers, and field managers were proud of their accomplishments. They boasted they had "made the desert bloom."

What is more, the company was by far the largest industrial employer in Iran. It employed more than 63,000: 2,700 senior staff—mostly Britons; 4,700 junior staff—1,500 of whom were Indians, Pakistanis, and "Palestinians"; and more than 53,000—mostly artisans, skilled, semi-skilled, and unskilled workers—in the refinery, oil fields, and the docks. The fields alone employed more than 21,000. The company also used more than 14,000 contract laborers—almost all unskilled—for seasonal work, especially for road construction. Abadan, with a population of 115,000, contained 30,000 company employees. Another 10,000 earned their living indirectly through the company—as repairmen, shopkeepers, and small businessmen.

Year	Crude Oil Production [11] (thousands of barrels per day)
1913	5
1914	6
1915	10
1916	12
1917	19
1918	18
1919	25
1920	33
1921	45
1922	61
1923	69
1924	88
1925	96
1926	98
1927	108
1928	118
1929	115
1930	125
1931	121
1932	135
1933	149
1934	150
1935	157
1936	171
1937	191
1938	214
1939	214
1940	181
1941	139
1942	198
1943	204

(continued on next page)

Year	Crude Oil Production (thousands of barrels per day)
1944	278
1945	357
1946	402
1947	424
1948	520
1949	560
1950	664

This dramatic growth did not necessarily endear the company to the public. On the contrary, over the years the public accumulated an ever-increasing list of grievances against the company. It suspected the company of irregular bookkeeping since it refused to both publish proper annual accounts and define what it meant by royalties based on "net profits." Instead, it calculated royalties in an opaque manner—4 shillings per ton of oil exported (equivalent to 20–25 cents a barrel), plus 20 percent of dividends distributed to "ordinary shareholders"—after taking deductions for taxes to the British government and for sums put in reserve for future investments. The Foreign Office admitted the company was "reluctant to divulge even to us the profit element per barrel in Persian operations much less the basis on which it is calculated." [12] It also admitted in 1949 that it was in the dark as to whether the 20 percent was on gross or net profits—that is, before or after tax and other deductions.[13] Either way, the sum was deemed grossly unfair, especially after 1943, when Venezuela signed the first of the 50/50 deals receiving half of annual profits. Mexico had gone even further in 1938–40, nationalizing the local British and American–owned oil company. Mexico had been lucky in its timing, since America and Britain could hardly afford another major crisis right on the eve of World War II. They had no choice but to accept "fair compensation"—a term much favored later by Mossadeq.[14] Iranian complaints against the AIOC became more vociferous in 1950 when Aramco—the American oil company in the Persian Gulf—signed 50/50 deals with both Kuwait and Saudi Arabia. Daniel Yergin describes these 50/50 deals as a "watershed"—even a "revolution"—in the history of world petroleum.[15]

By the late 1940s, Iranian newspapers—even establishment ones such as *Ettela'at*—frequently pointed out that over the years the AIOC had given Iran a measly £105 million in royalties, but as much as £170 million in taxes to the British government, £115 million in dividends to British shareholders, and invested more than £500 million in its operations outside Iran.[16] An internal AIOC memo shows that in 1949 alone, the company paid the British government £22.8 million in taxes, distributed £7.1 million in dividends to shareholders, and put £18.4 million in reserve, but gave Iran only £13.5 million in royalties.[17] Another internal memo admitted that the company had shortchanged royalties by putting large sums into reserve.[18] Of course, all royalties were paid in sterling, thus binding Iran firmly into the sterling area and thus making it vulnerable to the vagaries of the British pound. A confidential Foreign Office memorandum in 1949 advised that Iran should be discouraged from buying goods from the United States, since such purchases would require dollars, thus draining sterling: "A point to bear in mind," the memo explained, "is that any excessive purchases in the Western hemisphere create a new dollar drain for us so that it is dangerous for us to encourage more than absolutely essential dollar purchases by Persia."[19] Some also suspected the company sold oil to America at discount to diminish the wartime debt owed by Britain to the United States. It is not for naught that the Persian word *este'mar* (colonialism-imperialism) is derived from the Arabic term *estesmar* (economic exploitation).

Grievances were not limited to royalties. The company ran a tight ship from Britannic House in London. It treated geological explorations as well as annual accounts as state secret—especially from the Iranian government. It sold fuel to local consumers at world prices, but to the British Navy and Air Force at undisclosed discount rates warding off all inquiries by claiming these valuable customers could turn elsewhere.[20] It burned natural gas instead of piping it to urban centers. It avoided customs dues on imported goods—even on such household goods as refrigerators, watches, furniture, and musical instruments. It caused massive ecological damage by cutting down trees for roads and pipelines. It was rumored its well across the border in Iraq siphoned off oil from Qasr-e Shirin. It struck deals with local tribal chiefs, signed separate oil concessions with the Bakhtiyari khans, and extended political protection to Sheikh Kha'zal of the Ka'ab tribe. What is more, the company lobbied hard to place friendly officials in crucial positions—in Tehran as well as in the local administration. Its field officers, helped by British consuls throughout Khuzestan, did their very best to influence the choice of provincial governors, police chiefs, local mayors, and even tribal leaders. Such forms of meddling were so sensitive that the company continues to keep them classified even to the present day. One of the very first books on the oil industry published in Persian was aptly titled *Black Gold or Iran's Calamity*.[21] Long before others, Iranians at least, some Iranians had begun to depict oil as a curse rather than a blessing.

The company further alienated the public in other ways. It restricted the number of Iranians promoted to managerial positions. For years, it imported semiskilled labor from

India and Palestine. It preferred to hire temporary contract laborers—especially from the local Arab tribes—rather than give job security to full-time Persian-speaking workers. It failed to provide decent housing for native employees: many refinery workers lived in shantytowns; oil-field workers in desert tents. It ran Abadan as a company town with each grade of employee allocated to special districts and facilities. It was rumored—in this case falsely—that British facilities displayed signs warning DOGS AND IRANIANS TO KEEP OUT. In 1949, a group of British employees sent a confidential letter to the Foreign Office complaining that management harbored "racist" attitudes, discriminated in housing, and in the last fifteen years had hired few Iranians while doubling its European staff.[22] MI6 warned the British ambassador that the company was highly unpopular since it considered "everyone east of Calais to be a wog." The ambassador replied that such complaints should be addressed to the commercial attaché.[23] Professor Laurence Elwell-Sutton, who had worked for the company before entering the Foreign Office, wrote in his classic work entitled *Persian Oil* that the AIOC resembled a typical "colonial" enterprise—its newspapers ignored the host country, its officials rarely ventured outside its own installations, and its rules and regulations tended to encourage "a racial bar." "Segregation," he wrote, "was almost complete, whether in major matters like employment or accommodation, or in the use of buses, cinemas, and clubs":

> The distinction was emphasized by trivialities such as nomenclature borrowed from India—the Britons were "sahibs," their wives "memsahibs," terms that excluded even those Persians who had the same grade as their British colleagues. . . . The rarity was the Briton who made a genuine attempt to mix with Persians on his own, and he

was regarded as wrong in the head. Even to meet a senior grade Persian was odd; and as for calling on a Persian of lower grade, that was unheard of. The most tragic were a few English girls who had married Persian students in England and now found themselves virtually ostracized by their British compatriots. . . .

With this attitude towards Persians who were nominally their social equal (some would say superior), it is not difficult to imagine the prevailing British view of the workers, the 50,000 wage-earners with whom they were in contact every day of their lives. They were, it seemed, a race apart, "wogs," "bastards," "lousy —s." The only way to handle them, so one was told, was to browbeat them, to cow them into submission. . . . This racial antipathy is to be found even among quite intelligent people here.[24]

Not surprisingly, the company's dealings with labor were wrought with difficulties that periodically erupted into spectacular general strikes. On May Day, 1929, 11,000 refinery workers—coordinated by the underground Communist Party—struck, demanding the eight-hour day, better wages and housing, union recognition, equal pay for Iranian and Indian employees, and paid annual holidays including May Day.[25] Strikers chased the governor and the police chief into the city fire station. The British rushed gun boats to Abadan. Order was not restored until the government declared martial law, dispatched Army reinforcements, and arrested twenty-nine ringleaders.[26] Another 500 workers were fired. The British government thanked the shah for his "speedy and effective handling" of the situation.[27] The company, meanwhile, blamed office workers and "Armenian agitators," even though most of the arrested were foremen, fitters, and carpenters with impeccable Muslim names. Five remained incarcerated until 1941.

An even more spectacular crisis broke out in 1946—this time coordinated by the Tudeh (Masses) Party, the heir to the Communist Party. It began on May Day when a rally of 80,000 in Abadan repeated the 1929 demands, adding pay for Friday—the Muslim day of rest—and the strict implementation of the country's recently passed Labor Law. One woman speaker denounced the company for spending more on dog food than on wages and demanded the takeover of the oil industry: "Oh brothers, the production of oil in our land is like jewels. We must try to get these jewels back. If we don't we are worthless." [28] This was probably the first call for nationalization heard in public.

The crisis escalated in July when the company, eager to maximize profits rescinded Friday pay. This sparked a massive general strike throughout Khuzestan. The strikers, totaling more than 65,000, included refinery and field workers; clerical and manual workers, artisans, and technicians—including Indians; shopkeepers and students; firemen, truck drivers, railroad and dockworkers; even chauffeurs, servants, and cooks employed in British households. It was by far the largest industrial action seen in the Middle East. British officials reported that the strike gave the Tudeh "complete control over the industrial regions of Khuzestan"; that the leaders were mostly "drivers, fitters, and plant attendants"; that the mass meetings in Abadan were by far the largest in the city's history; that more than 75 percent of the labor force had enrolled in the Tudeh unions; and that the Arab chiefs were worried the Tudeh was "poisoning irretrievably the minds of their ignorant tribesmen." [29]

The British rushed two warships to Abadan and an Indian brigade to Basra. "One of the remarkable things about the whole strike," wrote the consul in Ahwaz, "was its wonderful organization. Of course, the perfection of the AIOC's communications made it easy: the Tudeh just collared all, or almost all, of the telephone network." [50] A senior official at the Ministry of Fuel advised the company to improve work conditions and remarked: "I cannot get it out of my mind that the Tudeh Party, though admittedly a revolutionary party, may be the party of the future in Persia which is going to look after the interests of the working man." [51] A Labour Member of Parliament, after his tour of the oil facilities, warned that "it was time to sit up and listen when you hear fourteen-year-old children talking about how the 'liquid gold' should belong to us and not to the British." [52] He added such sentiments were "permeating the Middle East."

The strike did not end until the government declared martial law and carried out mass arrests, but, at the same time, persuaded the company to both give Friday pay and raise the minimum wage. Company negotiators told Britannic House that the choice was either continued strike or £1 million for Friday pay. [53] Philip Noel-Baker, the British secretary of state, confided to his colleagues that the entire crisis had been caused by the company's intransigence over Friday pay. [54] Similarly, an AIOC whistleblower told the Foreign Office that the general strike should be blamed entirely on company "diehards" who failed to appreciate the daily problems of workers and had no experience of dealing with organized labor. He added that their "knowledge of trade unionism is limited to the repetition of worn-out jokes that went out with crinolines." [55] The AIOC later claimed the strike ended only because "government took strong measures to restore order." [56]

In the aftermath of the strike, the State Department appointed a labor attaché to Tehran, and the British embassy sent its own labor attaché on an investigatory tour of Khuzestan. He wrote back that although native workers were mostly "illiterate," "lacked confidence and quick reactions," and failed to remain on their jobs for any length of time, they were "eager to learn," "took kindly to high speed and automatic production," and were well suited to become "welders, carpenters, fitters, and machine operators."[37] He added that they bore genuine grievances against the company: bad housing, poor medical facilities, cattle-like practices, refusal to tolerate trade unions, and retaliation against union organizing. Technically the company did not fire union organizers. Instead it gave local authorities a list of such organizers, who were promptly arrested. After seven days, according to the Labor Law, the company could lawfully lay them off on grounds they had been absent without proper leave. The attaché cryptically noted: "The figures show that 25% of employees above the skilled category are non-Iranian. It must be an unwelcome reflection to the Iranian that so few of his nation are considered capable of filling Staff appointments." He ended the report by warning it would be "dangerous to assume that the present easing of tensions is anything but a temporary lull":

> Workers' organizations or any form of authoritative representation do not exist. During the heyday of Tudeh in Khuzestan there was both a Trade Union and a highly organized system of Tudeh Shop Stewards and spokesmen. The structure was imposed on the workers who were, however, quite willing to support self-appointed leaders who, in addition to bringing novelty and excitement, were fortuitously able to claim credit for certain concessions that were granted by the Company to its employees. These leaders have now either been arrested or have fled. The Company denies victimization.

A U.S. Senate committee came up with this conclusion:

July 1946 saw 50,000 Iranian employees of the Anglo-
Iranian Oil Company in Abadan leave their work in the
greatest strike in Iran's history. It seemed on the surface to
be a dispute between a foreign company and its workers,
but actually it was a grave power conflict involving oil,
and, for a time, the very future of Iran itself. This strike
climaxed a campaign to organize the AIOC employees
into Tudeh-controlled labor unions. The July work stop-
page had the antecedents in an unsuccessful strike of 7500
AIOC men in May 1945 for more pay and better working
conditions, the strike in May 1946 of 7500 Agha Jari field
workers that was won as a result both of good organization
and intervention by the Government in response to Tudeh
pressure and power, and the successful gain-solidifying
strike of Tehran tank installations and service workers in
June 1946. By the time of the Abadan strike Tudeh had
managed to secure effective control over the AIOC employees and Iranian organized labor in general.[38]

The company's relations with even its own British employees were fraught with difficulties. At the height of the
war, a whole contingent of employees returned to Britain without permission, complaining that work conditions
threatened their "mental health." The British government
contemplated prosecuting them for undermining the "war
effort" but thought better of it. A Tory woman dispatched
from London lectured them on how lucky they were not to
be in a Japanese prisoner-of-war camp. Some retorted that
she should visit the local British cemetery. Others suggested
"more dramatically of decoying her into some dark corner
and dealing with her in the proper Japanese fashion."[39] In
the Ministry of Fuel in London there were far-fetched rumors of "a Jewish-communist plot to sabotage" the AIOC.[40]
After years of ignoring criticisms, the company in 1951

issued a brochure flaunting its "contribution to the country's and surrounding community's welfare," and "turning a salt desert inhabited with a few Arabs and palms into a gigantic industrial complex."[41] It boasted that over the decades it had built 21,000 homes, 35 medical clinics with 90 nurses, 2 hospitals with 850 beds, 1 nursing school, 33 primary and 3 secondary schools with 13,000 pupils, 1 technical college with 1,200 students, 1 workshop with 3,000 apprentices, 19 football fields, 21 swimming pools, 34 cinemas, 1 stadium, 40 clubs, and numerous parks, libraries, and bathhouses. It took credit for increasing the literacy rate in the labor force, and diminishing the numbers dying from malaria, cholera, typhoid, and the plague. It stressed that its contributions to Iran were not limited to royalties but included customs revenues as well as wages and salaries paid to local employees who in turn paid taxes to the central government. These sums, including the swimming pools, supposedly compensated for meager annual royalties. Elwell-Sutton could not resist commenting that the company's "civilizing mission" provided no social insurance, no minimum wage for contract laborers, and no housing for most unskilled workers. He added that the much-flaunted company schools met the needs of only a small percentage of the population.[42] He could have added that these schools, although originally built by the company, were in actual fact financed and managed by the ministry of education. The brochure also claimed the company had made sincere attempts to Persianize the staff. But a confidential memo noted:

It is noteworthy that Persians have been given senior appointments in administration rather than in technical posts. The reason given is that risks cannot afford to be taken in the latter, that as yet no Persians have emerged with sufficient ability to shoulder higher technical responsibilities,

that all reports, logs, etc, must be prepared in English, and
that the entire technical background of the industry is in
English. In administration, on the other hand, some men
of sufficient ability have merged and the Company is prepared to risk giving Persians jobs which are often somewhat above their capabilities. This occasionally results in
resignations as Persians apparently often cannot face high
responsibilities for long.[43]

The specific grievances against the company cannot be
separated from the general animosity toward the British
Empire. This anti-imperialist sentiment had been growing
steadily since the 1820s, when Iran had found itself wedged
in between two expanding empires—Russia from the north
and Britain from the south. To use the language of the time,
Iran had become a pawn in the Great Game. The Russians
expanded southward into the Caucasus and Central Asia; and,
having defeated Iran in two short wars, extracted not only
economic concessions but also large chunks of territory in the
north. Similarly, the British, having established a firm foot-
hold in India—their imperial jewel, moved into Afghanistan
and the Persian Gulf. Iranians dubbed Russia their northern
and Britain their respective southern "neighbors."

The shahs tried to retain some semblance of independence
by playing off the two powers. This later became known as
the policy of positive equilibrium. They granted each parallel trading privileges, economic concessions, extraterritorial
rights, and overt political influence—in the choice of ministers, governors, and, at times, even heirs to the throne. Their
diplomats in Tehran were deemed to be the real power behind the throne, their provincial consuls the real force behind the governors, and their commercial houses as unfair
competitors undermining native merchants. By the 1890s,
Lord George Curzon—the future viceroy of India—found

during his grand tour of Iran a widespread and deep-seated distrust of the two imperial powers. He ended his *Persia and the Persian Question* with the observation that the public imagined the foreign hand to be lurking behind most significant developments.[44] Similarly, Sir Reader Bullard—the British ambassador during World War II—wrote: "In Persia one can not take a drink without being accused of acting under British or Russian influence." He added that although both Britain and Russia were "blamed" for the country's problems, the latter was rarely mentioned since they "might be a little tough."[45]

Although this "paranoid" or "conspiratorial" style of politics had its origins in the nineteenth century, it blossomed in the twentieth—with a brief interlude in 1905 and 1906, when Britain supported the constitutional movement. But the brief interlude ended abruptly in 1907 with the Anglo-Russian Agreement carving up Iran into "zones of influence." Britain took the southwest, Russia the north. They further consolidated their hold in 1914 with the British occupying the whole of the south, including the oil regions. The British government later, without any trace of irony, presented Iran an itemized bill for having occupied the south. The bill totaled 313 pounds, 17 shillings, and 6 pence.[46]

After World War I, Curzon—now foreign minister—not only barred Iran from Versailles but also persuaded, with the help of special subsidies, the Iranian prime minister, Vossuq al-Dawleh, to sign the notorious Anglo-Persian Agreement of 1919. This turned Iran into a vassal state. Harold Nicolson, who at the time served in the British Legation in Tehran, wrote that Curzon wanted not only to create a "chain of vassal states from the Mediterranean all the way to India" but also believed that God had created British imperialism and the British upper class as an instrument of his "Divine Will."[47] A London newspaper mocked that Curzon "seems to be under the impression that he discovered Persia and that, having discovered it, in some mysterious way, he owns it." [48] A British visitor to Tehran reported: "Lord Curzon's statements that he was Persia's best friend resulted in provoking an outburst of fury, derision, and contempt throughout the country, where he is considered to be Persia's greatest enemy and would-be oppressor." [49] Not surprisingly, the Anglo-Iranian Agreement was received in Iran with mass protests, petitions, bazaar strikes, street demonstrations, and even assassinations. The British Legation used blunt language to describe the mood in Tehran:

> It does not appear to be realized at home how intensely unpopular [the] agreement was in Persia and how hostile public opinion had become to Vossuq's Cabinet before it fell. It was believed that agreement really aimed at destruction of independence and that Vossuq had sold their country to Britain. Secrecy with which agreement had been concluded, fact that Majles was not summoned and attempt created to pack Majles by resorting to most dishonest methods . . . all added to conviction that Great Britain was in reality no better than the hereditary foe, Russia. . . . The feeling grew that Britain was a bitter foe who must be rooted out of the country at any cost. Revolts in Azerbaijan and Caspian provinces were due to this feeling and to it was spread of Bolshevik propaganda, for it was thought that Bolsheviks could not be worse and might, if their profession of security justice for the downtrodden classes were sincere, be much better.[50]

From an external point of view Great Britain was generally regarded as the enemy, Russia as the possible friend. Although the obvious Russian efforts to diffuse Communist ideas and propaganda caused certain uneasiness, the apparent generosity of canceling Persia's debt to Russia, of returning all Russian concessions acquired in Tsarist times, of handing over the Russian Banque d'Escompte to the Persian Government and surrendering Capitulations had made a profound impression, and the Russian-inspired idea that Persia had everything to gain by association with a Russia purged by the fires of revolution and everything to lose by succumbing to the imperialist and colonizing ambitions of Great Britain, was sufficiently plausible to gain many Persian adherents . . . particularly in the ranks of those whose ill-doings had brought them into conflict with the British military and other authorities in Persia during the British occupation.[51]

The passage of time did not diminish anti-British sentiments. A contemporary Iranian historian recently made the wild accusation that British food exactions to feed its army of occupation during World War I resulted in 10 million dead— half the population.[52] He accuses the British government of "covering up" this "genocide" by systematically destroying annual reports. In fact, no annual reports on Iran were written from 1913 until 1922; the British expeditionary force of some 15,000 would not have required that much grain; and although as many as 2 million may have lost their lives in these years, the vast majority died not because of food exactions but from cholera and typhus epidemics, from a series of bad harvests, and, most important of all, from the worldwide 1919–20 influenza pandemic.[53] Nevertheless, such wild accusations received much traction.

The suspicion that Britain was the "hidden hand" did not diminish even after the emergence of Reza Shah, who, after a military coup in 1921 and the establishment of his new Pahlavi dynasty in 1925, did much to reduce foreign— especially British—influence. He scrapped the 1919

Anglo-Persian Agreement; signed a neutrality treaty with the Soviet Union; eased out British military and financial advisers; reduced the number of foreign consulates; ended all nineteenth-century extraterritorial privileges known as Capitulations; took over the British-owned Telegraph Company and Imperial Bank; and preferred to hire technicians from France, Germany, Italy, Czechoslovakia, and Switzerland—anywhere but Britain.

What is more, Reza Shah in 1932, after prolonged and fruitless negotiations with the oil company, canceled with much fanfare—with fireworks, national holidays, and street celebrations—the D'Arcy Concession. The crisis was precipitated by the Great Depression, which had brought about a steep decline in company profits and thus in Iran's royalties. Profits had fallen from £6.5 million in 1930 to less than £3.1 million in 1933; royalties from £1,288,000 to £306,800. The shah lodged a number of complaints: overall royalties were pitiful—between 1905 and 1932, the company had made more than £171 million in profits but given Iran less than £11 million in royalties; the recent fall in profits as well as in sterling had made royalties not only pitiful but also unpredictable; company books were kept secret; Iranians were not being trained for responsible positions; and the Iranian government—unlike the British one—had no representation on the company board of directors.[54]

Despite these stances, many Iranians continued to see Reza Shah as a British "agent." They did so in part because British military officers had financed his 1921 coup; and in part because the new oil concession signed in 1933 after the much taunted cancellation turned out to be highly favorable to the AIOC. Iran agreed not to renege or unilaterally change the new agreement. It also extended the concession for another thirty-two years—from 1961 to 1993. In return, the company promised to train more Iranians; relinquished some territory (territory it knew contained no oil); made allowances for the decline of sterling relative to gold; agreed royalties would not fall below £750,000—the average in 1920–30 had been £825,000; and made small adjustments to the complex formula for calculating royalties. By the new formula, Iran would receive 4 shillings per ton of oil produced, plus 20 percent of dividends distributed to ordinary shareholders. This percentage, however, still did not take into account the large sums both paid in British taxes and put into the company's reserves.

Reza Shah's sudden retreat provided fodder for the rumor mills. Some suspected the whole crisis had been a British ruse to prolong the concession. Some suspected he had been intimidated by tacit as well as explicit threats—Britain had moved battleships into the Gulf, toyed with secessionist movements among Arab tribes, and threatened to take "all such measures as the situation may demand."[55] Some insinuated that secret funds had been channeled into his private bank account in London. Others concluded that the incident proved once again that Reza Shah was merely a British "tool." Hassan Taqizadeh, a member of the negotiating team and veteran statesman often tarred with the British brush, later told Parliament that the shah for unknown reasons had personally intervened in 1933 and ordered the negotiators to settle on these unfavorable terms.[56] In a private conversation with the *Guardian* (Manchester), he confessed he had been taken aback by the shah's sudden settlement. The only explanation he could offer was either "AIOC pressure" or a "private deal."[57] Thus Iranian nationalism took the shape of deep distrust of both the British and the Pahlavi dynasty.

By midcentury, popular historians claimed to detect the British "hidden hand" behind most crucial events in their country's past—not just in the 1921 coup and the

Constitutional Revolution of 1905, but also in the murders of Aleksandr Griboedov, the Russian emissary, in 1829; of Amir Kabir, the reformist minister, in 1852; of Nasser al-Din Shah in 1896; and of Robert Imbrie, the U.S. vice-consul, in 1924 supposedly for seeking an oil concession in the north on behalf of an American company.[58] In the words of a contemporary historian, twentieth-century Iranian politics has been conspicuous by its paranoid style—especially the search for British conspiracies.[59]

Anti-British sentiments increased even more after Reza Shah's abdication, in part because of the Allied invasion, and in part because the Allied occupation necessitated daily British involvement in internal Iranian affairs—in the choice of ministers in Tehran; in the appointment of governors in the provinces; in the election of deputies to the Majles; in the negotiations with local tribal chiefs; in the buying of food supplies from landlords; in the recruitment of local labor; and in the selection of military commanders, police chiefs, town mayors, and even village heads in Khuzestan. To oversee the occupation, Britain opened consulates in almost every city—in Mashed, Rasht, Tabriz, Kermanshah, Isfahan, Shiraz, Kerman, Bushire, Ahwaz, Khorramshahr, and Bandar Abbas. British presence seemed all-pervasive.

Not surprisingly, Britain became identified as part and parcel of the national power structure. Bullard, the British ambassador who rarely minced his words, admitted that Britain rather than the Soviet Union bore the brunt of complaints about wartime deprivations—inflation, food shortages, transport dislocations, and the breakdown of authority.[60] He typically explained this by way of "national characteristics": "It is regrettable but a fact that the Persians are ideal Stalin-fodder. They are untruthful, back biters, undisciplined, incapable of unity, without a plan. The Soviet system is equipped with a complete theoretical scheme for everything from God

to galoshes."⁶¹ This pervasive suspicion of Britain was no-
ticed by a personal emissary sent by President Roosevelt to
take stock of the general situation once America joined Britain in the occupation of southern Iran. He reported back to
Washington:

> The Iranians distrust the motives of both Britain and
> Russia and believe that the future existence of Iran as an
> independent nation is threatened. . . . For the most part
> the attitude of the Iranian officials, and indeed of the Ira-
> nian people who are in a position to appraise conditions,
> is one of intense bitterness towards Great Britain. This
> bitterness towards Britain is so emotional that it has al-
> most completely wiped out the meaning of 400 years of
> uninterrupted British-Persian friendship. Towards Rus-
> sia there is less bitterness. . . . The Iranians openly charge
> and believe that Britain has been guilty of conduct akin to
> that of the Nazis in Europe. If the Iranians had to decide
> today between Britain and Russia they would in my opin-
> ion unquestionably choose the Russians.⁶²

In other words, for most Iranians the main national enemy
was Britain. This may be difficult for most Americans and
Britons to comprehend—especially during the Cold War.

Mossadeq

Muhammad Mossadeq (Mossadeq al-Saltaneh)—the champion of oil nationalization—was well placed to emerge in
the turbulent years of World War II as the icon of Iranian
nationalism. The scion of an old patrician family related to
the Qajar dynasty that ruled the country from 1796 to 1925,
he had been prominent in politics ever since the early part
of the twentieth century. His mother, Najm al-Saltaneh,

was the granddaughter of Fath Ali Shah and the sister-in-law of Muzaffar al-Din Shah. Mossadeq himself married Ziya al-Saltaneh, the granddaughter of Nasser al-Din Shah and the daughter of Tehran's Imam Jum'eh (Friday Prayer Leader). They remained married for the rest of their long lives. His own father, Mirza Hedayat, had been finance minister and came from the famous Ashtiyani family that had provided both the Safavids and the Qajars with trained *mostowfis* (accountants—administrators). These *mostowfis* were in many ways comparable to the mandarins in China. Thus Mossadeq was related either directly or through marriage to the main aristocratic families that had ruled the country before the establishment of the Pahlavi dynasty—families such as the Imam Jum'ehs, Hedayats, Daftaris, Matin-Daftaris, Bayats, Dibas, Aminis, Qavams, Vossuqs, Alams, Zolfaqaris, Sami'is, Mostowfis, and Farmanfarmas.

Although from a patrician family, Mossadeq himself was not fabulously rich. The British press liked to bill him as one of the very richest men in Iran. In actual fact, he owned only one village—Ahmadabad, eighty-five miles outside Tehran—and two houses in Tehran. He lived frugally—he was reputed to own only two suits—and gave surplus money to a charity hospital his mother had established in Tehran. He personally managed Ahmadabad as a model farm and lived there in a simple two-floor house. After World War II he installed in it a generator to provide electricity—but only in the evening until nine p.m. The house relied mostly on candlelight.

Tutored at home, Mossadeq inherited the title al-Saltaneh in 1895 when his father died. At the time he was only thirteen. He spent four years apprenticed to his elder brother as a court *mostowfi*; and then was appointed *mostowfi* of the province of Khurasan. His memoirs reveal a tinge of nostalgia for the old administrative system:

There was always a reasonable balance between revenues and expenditures. The public servants of the country were not particularly well informed; nor did they have all the expert knowledge needed for a good modern government. Nevertheless, they managed to administer the country in their own way, according to their own peculiar sense of wisdom and disposition; and by their faith in the survival of the country. They did manage to turn the wheels in the right direction without the need to beg for money from foreigners.[63]

As a young aristocrat sympathetic to the constitutional cause and as a secret member of the liberal Society of Humanity, formed mostly of Ashtiyani families, Mossadeq was, at the age of twenty-five, elected to represent the "nobility" of Isfahan in the first Majles—the first electoral law that divided the population into classes. Not meeting the required age of thirty, he was unable to take his seat. He spent the next decade working in the finance administration and studying in Europe—first finance at the school of political science in Paris and then law at Neuchâtel University in Switzerland. He wrote his thesis on the role of wills in Shi'i law. He returned home on the eve of the outbreak of World War I. While in Europe, he developed ulcers and stomach ailments that would plague him for the rest of his life. His fainting spells, for which he became famous, were due to his inability to eat full meals. This ailment may have also contributed to his reluctance to socialize even though he was very gregarious, witty, and engaging. His son reminisces that he rarely "socialized" and had "few friends of his own age."[64]

During World War I, Mossadeq built up a reputation as a reformist intellectual. While teaching law at the School of Political Science in Tehran, he wrote three handbooks: *Capitulations and Iran*, arguing for the abolition of these nineteenth-century concessions; *Procedural Orders in Civil Courts*, advocating judicial reforms; and *Joint Stock Companies in Europe*, spelling out rights of private corporations in the West. He also contributed articles to *Majaleh 'Elmi* (Scientific Journal), a literary magazine favoring reform, and to *Seda-ye Iran* (Voice of Iran), a nationalist periodical opposed to the Anglo-Russian occupation. Some clerics criticized him when he published a piece favoring the adoption of the Western concept of a statute of limitations. It was deemed to contradict the *shari'a*. In his reminiscences he wrote, "I was perturbed that, after all the education I had received, I was not able to express my opinions, and was being subjected to misplaced and unjustified criticism. I wondered how on earth I could use my knowledge to serve my country." [65] In later years, he published two additional books: *Parliamentary Law in Iran and Europe* and *Principles of the Laws of Taxation Abroad and in Iran Before the Constitutional Movement.*

In the post–World War I era, when cabinets lasted on average less than four months, Mossadeq held a series of high posts: justice minister (1919), governor of Fars (1920), finance minister (1921), governor of Azerbaijan (1923), and foreign minister (1923). He was also elected from Tehran to the fifth and sixth Majles (1924–1928). From these positions, he enhanced his reputation as an outspoken and incorruptible politician. As finance minister, he trimmed waste, sinecures, and even the court budget.[66] As Fars governor, he denounced the 1921 coup led by Sayyed Ziya Tabatabai and Col. Reza Khan—the future Reza Shah. He had to take refuge with the Bakhtiyari tribes. He also denounced the 1919 Anglo-Iranian Agreement, accusing Premier Vossuq al-Dawleh, who happened to be his relative, of trying to turn Iran into a "British protectorate." [67] The British Legation labeled him "a demagogue" and "windbag who talks a lot of nonsense." [68] He initially supported Reza Khan becoming premier and commander-in-chief, expecting him to initiate extensive reforms; but opposed him becoming monarch on the grounds that such concentration of power would make a mockery of the constitution. He was one of the few deputies willing to openly oppose the offering of the crown to Reza Khan.

For much of Reza Shah's reign Mossadeq was confined to Ahmadabad. He was not permitted to speak, write, or travel outside the village. He was even imprisoned and banished to northern Khurasan in 1940. This internal banishment, however, lasted only fifteen days. Ernest Perron, a Swiss childhood friend of the crown prince who happened to be a patient of Mossadeq's son, a doctor, interceded and persuaded the shah to return Mossadeq back to Ahmadabad. The Anglo-Soviet invasion a few months later ended Reza Shah's reign.

Mossadeq reentered politics in the fourteenth Majles— the first to be freely elected since 1925. Competing for the twelve most prestigious seats in Tehran, he swept in first in a race of more than thirty prominent candidates—many of them courtiers, religious dignitaries, and wealthy landlords. Having a lively press and electorate, the capital's twelve seats were the most prestigious in the country. The young shah, fearful of an assertive parliament, quietly offered Mossadeq the premiership on condition he "nullified" the elections. Mossadeq replied he would do so only if he could hold a referendum for a new electoral law limiting the undue influence of landlords and government officials, especially military commanders. He later revealed he suspected the shah's offer was a ruse to deprive him of his seat, since ministers could not also sit in Parliament. Sir Reader Bullard, the British ambassador, was also cool to the whole idea. He considered Mossadeq to be too "touchy" and "nationalistic." He also suspected the shah's real aim was to pack a new Majles with his own placemen. "I fear," he added, "that what the

Shah wants is not a better parliament but more subservient deputies."[69] This little-known backstage politicking was a harbinger of the future complex relationships between the shah, Mossadeq, and the British.

In the turbulent fourteenth Majles (1944–46), Mossadeq acted as the main spokesman for some thirty backbenchers who constituted a loose group known as the Fraksiun-e Monafardin (Independent Caucus). They distanced themselves from other caucuses formed by courtiers, tribal chiefs, Tudeh leaders, pro-British landlords from the south, and pro-Russian landlords from the north. Mossadeq's frequent speeches, always eloquent but sometimes long, enhanced his national reputation. He tried to prevent Sayyed Ziya from taking his seat from Yazd—a town under British occupation. He explained he was breaking his long silence on the 1921 coup because of the urgency of drawing attention to the continued danger of British imperialism. Mossadeq, like many Iranians and even British diplomats, saw Sayyed Ziya as the most Anglophile of the old-time politicians. Unbeknownst to them, Sayyed Ziya, while in exile in Palestine during the war, had established contacts with fascist Italy, receiving money and promising an oil concession in northern Iran.[70] Sayyed Ziya was more a right-wing opportunist than a British "agent."

Mossadeq also expressed some admiration—couched in subtle warnings—for the young shah. He thanked him for cutting short his internal exile and reminded him that his oath of office taken before Parliament was to the written constitution. He also reminded the deputies that their oath was not to the person of the shah but to the constitutional monarchy. The constitution, he stressed, clearly stipulated the monarch's role was purely ceremonial. "If the shah," he warned, "gets involved in politics then he can be held responsible. If he is responsible, then he can be held accountable."

He often repeated the saying "The Monarch Should Reign, Not Rule." In many ways he was an Iranian version of a nineteenth-century English Whig. Contrary to his reputation as an angry Anglophobe, he had great admiration for Britain precisely because he saw its constitutional monarchy as the integral part of its parliamentary democracy. "The English nation," he argued "is the most self-sacrificing, most understanding, most patriotic of all nations precisely because it has enjoyed freedom for centuries." [71] Unable to distinguish between his opposition to British imperialism and admiration for their constitutionalism, American policymakers found him erratic and inconsistent. Averell Harriman—Truman's special emissary to Iran—had trouble understanding how Mossadeq could vehemently denounce the British oil company yet send his grandchildren to England for schooling.[72] This reinforced Harriman's view that Mossadeq was a character straight out of *Alice in Wonderland*. The problem, however, lay less in Mossadeq than in American perceptions.

Mossadeq also favored many of Reza Shah's reforms—including his extension of rights to women as long as they retained the choice of wearing the veil. He also continued to call for a new electoral law with one-day balloting, with independent monitors to check the influence of landlords and government officials, with more weight given to literates since "illiterates could be easily manipulated by landlords," and with increased representation for the urban centers, especially Tehran." [73] He proposed to increase the capital's representation to twenty-five. He noted that for twenty-five years there had been no occupying powers in Iran yet there had been no "free elections." When the House refused to discuss electoral reform, he walked out, denouncing it as a "den of thieves" who had bought their seats. The following day, a crowd of university students carried him back to the chamber. In the ensuing melée the police killed one student.

Mossadeq's close bond with the university students was
forged in these early years of the fourteenth Majles.

Mossadeq's main interest, however, lay in foreign policy.[74]
He argued that past politicians, including the Qajar monarchs, had blundered in thinking they could mollify the two
"neighboring" powers by giving them equal concessions.
He equated this to an amputee who imagines he can balance the loss of one arm by giving up the other. He termed
it the policy of "positive equilibrium." Some, he also argued,
tried to balance the two by tempting in a third power, such as
France, Germany, or the United States. Such policies, however, had merely whetted predatory appetites. The logical
result had been the 1907 partition of Iran. Similar danger
loomed again, since foreign armies were in actual occupation of the country. To prevent a repeat of history, Mossadeq
favored strict neutrality, arguing that the major powers
would be willing to leave the country alone if they were assured that none would enjoy special advantages. He called
this the policy of "negative equilibrium"—the Iranian version of neutralism and nonalignment. In arguing his case,
he singled out the 1933 oil agreement. He denounced it for
extending the D'Arcy Concession, giving the foreign firm in-
ordinate influence in internal politics, and, most dangerous
of all, enticing others to seek similar concessions.[75]

Mossadeq found the opportunity to articulate this policy
as early as September 1944, when the Soviet Union publicly demanded an oil concession in northern Iran. But this
demand—which some pinpoint as the very start of the
Cold War in Iran—was itself prompted by rumors in the
Majles that representatives from Western companies were
in Tehran actively seeking secret new oil deals. These rumors were soon verified by the Foreign Office and State Department. In September 1943—a full year before the Soviet

demand—Standard Vacuum, owned jointly by Standard Oil of New Jersey and Socony-Vacuum, had quietly initiated negotiations for a concession in the southeastern province of Baluchestan. It had done so in opposition to the U.S. minister in Tehran, who felt such negotiations would threaten Allied relations, but with the support of Washington, worried that American home resources were fast depleting.[76] Hot on the footsteps of Standard Vacuum came Sinclair Oil and Royal Dutch Shell—the Foreign Office and the State Department treated Royal Dutch Shell as British.[77] Their negotiations soon expanded from Baluchestan to other parts of Iran, including the provinces on the Soviet border. The British expressed concern that the Americans were trespassing into their territory. They were also "most anxious for Shell to get a concession since it would provide [a] valuable source for sterling."[78]

The British embassy reported that the American ambassador as well as Herbert Hoover, son of the former president, were actively lobbying on behalf of the U.S. companies and urging them to outbid Shell by offering a 50/50 deal. A Foreign Office expert later commented cryptically that the whole crisis could have been avoided if "the parties had followed the advice of doing a secret deal with the Americans."[79] The State Department, for its part, warned that British interests were becoming "most importunate" and urged more should be done on behalf of the American companies.[80] The U.S. embassy reported that the shah and prime minister both favored the American companies and intended to give Standard Oil a concession in the north—but only after the war, when Soviet troops had left Iran.[81] In July 1944, the American charge d'affaires urged the secretary of state to take a strong stand over the issue not just because of the importance of Iranian oil itself but also because of the

potentialities of the local markets for American goods and
for the "long-range protection of our oil concessions on the
Arabian side of the Persian Gulf."[82]

The Soviet demands—coming three months later—
caused considerable soul searching. The British consul in
Mashed later wrote in his memoirs that what had turned
"Russia from hot-war ally to cold-war rival" was the "vig-
orous American intervention to capture the Persian market,
especially the efforts of Socony-Vacuum to secure oil pros-
pecting rights."[83] Another Foreign Office expert complained
privately the State Department had "done its best" to "create a scare about the Soviet menace" with a series of "sen-
sational reports."[84] The U.S. embassy speculated that the
probable aim of the Russians was not to actually get the
oil for themselves but to "keep others out of the north."[85]
Similarly, George Kennan, the American charge d'affaires
in Moscow and architect of the policy of containment during
the Cold War, informed the secretary of state:

> The basic motive of recent Soviet action in northern Iran
> is probably not need for oil itself but apprehension of po-
> tential foreign penetration in that area coupled with the
> concern for prestige. The oil of northern Iran is important
> not as something Russia needs but as something it might
> be dangerous for anyone else to exploit. The territory lies
> near the vital Caucasian oil center which so closely es-
> caped complete conquest in the present war. The Kremlin
> deems it essential to its security that no other great power
> should have even the chance of getting a foothold there. It
> probably sees no other way to assure this than by seeking
> greater political and economic control for itself.[86]

In short, what triggered the first Cold War crisis in Iran
was not the Soviet oil demand in 1944 but the secret bids by

American and British companies in 1943 to obtain their own oil concessions—especially in northern Iran.

The Iranian government tried to diffuse the crisis by promising to grant no oil concessions until after the war. The Soviets, however, suspected—rightly—this to be merely a ruse. They persisted with their oil demand; delayed withdrawing troops; encouraged Kurds and Azeris to stage ethnic revolts; helped them set up provincial—not secessionist—governments; and insisted on having a prime minister in Tehran they could work with. They even named Ahmad Qavam (Qavam al-Saltaneh) as such a prime minister. A statesman in and out of high office ever since the 1905 revolution—the proclamation granting the nation a constitution had been in his masterful calligraphic handwriting—Qavam had the aura of being the most skillful, pragmatic, and scheming of all veteran politicians. He had wheeled and dealed with Britain, America, and Russia—both Tsarist and Soviet. Coming from the same social background as Mossadeq—they were distant cousins—Qavam was in many ways the exact opposite. While Mossadeq was deemed honest and straightforward, Qavam had the reputation of being slippery and Machiavellian. While the former was an orator who enjoyed the public arena and the limelight, the latter liked to work behind the scenes making secret and opaque deals. While the former was considered incorruptible, the latter relished the aura of being able to offer all things to all men. While the former lived an austere life, the latter flaunted his high life and landed wealth, especially his tea plantations in Gilan. While the former was seen as a "man of the people," the latter was reputed to be so haughty, his office had no visitors' chairs so that all—even members of the royal family—had to stand in his presence. What is more, while the former championed the policy of "negative equilibrium," the latter in many ways epitomized that of "positive equilibrium." Vossuq al-Dawleh, the premier responsible for the notorious 1919 Anglo-Iranian Agreement, happened to be Qavam's older brother.

Although Mossadeq drastically differed from Qavam on foreign policy, he nevertheless voted to elect him prime minister in 1946 on the grounds that only Qavam was capable of negotiating a Soviet withdrawal. But to tie Qavam's hands, Mossadeq sponsored a bill forbidding all government officials—premiers as well as ministers and undersecretaries—from negotiating oil agreements with any foreign entities. This became known as Mossadeq's law. In introducing the bill, Mossadeq declared that he was fully in favor of developing the oil industry and exporting petroleum to all countries that needed it—including America and the Soviet Union, but that the development had to be "in our national hands." The implication of this statement was not missed at the British embassy.

Qavam submitted his cabinet to Parliament on the very last day of the fourteenth Majles. A few hours later he flew off to Moscow to negotiate with Stalin and Molotov. He informed them that because of the recent law he could not sign any oil agreement but could propose such an agreement to the next Majles when it convened. He also pointed out that another recent law stipulated that elections for the next Majles could not be held until all foreign troops had evacuated Iran. The British embassy in Moscow—which seems to have had access to these private conversations—reported that Britain was "lucky" that these recent laws, especially Mossadeq's bill, had "tied Qavam's hands." [87]

Qavam soon obtained an agreement. The Soviets agreed to withdraw troops within forty days, thus leaving the ethnic rebels to the mercies of the central government. Qavam, in return, agreed to submit a proposal for the formation of a Joint Soviet-Iranian Oil Company to the next Parliament within seven months of its convening. The proposal—covering all the northern provinces—came close to a 50/50 deal. In the first twenty-five years, the Soviets would hold 51 percent of the stock, Iran 49 percent. In the following twenty-five years, the percentages would be reversed. The Soviets would provide all the technicians and equipment.

The proposal caused consternation in the British and American embassies. The British warned that such a venture would increase Soviet influence throughout Iran; that they would dump surplus oil on the international market; that they would train local technicians; that they—unlike the AIOC—were not a business enterprise constrained by financial pressures; and that they could undermine the AIOC by cutting prices and attracting labor with better wages, housing, and work conditions. They also warned that these installations could eventually be passed into Iranian hands.[88] The Americans, meanwhile, feared that such a Soviet deal could kill "all possibility of an American oil concession, and, most important of all, threaten America's immensely rich oil holdings in Saudi Arabia, Bahrain, and Kuwait."[89]

Bullard, the outgoing British ambassador, warned that "appeasement" in the north would "in the last analysis threaten our vital oil supplies in the south."[90] Similarly, Sir John Rougetel, the incoming ambassador, reported that his American counterpart had received "instructions from the US oil companies as well as from the State Department to strongly oppose the Soviet deal."[91] He added that American geological experts were convinced there were vast oil reserves in northern Iran. The Foreign Office's final recommendation was that "Britain and the US should persuade the Iranian government to reject the agreement, and, at the same time, encourage it to give a concession to Shell for the south and invite [the] US to participate in such a concession."[92]

While the two Western powers encouraged Iran to reject

the Soviet deal, some had the foresight to realize that rejection could set a dangerous precedent and potentially threaten other oil interests. Qavam informed the American ambassador "in utmost confidence" that the Soviet agreement was long overdue since in the past Britain had been overly favored.[93] He promised the Americans an oil concession in Baluchestan, dismissing British bids for such a deal with the argument that the latter had got all the concessions they deserved. The American ambassador reported "this bears out his long record of favoring American enterprise in Iran."[94] He added that there were some UK diplomats who were greatly worried that if the Soviet deal was rejected, Iranians might contemplate nationalizing the British oil company.[95] The British ambassador himself warned London that "even though a Russian concession in the north is wrought with difficulties, its outright rejection could lead the Russians to try to secure AIOC cancellation, and they could well prove successful." Despite these warnings, the US eventually came down firmly against any Soviet concession arguing that such a deal would divide the country into "spheres of influence" as in 1907, and end up putting "more rather than less pressure against both British and eventually American petroleum positions in the Persian Gulf."[96]

Qavam did not submit the Soviet proposal to Parliament until late October 1947—almost a year after the Soviet withdrawal. The delay was caused by intense jockeying between the shah and prime minister over the control of the fifteenth Majles elections. Constituencies under martial law, such as reoccupied Azerbaijan and Kurdestan, not surprisingly elected court favorites. Those controlled by the interior minister elected Qavam supporters. And the many "rotten boroughs" scattered throughout the country returned their usual local notables—many of them in the south being pro-British landlords and tribal chiefs. Mossadeq, who had headed the

previous winners list in Tehran, as well as most of his adherents, were kept out. Qavam submitted the proposal to Parliament without either approving or disapproving it. After a
series of closed sessions, the deputies voted overwhelmingly
to reject it. They also voted not to hold Qavam accountable,
since he had not actually signed the agreement but had
merely agreed to submit the proposal to a future Parliament.

The British embassy was surprised that the Soviets received the rejection "remarkably well."[97] They seemed to
lick their wounds, withdraw into their shell, and take little
interest in the country in the next few years.[98] Qavam, however, lost control of the Majles and was forced to resign two
months later. In rejecting the Soviet proposal, the Majles
had passed a resolution forbidding the government to grant
a northern concession to any foreign entity. It also urged the
government to "initiate negotiations to redeem the rights
of the nation over the resources of the country, both below
and above the ground, especially regarding oil in the south."
Again the import of this resolution was registered by some
in the Foreign Office.[99] The Soviet withdrawal had been
brought about not by A-bomb threats as some at the time
claimed but by Qavam's old-fashioned juggling act. And the
Soviet agreement had been sabotaged not so much by design
as by the general sentiment that vital resources should be
under national sovereignty. Even some Tudeh leaders, while
outwardly supporting the Soviets on account of "socialist
solidarity," had privately from the very beginning expressed
misgivings over the whole issue of giving a concession to a
foreign power.[100]

The most far-reaching fallout from the rejection of the
Soviet concession was the launching of negotiations to revise
the 1933 agreement with the Anglo-Iranian Oil Company.
Some in Britain, however, missed the significance. The British ambassador dismissed the resolution as "imparting to the

act a more general complexion," and a "typical Iranian way of softening the rebuff to Russians." Likewise, the oil company felt confident it enjoyed "goodwill throughout in the country"—after all, it reassured itself, it had just generously donated £150,000 to Tehran University.

The new negotiations were launched by Qavam himself in November 1947, just one month after the Majles resolution. They were continued—of course, behind closed doors—by his three immediate successors: Ibrahim Hakimi (January to June 1948), Abdul-Hussein Hezher (June to November 1948) and Muhammad Saed (November 1948 to March 1950). These negotiations eventually, in July 1949, produced the highly controversial Supplementary Agreement, also known as the Gass-Saed Agreement—named after Saed, who signed on behalf of Iran and Neville Gass on that of the company. The agreement, of course, required parliamentary ratification.

In the long, drawn-out negotiations, the AIOC initially rejected a 50/50 deal, dismissing it as "exorbitant" and claiming it was "impossible to calculate" since the company derived profits from many other sources. "The Company," the Foreign Office reported, "thinks the 50% formula is unworkable and would give Iran 33 shillings per ton—a figure far beyond even the highest bids of speculators in Middle Eastern oil concessions." [101] The company instead offered to improve the 1933 concession by raising payments from 4 shillings to 6 shillings per ton of exports; and by calculating Iran's 20 percent share of profits before British taxes—not after, as done since 1933. The company also promised that annual royalties would not fall below £4 million. At one point, it threatened to withhold royalty payments until the prime minister speeded up the submission of the agreement to Parliament.

Max Thornburg, a former adviser to Standard Oil and the

State Department who had been employed by the Iranian government as an economic consultant since 1946, urged the prime ministers not to sign. "The proposals," he argued, "were drafted so obscurely and so ambiguously that no one in the world could have known where the Persian government would have been left if it had signed the agreement." [102] He recommended holding out for the "50/50 principle," and himself took a rushed trip to London to "make clear to the AIOC board of directors that what faced them in Persia was not mere stubbornness or Oriental bargaining shrewdness but a rising tide of inflamed hostility among the people of the country toward not only the Company but whatever elements of responsible government still existed." He admitted that his London trip had not been a success.

Even members of the British government expressed—of course, in private—dismay at the AIOC. A senior minister in the Labour cabinet feared that Britain ran the risk of appearing "too imperialistic," since the existing division of profits was "too unjust" and the position of the oil company was "too intransigent." [103] He added that even though the AIOC was a private company, it was too important to be left to its own devices. The U.S. State Department was even more critical, arguing that the AIOC should follow the Venezuela model based on the 50/50 deal. George McGhee, the assistant secretary of state, went so far as to describe the Supplementary Agreement as a "raw deal." He dismissed as "spurious" the company claim that it would not be able to calculate such division of profits. He also noted that production costs in Iran were far less than in Venezuela.

The oil company view was summed up by an unsigned article in *The Economist*. The author was probably Elizabeth Monroe, professor of History at London University. The article argued that the company offer was highly generous— guaranteeing annual royalties of £22 million, but that Iran had refused because its "ignorant townspeople had been led astray by its corrupt and avaricious rulers."[104] This became the British mantra throughout the crisis.

Years later, Sam Falle, a Foreign Office expert on Iran, admitted that the failure of these early negotiations was in part because of the "stubborn" attitude of the company's "Scottish management," and in part because of the British government's need to extract as much tax money as possible from the oil industry. He later wrote that Britain had been sitting on a smoldering "volcano."[105] Sam Falle was nicknamed Sam the Red within the diplomatic service because he felt that the age of empire had ended. George Middleton, the British charge d'affaires in 1952, later admitted the company had refused to take the nationalization campaign seriously because it was convinced the Iranians were incapable of running the facilities—a conviction that proved to be false.[106] It was in describing these early bargaining tactics by the British oil company that Dean Acheson, the U.S. secretary of state, made his famous statement: "Never had so few lost so much so stupidly in so short a time."

Nationalization Campaign

Mossadeq again reentered politics in the sixteenth Majles elections. He campaigned on two main themes: free elections and oil nationalization. His closest advisers were twelve young, mostly French-educated, professionals: Dr. Ali Shayegan, Hussein Fatemi, Hussein Makki, Abdullah Moazemi, Baqer Kazemi, Karem Sanjabi, Kazem Hassebi, Ahmad Zirakzadeh, Ahmad Razavi, Mahmud Nariman, Allayar Saleh, and Shams al-Din Amir-Alai. They constituted his inner circle (*dowreh*). Many remained with him through thick and thin until the very end in August 1953—and some even beyond.

Shayegan, a professor at Tehran University, was

Mossadeq's lawyer. He had known Mossadeq since his childhood—his father had befriended Mossadeq when the latter had been governor of Fars. The son of a minor cleric in Shiraz, Shayegan was a *sayyed*, although he rarely used the title, which denoted he was a male descendant of the Prophet. He had been among the first batch of students sent to France by Reza Shah. He returned with a law degree from the University of Lyon and taught at Tehran University, where he eventually became dean of the law faculty. Although one of Mossadeq's closest advisers, Shayegan had served Qavam as his minister of education in 1946. He continued to keep in touch with him. Such contacts could always come in handy.

Fatemi, the only National Front leader to be executed after the coup, was the editor of *Bakhtar-e Emruz* (Today's West)—the organ of the National Front. Son of an ayatollah in Na'in and a *sayyed* who also rarely used the title, Fatemi had attended an English missionary school in Isfahan and worked briefly in the British consulate before going to France to study journalism. He was the only newspaper editor with a degree in journalism from Europe. His elder brother was a prominent pro-British politician who, for a while, had been mayor of Isfahan and had created yellow unions to fight the Tudeh Party. Even though Hussein Fatemi had impeccable anticommunist credentials, a top British diplomat categorized him as a "Moscow trained ideologue" because of his tendency in discussing the oil issue to cite "endless facts and figures." [107] The same diplomat often complained that Mossadeq had the tendency to avoid specifics and talk only in generalities.

Makki, an orator, entered the fifteenth Majles as Qavam's protégé but soon became Mossadeq's emissary delivering his messages on the oil issue. As such, he led a long filibuster against the Supplementary Agreement so that the bill would not be voted on until the sixteenth Majles, where Mossadeq hoped to have more supporters. He soon edited a collection of Mossadeq's earlier speeches. The son of a bazaar merchant, Makki later turned to history writing and became famous for his conspiratorial explanations of twentieth-century Iran. He wrote a series of bestsellers entitled *Tarekh-e Best Saleh* (Twenty-Year History), *Ketab-e Siyah* (Black Book), *Modarres: Qahreman-e Azadi* (Modarres: The Hero of Freedom), and *Khaterat-e Siyasi* (Political Memoirs). He was one of the few among the twelve without a Western degree. He was also one of the few who later broke from Mossadeq. Months before this defection, the British embassy predicted that Makki—because of his "opportunism"—would "undoubtedly desert" Mossadeq if he could obtain "acceptable terms from his successor."[108]

The other nine were all members of the Iran Party. The party had grown out of the Engineers Association in 1944 and modeled itself on the moderate Socialist Party in France. The Engineers Association itself had been launched in 1942 soon after Reza Shah's abdication. Moazemi, a French-educated law professor, came from a landed and titled family in Golpayegan. He had represented that constituency in the fourteenth Majles, where he had joined the Independent Caucus. Kazemi, educated in United States, also came from a wealthy titled family. He sat in the fourteenth Majles and had a long career in the diplomatic corps serving both as ambassador and foreign minister. Sanjabi, another French-educated law professor, had been among the first batch of state scholars sent to Europe. He came from the leading Kurdish Shi'i tribe in Kermanshah. During World War I, the Sanjabis had given refuge to the national leaders who had refused to accept the Anglo-Russian occupation.

Hassebi, Mossadeq's main adviser on technical matters, came from a modest bazaar background. He also had been among the first batch of students sent to Europe. He had studied first civil engineering in France, then petroleum engineering in Britain and Czechoslovakia. Teaching geology at Tehran University, he had been a founding member of the Engineers Association. He lived modestly outside Tehran, commuting to the city by bus. When he joined the cabinet, Mossadeq ordered him to install a phone in his home so that he could be reached. The British embassy described him as "fanatically anti-British" and "one of the worst" with "a crazy look in his eyes." [109]

Zirakzadeh, another founding member of the Engineers Association, also taught at Tehran University and had studied mechanical engineering in Paris. Razavi—another *sayyed* who did not use his title—came from a wealthy landed family in Kerman and represented that constituency in the Majles. Like many of his colleagues, he had studied in France and had been a founding member of the Engineers Association. He made a name in the fifteenth Majles by audaciously denouncing the armed forces for inefficiency, corruption, and political meddling. Nariman—another *sayyed* who forsook the title—was a career civil servant and former mayor of Tehran. Son of the manager of the Imperial Bank, he had studied economics mostly in Switzerland. He served as Mossadeq's main adviser on financial matters. The British embassy deemed him "perverse" and "self-opinionated." [110]

Saleh, Mossadeq's main adviser on relations with the United States and ambassador to Washington, was a senior civil servant who had sat in a number of cabinets after 1941. The son of a wealthy landed family in Kashan, he represented that constituency in the sixteenth Majles. As a young student at the American school in Tehran, he had distributed leaflets denouncing the 1919 Anglo-Iranian Agreement. Finally, Amir-Alai, a Mossadeq family confidant, came from an aristocratic Qajar family and had a long career in the ministries of justice, finance, and interior. A graduate of the Tehran

Lycée, he had attended the University of Montpellier. He, like many of the others in the group, was a long-standing member of the Iran Party.

In short, Mossadeq's inner circle was formed predominantly of young French-educated professionals from the Iran Party. The British embassy described the Iran Party as "middle class," "nationalistic," and constituting Mossadeq's "inner core." [111] It added: "They represent the views of a large section of the electorate and there is no doubt that in a free election they could win a large number of seats." Years later, Falle of the Foreign Office wrote in his memoirs that Mossadeq's main support came from the middle class but he enjoyed "tremendous popular support because he was a brilliant demagogue and a sincere and honest patriot": "He was non-violent and really was a powerhouse because people loved him, wanted him, and saw him as a sort of Iranian Mahatma Gandhi." [112]

Mossadeq reentered politics on October 15, 1949, with a dramatic scene highlighting ballot rigging in the sixteenth Majles elections. He led a peaceful procession from his house in northern Tehran at 109 Kakh Street (Palace Street) to the nearby royal Kakh Marmar (Marble Palace) protesting ballot stuffing by the interior ministry and the armed forces. He announced the demonstration had only one slogan— silence—and would scrupulously observe Gandhi's principle of nonviolence. *Ettela'at*, the establishment paper, claimed the demonstration numbered only 180. Photos, however, show several thousand.[113] Most were clean-shaven and wearing ties, white shirts, and business suits. When an unshaven man shouted he had dreamt Mossadeq would soon establish a republic, Mossadeq had him removed and later described him as a police agent provocateur.[114]

At the palace gates, the court minister, Hezher, after some bargaining, permitted twenty into the royal gardens.

Mossadeq had threatened to take *bast* (sanctuary) at a major mosque or shrine—such a *bast* had sparked the famous constitutional revolution. The new protest became known as the Palace Garden Sit-In. Lasting four full days and nights, it ended only when the shah, threatened by a hunger strike, promised fair and honest elections. Shayegan wrote that their aim was to transform the "defective" and "sham" democracy into a real one by strengthening the electoral system, restricting martial law, keeping the armed forces out of the whole process, and strengthening the independence of the press.[115]

The twenty included Mossadeq and seven close associates: Shayegan, Fatemi, Nariman, Makki, Sanjabi, Amir-Alai, and Zirakzadeh. Another six were prominent gadfly politicians who first supported but then opposed Mossadeq: Dr. Muzaffar Baqai, a French-educated philosopher from a well-known Kerman family; Sayyed Abdul-Hussein Haerizadeh, a former judge and critique of Reza Shah in the fourth, fifth, sixth, and fourteenth Majles; Abdul-Qader Azad, a veteran politician who had spent ten years in Reza Shah's prisons and now edited *Azad* (Freedom); Ahmad Maleki, the long-time editor of the muckraking *Setareh* (Star); Abul-Hassan Amidi-Nouri, a trial lawyer and editor of another muckraking paper, *Dad* (Justice); and Abbas Khaleli, editor of *Eqdam* (Action), who had fled Iraq in the early 1920s after the anti-British revolt. The other six were less-known figures—many of them professionals.[116] Thus the group reinforced the image that Mossadeq's circle was formed predominantly of middle-class professionals with some of them coming originally from prominent families—some of whom had been active in politics before Reza Shah.

Immediately after the sit-in, the lead protestors met in Mossadeq's home and announced the formation of the Je'beh-e Melli (National Front).[117] They elected Mossadeq as chairman and Shayegan, Nariman, Amir-Alai, and Sanjabi as a temporary executive committee. They also elected a publicity committee formed of Fatemi, editor of *Bakhtar-e Emruz*; Zirakzadeh, editor of *Iran*—the Iran Party organ; Khaleli, editor of *Eqdam*; Muhammad Reza Jalali-Naini, editor of *Keshvar* (Country); Amidi-Nouri, editor of *Dad*; Maleki, editor of *Setareh*; and Baqai, who soon launched his own paper, *Shahed* (Witness). Fatemi was assigned the task of drawing up the statutes and platform for the whole organization.

The platform stressed the need for honest elections, a free press, the end of martial law, and proper implementation of the 1906 constitution. The statutes invited "patriotic organizations," not individuals, to join the National Front. It explained that the National Front was not a conventional party formed of individual members but a broad alliance of like-minded associations.[118] This conformed to Mossadeq's long-standing position that structured parties with strict discipline and elaborate programs were not suited for Iran. Moreover, he saw himself as the spokesman for the whole country—not just for any one particular party.

In the weeks to come, the National Front accepted into its fold the Iran Party and a number of professional organizations, led by the Lawyers Guild, the University Professors Association, the Engineers Association, and the Union of Bazaar Guilds and Tradesmen. And in the months to come, it gained the support of Baqai's Toilers Party (Hezb-e Zahmatkeshan) and Ayatollah Sayyed Abul-Qassem Kashani's Assembly of Muslim Warriors (Majmah-e Musulman-e Mojaheden).

Baqai had formed the Toilers Party by joining together with Khalel Maleki, a former Tudeh leader. An old-time Marxist educated in the Weimar Republic, Khalel Maleki saw himself as a militant but anti-Soviet radical. He had broken with the Tudeh and the Soviets over the oil demands and the ethnic rebellions in Kurdestan and Azerbaijan. He

has been described as the Iranian Tito. Thus, the Toilers
Party from its very inception contained two very different
elements: Khalel Maleki with his university-educated Marxists; and Baqai with his personal following both from his
hometown of Kerman and from the lower segments of the
Tehran bazaar—especially from *lutis* frequenting traditional
zurkhanehs (gymnasiums). For some, *lutis* were toughs no
better than *chaqukeshan* (cutthroats). For others, they were
well-built lads protecting their neighborhoods.[119] It was rumored that Baqai had a special fondness for these lads. The
British embassy claimed that Baqai's "main contribution to
Persian politics has been a gang of toughs who have been
used to intimidate National Front opponents and break up
their premises."[120] The Toilers Party mustered at its height
no more than five thousand members.

Ayatollah Kashani was the most prominent cleric active in
politics. Better known for political activities than theological
standing, Kashani implicitly ignored the advice given to all
clerics by Grand Ayatollah Sayyed Hussein Boroujerdi—the
paramount theologian—to shun politics. The son of a senior
cleric in Najaf, Kashani had been educated there and participated in the famous 1920 Shi'i revolt against the British. His
father was reputed to have been "martyred" in that revolt.[121]
After 1920, Kashani had found refuge in Iran together with
a number of Shi'i clerics. As member of the Constituent Assembly in 1925, he had voted to bestow the crown on Reza
Shah but then kept a low profile for the rest of his reign. He
was interned in 1944–45 by the British for having links to
the Germans. He was rearrested in 1946 by Qavam for organizing protests against the rigging of the fifteenth Majles
elections. He was rearrested once again in February 1949
when a photographer working for his paper, *Parcham-e Islam* (Flag of Islam), shot and wounded the shah. The shah
took quick advantage of the assassination attempt to declare

martial law, convene another Constituent Assembly, and obtain the authority both to dissolve the Majles and to establish a senate—half of whose sixty members he could name. He also took the opportunity to outlaw the Tudeh Party and issue arrest warrants not only for Kashani but also for a number of prominent opponents, including Qavam.

This time Kashani was exiled to Beirut. He was not permitted to return until June 1950, after winning a seat in the sixteenth Majles. In his absence, his electoral campaign was managed by his seven sons and Sayyed Shams al-Din Qonatabadi, a preacher-turned-businessman. Kashani's main constituency lay in the Tehran bazaar, especially among bakers and confectioners. His proclamations freely used secular terminology—terms such as "colonialism," "imperialism," "national sovereignty," "economic exploitation," "democracy," "nation," "free elections," and "respect for the 1906 constitution." They denounced the "regime" for "corruption," "luxury," "subservience to foreign powers," and failure to adequately oppose the imperial powers on such issues as Palestine, Kashmir, Algeria, Tunisia, Egypt, and even Ireland.[122]

Kashani was distrusted by apolitical clerics such Boroujerdi, as well as by royalist ones such as Ayatollah Sayyed Muhammad Behbehani—son of one of the two senior clerics who had supported the constitutional revolution. The British described the younger Behbehani as a court retainer.[123] Despite their differences, most clerics—including Boroujerdi and Behbehani—publicly welcomed Kashani's return. But a widely circulated pamphlet entitled "A Muslim Call" insinuated that Kashani received money from dubious Indian sources, "married a different woman every night," and collaborated with "adulterers, fire worshipers, and sodomites."[124] The British embassy described him as "a bitter enemy" but added that since "he and his sons were venal they can easily be detached from Musaddiq by any rival prepared to pay enough." [125] Kashani was as controversial in his own day as in later decades.

Kashani had tenuous ties with Fedayan-e Islam (Devotees of Islam)—one of the first real fundamentalist groups in the Islamic world. Formed in 1944 by Sayyed Navab-Safavi, a seminary dropout, members of the Fedayan-e Islam stood out because of two marked features. First, they demanded full implementation of the *shari'a* (Islamic law) in both private and public life. Obsessed with the issues of crime, alcohol, and women, they presented Islam as the "solution" to all of Iran's problems. "Criminals," the Fedayan insisted, "should not be coddled in 'rest homes' but should have their hands cut off, and if they persisted in their sins should be executed." [126] Second, they were willing to assassinate anyone they deemed to be un- or anti-Islamic. In 1946, they had knifed to death Sayyed Ahmad Kasravi, the country's leading historian, because he had questioned the Shi'i account of early Islam. The assassin was given amnesty because of the intercession of conservative politicians eager to use the group against the Tudeh. In 1949—a few weeks after the palace sit-in, the Fedayan shot to death Abdul-Hussein Hezher, the court minister, with the charge that he was an apostate—a secret Baha'i. This time the assassin was promptly hanged, producing the first "martyr" for the group. It was thought the Fedayan would not have carried out such assassinations without formal *fatwas* (edicts) from a senior religious authority, such as Kashani. But Navab-Safavi deemed himself such an authority qualified to issue death sentences. Although these and future assassinations gave the Fedayan much publicity, their inner core contained no more than a handful of zealots. Their total membership was less than a hundred. Most were young semiliterate apprentices in the Tehran bazaar. While some senior clerics, such as Behbehani, saw them as a useful tool against the left, others, notably Boroujerdi, saw them as an embarrassment. Boroujerdi soon banned them outright from the Qom seminaries.

In the sixteenth Majles elections held in early 1950, the National Front won eleven seats. Mossadeq headed the victor's list in Tehran. Kashani, Shayegan, Baqai, Makki, Haerizadeh, and Nariman followed. Moazemi, Saleh, Razavi, and Azad won in their home towns of Golpayegan, Kashan, Kerman, and Sabzevar. The eleven promptly formed their National Caucus (Fraksiun-e Vatan). Kashani rarely participated in parliamentary meetings, deeming them inappropriate for a cleric of his standing. Instead he sent emissaries with august messages.

The National Front carried far more weight than the caucus. It had the force of public opinion; an impressive array of newspapers, professional organizations, bazaar guilds, and middle-class associations; and could fill the expansive Baharestan Square outside Parliament with crowds totaling as many as thirty thousand. Consequently, few politicians dared to publicly oppose it—especially on the potent issue of oil nationalization. The British ambassador admitted that few deputies, even pro-British ones, were "willing to openly defend the new [Supplementary] oil agreement." [127] The Foreign Office added that recent prime ministers had been reluctant to bring the Supplementary Agreement to a vote. It added that even if Sayyed Ziya had been premier, he would be unwilling to sponsor it. [128] Even *Ettela'at*—funded by the court and run by the conservative Mas'oudi family—denounced the agreement and demanded a new one modeled on that of Venezuela. [129]

The National Front also received inadvertent and indirect support from the Tudeh Party. Although the Tudeh Party remained banned, it published an unofficial paper, *Besu-ye*

Ayandeh (Toward the Future), and set up an array of front organizations, each with its own paper—organizations such as the Peace Partisans, the Association Against the Imperialist Oil Company (later renamed the Association Against Imperialism), the Society to Aid Peasants, the Society against Illiteracy, the Women's Organization of Iran, and, most important of all, the Central Council of United Trade Unions. They received the endorsement of two clerics: Sheikh Ahmad Lankarani and Ayatollah Sayyed Ali-Akbar Borquei, known as the Red Ayatollah.

The British embassy reported that the Tudeh "dominated" the trade unions and gave Mossadeq "valuable support for his oil policy." It speculated that Mossadeq would accept Tudeh support as long as it suited him, since the latter was "the only organized political group which can lead and encourage the great mass of people to criticize and protest against prevailing conditions."[130] The Tudeh Party, for its part, supported the call for oil nationalization but criticized Mossadeq for being a "liberal bourgeois" with false illusions about America. Led by ultra-leftists during the early years of the oil crisis, the Tudeh viewed the National Front as representing not the "national bourgeoisie" but the "comprador bourgeoisie" linked to America. This ultra-left position was not abandoned until July 1952, when the Tudeh drew closer to Mossadeq and began to view him as a true national leader. However, some leaders of its youth organization continued to see him as being too close to the United States. Meanwhile, some National Front leaders continued to distrust the Tudeh for being too close to the Soviet Union.

With public support, the National Front elected six of its members—Mossadeq, Makki, Shayegan, Saleh, Nariman, and Haerizadeh—to a twelve-man Parliamentary Oil Committee assigned the task of examining the Supplementary

Agreement. Mossadeq was elected chair. The other six were unwilling to stick out their necks for the sake of Britain. The British ambassador later reported:

> By mid-June 1950, the National Front had acquired a moral ascendancy over the Majles and had achieved this simply by playing constantly and unscrupulously on xenophobia which is never far below the surface of most Persians. . . . When the Supplementary Agreement was placed on the agenda of the Majles members of the National Front secured places on the committee and Musaddiq was appointed its chair and Makki its rapporteur. Henceforth it was able to dominate the whole course of the oil question.[131]

This created political gridlock. The agreement needed Majles ratification, but before it could be ratified it needed the approval of the Oil Committee. Saed, who had signed the Supplementary Agreement, was forced to resign in March 1950—three months after the opening of the sixteenth Majles. His successor, Ali Mansur (al-Mulk), another old-time politician and prime minister under Reza Shah, lasted three months without signing or submitting the agreement to Parliament. The British embassy readily explained these delays by the supposed "Persian tendency to procrastinate." It claimed the Mansur administration needed "euthanasia," since it had failed to introduce social reforms, discipline the National Front, and, most important of all, submit the agreement to the Majles.[132] The embassy refused to admit to itself that the two premiers, as well as most establishment politicians, knew perfectly well the agreement would become even more unpopular once all its clauses were revealed.

At this point, the Foreign Office dismissed the National Front as a bunch of "noisy malcontents" trying to "bluff" the company into more concessions.[133] Sir Francis Shepherd, the new British ambassador, told the prime minister that the Supplementary Agreement was more than generous and that Iranian "greed" was preventing its ratification. "I told him," he flourished, "that the only thing I thought the Company might be willing to add to these concessions was perhaps the free medical treatment of certain deputies for the cure of hysteria."[134] Shepherd could compete with Reader Bullard, the wartime ambassador, in his use of blunt, nondiplomatic language. Having lived through the Indonesian independence struggle, Shepherd had been posted to Tehran with the promise that he would have an easy time in Iran since "we never have trouble with the natives there."[135] For some reason, the diplomatic service was under the impression that the "natives" in Iran did not have the habit of "beating the drums."

Unable to find thick-skinned politicians willing to sponsor the Supplementary Agreement, the shah—after much hesitation—turned to Gen. Ali Razmara, a no-nonsense man of action prepared to risk public antipathy. Razmara took office with the understanding he would submit the agreement to the Majles. The shah's hesitation came from his ingrained phobia about ambitious officers. His lifelong fear was that some officer would do to him what his father had done to the previous dynasty. He was especially wary of Razmara, who had a considerable following among younger left-leaning officers. The shah, in an earlier conversation with the British ambassador, had described Razmara as a "viper that must be crushed" because he was "disloyal, dishonest, and little better than a Russian agent."[136]

Razmara publicly opposed nationalization on the grounds Iran did not have the technical expertise to run the industry. At the same time, he quietly bargained for a better deal. The company dillydallied and eventually—after much pressure from the British and American governments and after the announcement of the 50/50 deal between Aramco and Saudi Arabia—made a verbal commitment to "consider" such a deal. The Foreign Office concluded that the Aramco deal had "killed" the Supplementary Agreement and that negotiations had to start again from "scratch." [137] The company's own labor adviser in London privately warned the Foreign Office that nationalization was now inevitable unless the company started fresh negotiations based on the 50/50 concept. He described his company directors as "helpless, niggling, without any ideas, confused, hide-bound, small minded, and blind." [138] George McGhee, the U.S. assistant secretary of state and himself an oil geologist, told the British foreign minister that Iran had "legitimate grievances"—especially about royalties being paid after taxes to Britain and after large sums had been put on reserve.[139] He estimated that Iran received as little as 37 cents per barrel, whereas Venezuela received as much as 77 cents.

These behind-the-scenes pressures, however, came too late. On March 7, before the company conceded its willingness to discuss a 50/50 agreement, the Fedayan assassinated General Razmara in the central mosque in Tehran. The Fedayan had taken Razmara's opposition to nationalization as evidence of him being a "British agent." Because of past tensions between him and the shah, rumors spread like wildfire that the palace had been behind the assassination. Homa Katouzian, a leading pro-Mossadeq historian, continues to accept the long, convoluted theory of how and why the shah—not the Fedayan—was really behind the assassination.[140] The shah, for his part, tried to take advantage of the crisis—as he had with the 1949 assassination attempt—to declare martial law, dissolve the two houses of Parliament, and call for new elections. But he was overruled by the leaders of the two houses—probably with the support of the

American and British ambassadors. Shepherd urged him to find a new premier instead and bring the Supplementary Agreement to ratification as soon as possible. He claimed the continued agitation against the oil company was distracting the country from its real problems and playing into the hands of the communists.[141] Max Thornburg, the American adviser, wrote: "A few days before Razmara's assassination the Company made a belated offer 'to discuss' a 50/50 arrangement. I was away from Tehran and knew nothing about this until after Razmara's death."[142] Unbeknownst to Thornburg, the British embassy at the very same time was trying to persuade the State Department to terminate his stay in Iran.[143]

The day after the assassination, Mossadeq got a unanimous vote in the Oil Committee rejecting the Supplementary Agreement. Simultaneously, he introduced into Parliament a one-article bill nationalizing the oil industry. It simply declared: "For the happiness and prosperity of the Iranian nation and for the purpose of securing world peace, it is hereby resolved that the oil industry throughout all parts of the country, without exception, be nationalized; that is to say, all operations of exploration, extraction, and exploitation shall be carried out by the government." A week later—on March 14—the Majles, with a large majority, accepted the bill. The discussions over how to revise the old agreement were now superceded with a far more radical demand. Despite the dire situation, the Foreign Office remained complacent. It claimed that the "nationalization cry" was not important, that Razmara had mishandled the Majles, that the deputies would accept the Supplementary Agreement once they "understood it," that the National Front had not really thought out the issue, and that public discontent was really directed at the shah—not at the oil company.[144]

To lower tensions, the shah called upon Hussein Ala (Mu'en al-Vezareh), his trusted court minister, to form a new

government and temper the National Front by offering it
some seats in the cabinet. Although Ala had been educated in
England and came from an old Anglophile family, the British
embassy deemed him a "little nigger in the woodpile" who
on some days echoed the views of the shah and other days
acted as the "voice of America." [145] Consulting Mossadeq, Ala
gave the justice ministry to Amir-Alai, and the education
ministry to Ahmad Zanganeh, a technocrat close to the Iran
Party. The British ambassador saw Ala as a "caretaker" to be
replaced soon by a more forceful personality—either Qavam
or Sayyed Ziya.[146] Just as Ala was putting together his cabinet
and wooing the National Front, the country was shaken by a
massive general strike throughout the oil industry.

The Oil Strike

The general strike of April 1951 matched that of July
1946. The latter had ended after the massive use of both
sticks and carrots. The government had declared martial
law throughout Khuzestan, arrested more than a thousand
"troublemakers," and ordered troops to shoot into groups of
demonstrators. Twelve had been killed outside the Kermanshah refinery. The local British consul received "the heart-
ening news that military commanders had instructions to
fire." [147] The oil company, meanwhile, dismissed eight hundred workers; recruited armed Arab tribesmen to surround
Agha Jari and attack the Tudeh headquarters in Abadan—in
which twelve would be killed and more than three hundred
injured; and created the Workers Consultative Committees
and the Central Union of Oil Workers to undercut the Tudeh Central Council of United Trade Unions as well as the
government-sponsored yellow unions—the Union of Iranian
Workers Syndicates (ESKI). What is more, the oil company
and the central government—both under pressure from

a newly appointed British labor attaché—had promised to implement the new labor law, which provided workers with a minimum wage, the eight-hour day, some semblance of job security, and paid holidays, including Fridays. Diplomats later admitted that "considerable pressure had to be exerted at the highest levels, even at the cabinet level, to get the company to liberalize its attitudes towards industrial relations." [148]

In the years immediately after 1946, the oil industry appeared tranquil—an appearance that proved to be deceptive. By late 1948, the British consul in Khorramshahr warned that although the local Tudeh organization had only one thousand active members the vast majority of oil workers would rally behind the party if the opportunity arose again. [149] He added that "most workers viewed the Tudeh as their defenders." [150] By late 1949, the British labor attaché in Tehran was reporting: "Disillusionment with ESKI has increased the sympathies of many for the Tudeh Party. Workers, students, and lower grade professional men who have hitherto claimed to be opposed to the Tudeh movement are now privately expressing anxiety at bad social conditions and are stating that the Tudeh is the only hope for improving the conditions of the people. The poorer classes were better off when the Tudeh was powerful." [151] The company's own union had "drifted" toward the Tudeh-led Central Union of Khuzestan Workers. [152] The head of the latter was chosen in fair elections to represent oil workers at the International Labor Office in Geneva. [153] British sources admitted that unions sponsored by the company and the government found themselves in "dif ficult positions" since they had to keep their distance from the popular campaign to nationalize the oil company. [154]

The campaign to nationalize the AIOC provided the Tudeh with an opportunity to regain its strength in the oil industry. Having created secret cells and underground unions, it waited for an opening. This came in March 1950—in the midst of the hot debates over the Supplementary Agreement—when the oil company, in its infinite wisdom and insatiable desire to cut costs, fired eight hundred workers, closed a plant in Kermanshah, and trimmed down housing projects. The British embassy reported that this caused "great embarrassment for the government," and that the company added insult to injury by refusing to discuss the issue with the labor minister in the presence of workers' representatives.[155] Saed, the prime minister, complained to the British ambassador that he dared not submit the Supplementary Agreement to the Majles in the midst of these cutbacks.[156]

The workers' representatives protested not only the cutbacks but also the company's general hostility to unions, inability to provide housing, failure to match its minimum wage with inflation, and the tendency to subcontract—subcontractors were not bound by the national minimum wage. The British labor attaché admitted that although 92 percent of artisans had decent housing with drinking water and electricity, more than 50 percent of skilled workers and 91 percent of unskilled workers lived in dismal conditions. Most unskilled workers lived in tents without proper wood flooring.[157] The British consul in Ahwaz had warned that this "failure of the company to fulfill its understanding [about housing] with the unions may encourage the unions to form a closer alliance with the Tudeh." [158] The British embassy noted the Tudeh had regained "sympathy among the general public" and had "overcome its earlier handicap of being regarded as a Russian tool." [159] It elaborated: "It is now common for the members of the Persian middle class to enquire 'what reason is there why I should not support the Tudeh Party'? Things could not be worse if they were in power and might be better."

Philip Noel-Baker, the British secretary of state, warned

that the AIOC was providing the Tudeh with "perfect" ammunition—especially since the company had just boasted £194 million in gross profits, £43 million in net profits, given out £14 million in dividends, and placed another £42 million in reserve. "The importance of Persian oil to the economy and defence of the United Kingdom and the Common-wealth," he argued, "is so great that we cannot afford to take the smallest chance of labour troubles or social unrest, the more so since the Company are making such large prof-its and have such large reserves." [160] His advisers, however, sidetracked him with the argument that it was best to let sleeping dogs lie. They argued that the Tudeh was not an immediate threat, that housing had improved, and that work conditions in oil were better than in other industries.

The "dogs," however, did not oblige. On March 21, 1951—the Iranian New Year—the company presented its labor force with a surprise gift in the form of drastic cuts in rental allowances. It declared the wartime housing crisis had subsided to such an extent that these allowances were no longer justified. There were also rumors—which proved well-founded—that the company had a five-year plan to lay off a large number of workers. A confidential memo ar-gued that because of "high costs of wages and the exactions of the minimum wage" the company needed to mechanize and lay off as many as eight thousand.[161] The company's chief manger in Khorramshahr warned superiors that such "short-sighted," "penny wise and pound foolish" cuts would provide "fuel" to the opposition, especially the Tudeh." [162] "Britannic House," he wrote, "needed to learn some lessons from this experience." The Foreign Office later wrote that some local managers had deemed these cost-cutting decisions from above as "ill-timed and ill-advised" and had "thrown up their hands in horror." In discussing the situation with the Americans, the Foreign Office wrote, "It is embarrassing that we should have to speak thus to the State Department but it is no use hiding the facts." [163] The cuts led some nationalists to the paranoid conclusion that the British were really in cahoots with the Tudeh to sow dissension throughout the country. Why else, they asked themselves, would the oil company time their cuts in the midst of the heated debates over the Supplementary Agreement?

The housing cuts prompted protests in the port of Bandar Mashur, with wives of dockworkers leading the protests. The protests soon spread to the oilfields of Agha Jari, Lali, and Naft-e Sefid, as well as to the repair shops, technical college, and refinery in Abadan. When the oil company announced that strike days would be deducted from annual holidays, the protests mushroomed into a general strike throughout the oil industry. Tensions further increased when the government declared martial law and dispatched twenty thousand troops into the province. Tensions increased furthermore when the British Navy stationed three warships off Abadan "to safeguard British industries." The Foreign Office confidentially told select Commonwealth countries that Britain was prepared to move troops into Abadan "with or without the request of Iran." [164] Tension increased even further when the chief of the Ka'ab tribe revived his Arab Union and reminded his followers that the original name of Khuzestan had been Arabestan. [165] The British consul in Khuzestan favored the Arab tribes on the grounds that they were the "underdogs." [166] Sympathy for minorities can be useful.

The crisis came to a head on April 12–16 when the military governor tried to arrest strike leaders and ordered troops to shoot into union rallies in Abadan and Bandar Mashur. These rallies demanded the nationalization of the oil industry in addition to better wages and living conditions. Two women and one child were killed in Bandar Mashur; nine workers in Abadan—another thirty were wounded.

The shootings turned the Abadan crowd into an angry mob that killed three Britons—two engineers and one sailor—and chased another thirty-five into the city's main cinema. Military reinforcement managed to "extract" them, but the angry crowd—led by company apprentices and technical students—ransacked the cinema and took over the technical college and the student hostel. Much of the British community fled the city. The Army had to use fourteen tanks, six armored cars, and forty trucks full of soldiers to reestablish some semblance of law and order. Its move into Abadan was hampered by demonstrators prostrating themselves before the tanks—one demonstrator lost a leg. A company official reported to London that the strikers were convinced that by prolonging the strike they were helping the campaign to nationalize the oil industry.[167] The conservative *Ettela'at-e Haftegi* (Weekly News) gave detailed accounts of these confrontations but condescendingly dismissed the protestors as "simpletons" who did not understand the true meaning of industrial actions.[168]

At its height the general strike involved more than fifty thousand—in the oilfields, in the repair workshops, in the docks, and, most important, in the Abadan refinery. The oil town as well as the oilfields had struck against its company "benefactor." What is more, the crisis threatened to spread to other parts of the country, including industrial Isfahan. The Tudeh organized solidarity rallies elsewhere and threatened sympathy strikes in major industrial centers. One of its proclamations declared:

> Workers are fined, discharged, and disgraced. They are, due to lack of proper accommodation, struggling with slow death in their mud and paper huts. Our peasants and farmers have been deprived of their possessions due to the tyrannies of big proprietors and landlords who are

directly supported by the oil company. The oil company requires cheap workmen to fill its tankers with our blood and oil, and send them all over the world thus filling the pockets of the British capitalists. For this plundering, the Company has accomplices in the name of king, minister, deputy, and governor-general. The British consul travels about and gives instructions to the governor-generals and the head of the government offices in Khuzestan. . . . The treacherous king is also a servant of the imperialists.[169]

The British embassy in Washington telegraphed London and Tehran: "The State Department says that many influential people in Persia were very much concerned about the strike. They thought it might spread dangerously. State Department shares this concern and wishes that Company should do what it can—including usual and extraordinary measures—to end the strike. . . . We are in favor of a new attempt to suppress the Tudeh." [170] The U.S. embassy in Tehran rushed its labor attaché to Khuzestan to investigate the whole situation.

The Foreign Office later wrote the "most devastating article" on the situation had appeared in the *Jerusalem Post*. It had been written by a Palestinian employed by the oil company. The company, according to the article, divided employees into three distinct categories: senior staff, formed of some 3,500 Britons and Europeans with a sprinkling of Iranians; junior staff, composed of some 6,000 Indians, Iranians, and Armenian-Iranians; and 60,000 to 70,000 "unnamed coolies" and "the poorest creatures on earth," many of whom lived without proper housing, without medical services, and without proper pay—some of their eight-year-old children had to work on road construction. The article continued: "Until recently I had only read about the exploiting of human beings. Now I see it with my own eyes. . . . The British told us 'We

British have had hundreds of years of experience of how to treat natives. Socialism is all right back home, but here you have to be master. The softer you are the more will be asked of you. Keep them in their place where they are now.' " The article concluded: "The Persians will stop at nothing to abolish the AIOC and to replace it by one of their own." [171]

The strike did not end until April 25—the same day Mossadeq navigated his nationalization bill through the Oil Committee. Workers returned to work when the company promised to rescind the housing decision and to raise the minimum wage as well as pay workers for the strike period. The Tudeh advised people not to give the authorities the excuse to shoot by congregating in the streets. Even though the strike was formally called off, the British consul-general for Khuzestan continued to advise British families to stay away. He complained that "labour staff is still showing increasing signs of insolence and truculence, and adopting a go-slow attitude." He added the general feeling among the British staff was "they may not be here in a few months' time."

In a postmortem on the whole crisis, the same consul began claiming that "the reasons for the strike were not clear," but then went on to list them as: "genuine grievances"; "Tudeh propaganda"; "desire for self-expression by apprentices"; and "spontaneous rioting precipitated by military violence." He ended with the warning that even though tempers seemed to have cooled, "inherent dangers" still lurked, especially since local "officials continue to suspect us of intriguing with Arab sheikhs." [172] The company named 130 "known communist trouble-makers" for arrest and deportation from Khuzestan.[173] The company blamed the whole crisis on "outside agitators" and the government—the latter for both being too high-handed and too conciliatory toward the strikers. The government, in turn, blamed the oil company, especially its labor practices. The British treasury calculated that the strike had drained its foreign reserves by as much as $347 million.[174]

The general strike had more profound effects on Iran. Premier Ala, in declaring martial law, claimed the strike "enflamed class warfare" and thus undermined the foundations of society.[175] The shah, in addressing the nation, warned that class antagonisms "poisoned social life" and "endangered the entire existence of the country." "The best way to alleviate them," he argued, "was to apply the laws of Islam and to live as true Muslims."[176] This would have been music to Kashani's ears. He admitted privately he had been tempted to invite British troops to "protect the oil fields and installations."[177] One senator exclaimed that class tensions had reached such a boiling point, they threatened to overwhelm the whole country. "The illiterate and uninformed classes," he declared, "have been led astray by high-sounding slogans and promises."[178]

Although the oil strike gave the nationalization campaign a major boost, Iranian historians, even those sympathetic to Mossadeq—or, one should say *especially* those sympathetic—have tended to gloss over it. Both Katouzian and Farhad Diba, in their separate biographies of Mossadeq, airbrush it out entirely.[179] Sepehr Zabih, who before becoming an in-house resident of the Hoover Institution had been an ardent supporter of the National Front, writes that Mossadeq "was swept into office on a wave of national acclaim" without mentioning the strike.[180] Fakhreddin Azimi, in his highly detailed description of the nationalist movement, allocates only one short paragraph to the strike, implying it was insignificant because it had ended before Mossadeq was actually elected premier.[181] Similarly, a detailed day-by-day chronology of Mossadeq's life drawn up meticulously by an ardent supporter has absolutely no mention of the oil strike.[182]

Ironically, the one person who recognized the importance

of the strike was Mostafa Fateh, the highest-ranking Iranian inside the AIOC. A veteran of the early labor movement, Fateh had studied economics at Columbia University and worked his way up in the oil company becoming, after thirty years, deputy director of labor relations. Nationalists deemed him pro-British; the British suspected him of harboring anti-British sentiments. In his *Fifty Years of Oil*—which remains the best account of the subject in Persian—he wrote that the strike pushed the country to the brink and thereby led to the nationalization of oil and the election of Mossadeq. "The whole country," he stressed, "was on the verge of a major upheaval." [183] He added the company's most vehement critics were its own local staff, for they were fully aware of its discriminatory practices. In private letters to the top management in London, he described Mossadeq as having a "quick mind," being pragmatic, serving "Iran's best interests," and not at all desirous of "destroying the oil industry." He noted that many who took part in nationalization demonstrations were Tudeh sympathizers; that the "Tudeh party was heartily supported by all the industrial workers because it was the only party which got them something"; and that Mossadeq skillfully used the fear of the Tudeh to maneuver his bill through the Majles, arguing that only he could implement it without major upheavals. Mossadeq, Fateh, continued, wanted a "quick takeover of the industry" because he was a "firm opponent of the Tudeh" and was "alarmed by the increasing power of the Tudeh." He ended his letters warning that the AIOC was on a collision course with the Iranian people. He advised that the best way to avoid disaster was for Britain to distance itself from the "corrupt ruling class"— especially from Sayyed Ziya and the shah, whose "one ideal in life is to be a dictator like his father." He even advised the company to think the unthinkable and accept nationalization. [184] In public, Fateh was taken to be a typical pro-British "agent." In private, he comes across as a very different person. Public appearances can be very deceptive.

Premier Mossadeq

The pace of events moved rapidly at the end of April. On April 25, the day after the general strike, Mossadeq submitted to the Majles a more detailed nationalization bill. Known as the nine-article bill, it called for the establishment of a twelve-man Mixed Commission—five deputies and five senators, as well as representatives from the finance ministry and the prime minister's office—to assist the government in implementing the original law. It set up a National Iranian Oil Company to replace the Anglo-Iranian Oil Company and to train technicians to "gradually replace" foreign ones. It also promised to deposit 25 percent of future profits in escrow at the National Bank "as fair compensation" to the previous owners and to continue to sell off oil at current prices to all regular AIOC customers. This nine-article bill was clearly designed to forestall legal problems the original one-article bill could have encountered in international law.

On April 27, Ala resigned. He did not want to appear opposed to nationalization. On the same day, the Majles president offered the premiership to Mossadeq; some think he did so under the impression Mossadeq would decline, since he had often done so in the past. In making the offer, the Majles president praised Mossadeq—who happened to be his relative—as a statesman who enjoyed the "house's full confidence because he came from one of the oldest and most distinguished families in Iran." [185] Falle of the Foreign Office admitted that Mossadeq came to power on a wave of "tremendous popular support": "He was sincere, honest, patriotic, nonviolent, brilliant, and the people loved him, wanted him and saw him as a sort of Iranian Mahatma Gandhi." [186]

The British embassy itself admitted—but much later, with the coup safely behind—that "in terms of class warfare, the movement led by Mussadiq was a revolutionary drive of the three lower classes against the upper class and the British who were identified with that class." [187]

Mossadeq accepted the premiership on the condition his nine-article bill was immediately passed into law. He stressed that his primary task would be to implement it fully and promptly. Of the one hundred deputies present, seventy-nine voted for him and his bill. Two days later, the senate followed suit with a unanimous vote. The British embassy reported that Mossadeq's election had taken many—including the shah—by surprise. The shah had sounded out Sayyed Ziya for the job, convinced the senate would never accept Mossadeq. Sayyed Ziya, however, told the British embassy he would take on the job only if he could dissolve the Majles, bar royal family members from politics, cut consumer taxes, hire British financial advisers, increase peasants' share of the crop, and obtain an oil settlement based on the 50/50 principle.[188] It is not clear whether he was merely asking for the moon knowing perfectly well that an Anglophile such as him would never be acceptable to the Majles, let alone to the general public. The shah may have completely misjudged the situation because of the severe physical pain he was suffering at the time. Officially he was suffering from "acute appendicitis." In reality, he had an intestinal tumor that was removed secretly by an American surgeon and a team of nurses rushed in from New York. The tumor turned out to be benign.[189] The nature of the operation was so secret that even recent biographers of the shah remain unaware of it.

A visitor from the Bank of England warned the Foreign Office that the nationalization issue was becoming so critical that it "could have serious effects on other Middle Eastern countries with oil concessions." Describing the "country as a complete madhouse," he wrote that there was "intense hatred for the company," "open denunciation of the concession," and "solid support [including among senior staff of the Bank and other educated Persians] in favour of nationalisation." He attributed all this to an "efficient propaganda machine" claiming the opposition controlled more than five hundred newspapers.[190] He added: "The feeling that the Shah is weak has justification, but, on the other hand, with the country completely behind nationalisation it is unrealistic to expect the monarch to turn entirely against the wishes of his countrymen, however misguided they may be."[191] A similar conclusion was reached by George McGhee, the U.S. assistant secretary of state, who rushed to Tehran to see if he could find ways of persuading the shah not to finalize the nationalization law.[192] In a long analysis entitled "Popularity and Prestige of Prime Minister Musaddiq," the U.S. embassy later admitted:

> There seems to be no question of the broad base if popular support for Dr. Musaddiq at the time he first took office as Prime Minister. As leader of the struggle against AIOC in a country where resentment and even hatred of the British is deep-seated, Musaddiq could count upon the support of the people from all levels of society with but few exceptions. For many months after oil nationalization the Prime Minister's popularity mounted. To the common people, Musaddiq was looked upon as a demigod. The phenomenon of Mossadeq was almost unique in Iran. The figure of a frail old man, in an Oriental country where age itself commands respect, who appeared to be successfully winning a battle against great odds, aroused the sympathy of almost all Iranians. In a country where political corruption had been the accepted norm, there

now appeared a man whose patriotism and financial honesty were unassailable.[193]

The shah put his signature to the nationalization law on May 1—fully aware of the symbolic significance of the day. In a May Day radio address to the nation, Mossadeq declared that on account of his age and health he never imagined he would one day become the country's prime minister. Hailing May Day as the world's "labor festival," he described workers "as dear to him as his own children" and beseeched them to be calm, orderly, and disciplined. He also beseeched journalists to be responsible and not abuse press freedoms.[194] In follow-up speeches, he argued that nationalization would take the wind out of communist propaganda, and that $120 million a year in oil revenues would improve economic conditions and thus alleviate social discontent.

Following parliamentary procedures, Mossadeq submitted to the Majles for approval his program as well as his cabinet. The Majles approved them with a vote of 99 out of 112. His program contained two short points: implementation of the nine-article law and reform of the electoral system. His cabinet was an amalgam of his own supporters and establishment politicians. His supporters included Fatemi, the journalist, as assistant premier; Baqer Kazemi of the Iran Party as foreign minister; Sanjabi, another Iran Party leader, as education minister; and Amir-Alai, yet another Iran Party member, as minister of economy. The interior ministry was given to Gen. Fazlullah Zahedi, who later played a prominent role in the 1953 coup. A career officer from the days of Reza Shah, Zahedi had been interned by the British in World War II for having ties to the Germans. He spent part of his internment with Kashani, with whom he established close relations. Also he had been appointed senator by the shah to counterbalance the rising power of his personal rival, Razmara. The other seven in the cabinet were mostly veteran politicians closely associated with the court.[195]

The British ambassador described the cabinet as "right wing," and in his very first meeting with Mossadeq—whom he depicted as "affable"—stressed the necessity of immediately removing all agitators from the oil industry.[196] He made the mistake of mentioning that the AIOC had already handed over to local authorities a list of 130 Tudeh organizers to be arrested.[197] This probably reinforced Mossadeq's conviction that the British were constantly and incessantly meddling in local as well as national affairs.

In launching his administration, Mossadeq made an impassioned speech to the two houses arguing that to implement the nationalization law he needed cooperative members on the Mixed Commission. He warned that "dark forces" were plotting to assassinate him, and, therefore, he would take sanctuary inside the Majles and carry a pistol. He collapsed before ending his speech. Western papers took this as "theatrics," but later events showed that such assassination plots were not imaginary. The speech had its intended effect. The lower house elected five National Front leaders—Shayegan, Moazemi, Saleh, Makki, and Hassebi—to the Mixed Commission. Similarly, the upper house elected six senators—all reputed to be anti-British. They were headed by Ahmad Matin-Daftari, Mossadeq's nephew and son-in-law. A French-educated lawyer, Matin-Daftari served as Mossadeq's main adviser on international law. He had been prime minister under Reza Shah and had been interned during World War II. The British embassy distrusted him as a "strict neutralist." It also dismissed the others as "negative," "stupid," "sly," "senile," "stubborn," and "extremists." [198]

The Mixed Commission promptly formed a Temporary Board to take over the AIOC installations in the name of the newly established National Iranian Oil Company. Makki, the orator, acted as chief spokesman for the board. On June 10, after a triumphant address to a cheering crowd of more than thirty thousand, Makki and the Temporary Board took possession of the company's headquarters in Khorramshahr. The NIOC had replaced the AIOC.

In a ceremony potent with symbolism and similar to dramatic shifts of power in newly independent countries throughout the world, the national flag was hoisted up as the company insignia was taken down. Nehru was one of the very first foreign leaders to send congratulations. He was soon followed by Lázaro Cárdenas, the Mexican president who had nationalized his own country's oil industry. As the installations were being taken over, AIOC top managers left, their technicians threatened to resign en masse, British para-troopers massed in neighboring Iraq, and the Royal Navy positioned nine warships near Abadan. For some in Britain, the lowering of the insignia marked another step in the dis-solution of the Empire. For many in Iran, the raising of the national flag showed the world that the country had finally gained true independence. Oil nationalization was for Iran what national independence was for many former colonies in Africa, Asia, Latin America, and the Caribbean.

2

Anglo-Iranian Negotiations

> For all Iranians—admirers and deprecators—he [Mossadeq]
> was the lodestone, the magnetic field, the lightning rod that
> lay both chronologically and intellectually at the center of
> Iranian politics of the twentieth century. Nearly everyone
> was pulled or pushed, attracted into or repelled out of the or-
> bit. Virtually no one passed through the period of influence
> unaffected by his presence.
>
> —Roy Mottahedeh, *The Mantle of the Prophet*

Control

Nationalization initiated a zero-sum struggle. For Mossadeq
and Iran, nationalization meant national sovereignty, and
national sovereignty meant control over the exploration, extraction, and exportation of oil. For Britain and the AIOC,
nationalization meant the exact opposite. It meant loss of
control over the exploration, extraction, and exportation of
the same oil. Political conflicts usually leave some room for
compromise; this left little such room. Either control had to
be in the hands of Iran—as Mossadeq insisted. Or, as Britain
equally adamantly insisted, control should remain in its own
hands—or, at least, out of the hands of Iran. If the struggle
had been over profit-sharing, compromise could have been
reached. After all, one can always cut up a cake in ways to
satisfy all. But since this struggle was over ultimate control, not over bread-and-butter issues, compromise was near
impossible.

During the twenty-eight turbulent months beginning with nationalization in April 1951 and ending with the coup in August 1953, the operative word underlying the whole crisis was "control." For Iran, control meant power to explore, produce, and export oil. This, in turn, meant influence over the pricing of oil in the world markets. Conversely for Britain, loss of control meant inability to determine the extraction, production, and exportation of oil. This consequently threatened a loss of influence over world oil prices. Although the emergence of the Organization of Petroleum Exporting Countries (OPEC) eventually produced such a shift of power in the 1970s, Britain and the AIOC, as well as the other Seven Sisters, deemed such a prospect absolutely unacceptable in the early 1950s. It is for good reason that economists see the emergence of OPEC as a major fault line in the twentieth century that divides the contemporary era from the age when Western companies had dominated the world market. By the end of the 1980s, most countries in the Middle East and North Africa, as well as in Asia and Latin America, had nationalized their oil, and thus gained influence over world prices. In the early 1950s, however, such a loss was seen as heralding the "end of civilization"—not only for Britain but also for consumers throughout the industrial world. It was feared that oil-producing states could be tempted to keep resources underground on the realistic calculation the value of such resources would increase in decades to come. Such fears inevitably brought the United States into the conflict—not as an "honest broker," as American diplomats liked to claim, but as a party with much at stake. The UK and the United States may have disagreed on minor details, but they agreed in their vehement opposition to nationalization.

The term "control" appeared constantly in internal government documents throughout the crisis. Long before the crisis had started, the Ministry of Fuel and Power warned the Foreign Office of the looming dangers if the Soviets obtained a concession in northern Iran: "The strength of British oil lies in the fact that we hold concessions all over the world, in which, we are ourselves developing the oil and controlling its distribution and disposal. It would weaken our position if countries began to develop their own oil. If Persia began to develop her own oil in the north, it might not be very long before she would want to do this in the south also. We should not encourage them to develop their own oil." [1]

Even before the nationalization bill had been drafted, the Foreign Office understood its long-term implications. In January 1951 it noted, "The financial aspect of the matter is not uppermost in Persian minds. The core of the matter is the Persian feeling that they have no control over the oil industry, their main source of revenue." [2] In March, it again noted at a top-level emergency meeting in London that the AIOC was "prepared to consider any arrangement with the Persian government so long as management remained in the Company's hands." [3] In April, it stressed, "Whatever new arrangements we arrive at, they should be such that we keep effective control of the assets in our hands. . . . We can be flexible in profits, administration, or partnership, but not in the issue of control." [4]

Soon after the bill was passed, the UK secretary of state made it clear to the United States that "control" of oil should remain in British hands, that "no arrangement should be made which would upset the world oil market," and that "it was better to have no agreement with Musaddiq than to have an unsatisfactory one." [5] At the same time, a series of top-level U.S.-UK meetings in Washington came to the consensus that "effective power should be kept over this valuable asset." The British representatives put it succinctly:

Under the present concession control rested with the Oil
Company. If nationalization came control would be with
the nationalizer. . . . The first effect of nationalization
would be to put control into Persian hands. Seen from the
United Kingdom point of view the present problem was
not solely one of the fate of a major asset. It concerns *the*
[emphasis in the original] major asset which we hold in
the field of raw materials. Control of that asset is of supreme importance. The point has already been made of
the importance of that asset to our balance of payments
and to our rearmament programme, but in the sphere of
bilateral negotiations the loss of this, our only major raw
material, would have cumulative and well-nigh incal-
culable repercussions. Moreover, it is false to assume an
identity of interest between the Western world and Persia over how much oil should be produced and to whom
it should be sold and on what terms. The Persians could
get all the oil and foreign exchange they need from much
reduced operations. For all these reasons the United Kingdom has to keep control of the real resources involved.
Finally, there is the consideration of Parliamentary and
public feeling in England which would not readily accept
a position where we surrender effective control of an asset
of such magnitude.

The Concession represents a very large asset which is
very much in our interest to preserve. It gives us great
power in the movement of raw materials about the world
and contributes one third to the total Anglo-Dutch production of oil. It also represents an element of the order
of magnitude of 100 million pounds in our balance of
payments.[6]

These meetings concluded it would be expedient to publicly accept the principle of nationalization, but design an

"arrangement" that would keep control out of the hands of Iran. A British delegate admitted the "problem" was how to pay "lip service to the notion" of nationalization while "keeping effective power of this asset in our hands."[7] An American delegate explained that the term "nationalization" would not be a problem because in the arrangement they had in mind "control of operations" would remain with the oil company.[8] A senior Foreign Office official later admitted the British had publicly accepted the principle of nationalization in order to facilitate negotiations.[9] Without apparent awareness of the contradiction, a State Department representative at the joint meeting declared that the United States could not "deny a country the right to nationalize," but, at the same time, assured his British counterparts his government fully accepted the AIOC main objective of "maintaining control." He recommended the group put together a proposal that would "shave" close between these two poles. This, in fact, became the main U.S. objective in the months ahead. The British delegates came away from the final meeting with the assurance that "Americans accept our cardinal point in our policy that we should maintain control."[10]

"Control" remained the operative word throughout the crisis. The Foreign Office warned that if nationalization succeeded, "We would lose control over the key thing, of use and direction of oil to the world markets. I don't believe the Persians are much concerned about share-holding and percentages. They want control."[11] Shepherd, the British ambassador, in a rare moment of candor admitted:

Thc hearl of the matter is the Persian feeling that they have no control over the main sources of revenue, once it is sold to the Oil Company. I confess that I sympathise with the Persians here: they feel that however inexperienced technically they may be in the intricacies of the

oil business, they should at least play some part in what
is going on in the production and refining of oil in their
country. They not only desire Iranianisation of the staff
of the company, but they want to participate in the actual direction of affairs. It is not enough to have a few
senior posts held by Persians. I feel sure nothing will satisfy them but some part in the direction of the concern as
far as operations within Persia are concerned. At present
time it is too easy for accusations to be made that the company is exercising an authority approaching that detest-
able thing "colonialism" in monopolizing the Southern
oil resources without considering national rights. This is a
feeling which it will be best to take into consideration. It
is not unique to Persia, and the examples of Mexican oil
and Argentine railways spring to mind. . . . I realize that
the appointment of Persian directors would present certain undesirable features and safeguards would have to be
worked out to prevent undue interference by the Persian
government.[12]

The Ministry of Fuel informed the AIOC that although
any settlement would involve some form of "nationalization," nevertheless it was important to restrict it so that actual
"control of future operations" would remain out of Iranian
hands.[13] At one point, the British went so far as to privately
toy with the idea of offering a 55/45 deal as long they kept
effective control.[14] In October 1951, Shepherd telegraphed
London that it "may be better to offer a 60/40 share so long
as AIOC can retain control."[15] He explained, "It seems very
unlikely we can do anything at all to meet Musaddiq. We
must keep effective control. We have explored a number of
devices by which we could disguise this hard fact but found
nothing that was not either too dangerous or too transpar-
ent for even the Persians to accept."[16] The British were

skeptical that concessions on other issues would satisfy Mossadeq, since "throughout the crisis he has been absolutely consistent. . . . There can be no doubt whatsoever that his fundamental objective is to remove the foreigner from any position in Persia other than that of a servant. He is first and foremost a Nationalist." [17] The Foreign Office reported that Fuad Rouhani—a respected oil expert whom it described as a "staunch supporter" of Britain—made it clear that "any arrangement acceptable to the Persians would have to provide it with overall control of the industry." [18]

The Persian Oil Working Party, an interdepartmental committee set up in London to handle the crisis, came to a similar conclusion early on: "Our primary object must be to retain effective control of operations in British hands before we accept the principle of nationalization." [19] The Working Party contained representatives from the Foreign Office, Treasury, Bank of England, and the Ministry of Trade as well as that of Fuel and Power. Its meetings were attended regularly by Sir William Fraser, the AIOC chair, who also had ready access to 10 Downing Street. The Working Party set itself two main goals: "ensure control of Persian oil supplies remain effectively in the hands of AIOC"; and "discourage other concessionary countries from following the Persian example." [20] It consistently stressed the need to retain "control over operations"; warned of "repercussions in other overseas countries"; and emphasized that "if other producing countries followed the Persian example, the effect might be that consuming countries will be forced to pay much higher prices for their oil." [21]

The Working Party in London was warned by a visitor from the British embassy in Tehran that Iranian politicians were reluctant to replace Mossadeq, since this would be seen as a British "victory." He further warned that the Iranian government was unlikely to accept any arrangements that would leave it without "overall control."[22] The Working Party even drew up a long list of British assets that would be threatened throughout the world if nationalization succeeded in Iran. The list included oil in Iraq, the Gulf, Burma, and Indonesia; major investments in the Commonwealth, including Pakistan, India, and Ceylon; copper, sulfur, and iron ore in Spain; tin and copper in Portugal; lead and rubber in Burma; teak, tin, and rubber in Siam; rubber in Indonesia; tin in Bolivia; copper and nitrates in Chile; and magnesium and nickel in Greece.[23] It was tempted to draw up a similar list of U.S. assets in the world.

The prime minister, Clement Attlee, in communicating with President Truman, strictly observed the strategy of paying lip service to nationalization while adding so many qualifiers as to make it meaningless. He did so in convoluted diplomatic language: "We have to agree on principle of nationalization . . . like Dominion status. It might well be that in negotiating an agreement in such a context a number of modifications would be introduced and that the resulting agreement would confer something that was, in fact, a good deal less than dominion status."[24] He warned Truman, "A breach of contract of this nature might well jeopardise other overseas contracts, not merely those held by British and United States companies for the development of Middle East oil resources, but contracts for other products elsewhere. . . . I am sure that we can count on the United States Government to exercise their influence to this and whatever it may be necessary."[25]

The British government instructed its Washington embassy both to "publicise the AIOC case" and to impress upon Americans that "unbridled and irresponsible nationalism posed grave danger for the Western Powers. For this nationalism is not based on any real national fervour, willing to accept unlimited discipline, sacrifice and labour; but is an attempt by the ruling class to divert attention from their own shortcomings by ascribing all ills to foreign domination." [26] Similarly, the Foreign Office warned the State Department:

Musaddiq would be content to see the industry running at a low level without foreign management. This raises a problem: the security of the free world is dependent on large quantities of oil from Middle Eastern sources. If the attitude in Iran spreads to Saudi Arabia or Iraq, the whole structure may break down along with our ability to defend ourselves. The danger of buying oil produced on a reduced scale had, therefore, potentialities with dangerous repercussions. [27]

Concluding that Mossadeq would not compromise on nationalization, British policymakers early on hammered out a hard-line strategy that they adhered to through thick and thin for the next twenty-eight months—the strategy of waiting out Mossadeq, confident he would not last long. They dismissed the nationalist movement as ephemeral. They told themselves and others that prime ministers in Iran on average lasted less than seven months. In public, they proclaimed that Iran lacked the technical expertise to run the complex industry. In private, they admitted that Iran had the expertise to refine enough for home consumption and even some extra for external sales but that a blockade could effectively stop exports. [28] In fact, the International Bank (later renamed the World Bank) in 1952 discovered—to its own surprise—that the nationalized company kept the oil installations in excellent order and produced more than enough for home needs. [29] The Working Party took care to regularly brief the opposition Conservative Party on the Labour government's hard-line strategy.

On May 1—the very day the nationalization law was

finalized, the British embassy in Tehran reported to the Foreign Office that prominent figures in Tehran did not "expect" Mossadeq to survive long because he "lacked constructive qualities." [30] Shepherd confidently predicted that Mossadeq would be replaced by Ala within "one week." [31] Even before Mossadeq had finished forming his administration, the British delegate to the top U.S.-UK meetings in Washington assured the State Department that the whole crisis would soon blow over and the situation would inevitably "change for the better." [32] Shepherd further reassured London that Mossadeq would "not remain in power much longer," that the "situation was more lunatic than ever," and that "we should be well advised to wait for Musaddiq to fall before making new offers." [33] Similarly, Professor Ann Lambton—a former press attaché in Tehran—strongly urged the Foreign Office to keep a "steady nerve" and wait for him to fall. She insisted, "Our own unofficial efforts to undermine him are making good progress. If we agree to discuss and compromise with him, the effort will strengthen him." She added that Americans who talk of compromise are "wrong and do not have the experience or the psychological insight." [34] She continued to give the same tough advice throughout the crisis.

In September, Ambassador Shepherd again assured London that the "opposition was growing," change of government was "essential," and others, notably Sayyed Ziya, were ready to take over. [35] Two months later, he reassured London once again that Mossadeq's government had so weakened that it was about to fall, and the only question was who would replace him. [36] The Ministry of Fuel contemplated new proposals to present to his successor. [37] The Foreign Office likewise cautioned that while "we wait and work for Mussadiq's fall" we should make sure we succeed in persuading America to continue to support us in opposing nationalization. [38]

The U.S. did not need much, if any, persuading. Even

before Mossadeq's election, McGhee, the assistant secretary of state, had rushed to Tehran to advise Britain to make "generous offers" to avoid such "undesirable consequences" as "nationalization"—"what ever that meant." [39] He assured the British ambassador he was there to "help combat the idea of nationalization." [40] He admits in his memoirs: "Both we and the British very much wanted to avoid nationalization of the AIOC concession. This would be bad for AIOC and Iran. It would jeopardize oil concessions held by the US, UK, and other firms around the world." [41] Years later, Falle admitted that the Americans often sounded a generous tone toward Iran in public but "could not afford an agreement that would start a vast series of renegotiations with all the world's oil producers." [42]

In the weeks after Mossadeq's election, the British ambassador in Washington reported that the U.S. position was very close to that of the UK, since the two "had a joint interest in the matter." "Mr. McGhee," he reported, "suggested accepting the pretence and the 'façade' of nationalization while maintaining effective control." [43] In other reports, he replaced "façade" with "cloak." He added that McGhee agreed that "whatever decisions were made control should be exercised by the UK," and the "essence of the problem was how to concede something to this emotional concept of 'nationalization' but sill enable AIOC to retain control of the oil operations." [44] McGhee himself in his memoirs explains that the obvious solution was to accept nationalization "as the expressed desire of the Iranian people," but, at the same time, "retain control" in the hands of the AIOC. [45] He speculated, "It may be possible to establish Iranian partial ownership without in fact diminishing effective British control of the company." [46] He never explained how this could be done.

At the same time, McGhee told representatives of the main American oil companies, including Aramco, Gulf, Socony, and Standard Oil of New Jersey, that to "salvage" operating contracts and "protect concession rights in other parts of the world" it might be expedient to accept some semblance of nationalization. But he assured them that the United States would not accept outright nationalization, since this would "have adverse consequences in other oil producing states." The representative from Standard Oil of New Jersey urged him to be more forthright in denouncing nationalization on the grounds that any such talk tended to discourage Americans from undertaking "operations anywhere in the world." The Socony representative recommended the use of force on the grounds that such a vital asset could not be allowed to be lost.[47] The Gulf Oil representative argued it would be better to lose Iran behind the iron curtain than to have Mossadeq succeed.[48]

The American companies expressed "fear that a soft American stance with respect to unilateral cancellation of concessions might weaken their own positions in the Middle East and elsewhere."[49] The Socony director told the AIOC chairman that he considered "nationalization" to be the same as unilateral "abrogation," and that such behavior threatened "international investments," "civilized countries," and the "well-being of the peoples of the world." "[The] AIOC," he affirmed, "is vital for the lives and welfare of other peoples."[50] These major companies consistently reassured the AIOC that they would not buy a drop of oil from Iran as long as the crisis lasted.[51] Herbert Hoover, who had taken an interest in Iranian oil in 1944, later admitted that if Mossadeq had succeeded, he would have posed a major threat to American oil interests as far afield as Venezuela and Saudi Arabia.[52]

The London *Times* applauded the *New York Herald Tribune* for realizing that "if this expropriation under the name of nationalization goes through American investment in Saudi Arabia will not be secure. . . . The whole precarious balance in the Middle East will be irretrievably upset." [53] William Fraser of the AIOC, after talking to his American counterparts, confidently told the British defense minister, "The other companies, including the Americans, are becoming increasingly apprehensive of the effects in other countries if Persians get away with their present actions. They see that what had been [the] sauce of the AIOC goose might well become sauce for their own gander. It is not only the oil companies which might be effected [sic]; the Egyptians, for instance, might think that this gave them a lead to nationalize the Suez Canal." [54]

The Foreign Office also felt confident that "major oil companies of all nationalities regard AIOC as fighting their own battle." [55] It explained that one important oil executive had been "so deeply impressed by the threat posed to American interests by what was happening in Persia that he had made a special trip to New York and Washington to make sure the implications were fully understood." [56] The Foreign Office added:

> The Chairman of Shell has asked to meet Fraser [the chairman of the AIOC and Iraq Petroleum Company] for a joint meeting to form a joint position. Other companies are, of course, deeply interested in Persian developments since these might have serious effects on their interests, in other parts of the world. Apart from there, the unilateral termination of productive concession is a serious matter which might have averse effects in other spheres besides oil, e.g. Chilean nitrate, Palestine potash, etc. Chairman of Shell came to see me . . . He takes a grave view of the Persian situation. His Company have an interest in Kuwait and in the Iraq Petroleum Company as well as their very large interest in Venezuela. The Sheikh of Kuwait has already demanded 50/50 and the Venezuelan government

is taking an unhealthy interest in the developments in Persia. . . . The American Companies, particularly in the Gulf, are also very disturbed.[57]

Even Americans previously critical of the AIOC were unanimous in their opposition to nationalization. Thornburg, the oil consultant employed by Iran, despite his objections to the Supplementary Agreement adamantly opposed nationalization. In a confidential memo to Mossadeq but leaked to the British, he insisted that Iran would not be able to afford compensation, lacked the technical knowledge to operate the industry, and ran a serious risk of unifying the other companies into an "anti-nationalization bloc."[58] After being pressured by the British to leave Iran, Thornburg went on a grand tour of North America, spelling out his views not only to the Overseas Writers Forum and Harry Luce of *Time*, but also to such influential figures as Nelson Rockefeller; Mrs. Roosevelt; Dean Acheson, the secretary of state; Gen. Walter Bedell Smith, the CIA director; Allen Dulles, the future director of the CIA; Gene Black, the head of the International Bank; Sumner Welles, a former senior diplomat who opened doors to influential senators; and Averell Harriman, the former governor of New York whom President Truman soon named as his special mediator between Iran and Britain.[59]

Walter Levy, another American consultant to Iran, repeated these same warnings. Claiming the industry would "disintegrate" within six months, he highlighted all possible difficulties: the power of the major companies, the lack of tankers, and the technical complexities of running the installations. A former Standard Oil employee, Levy had cultivated contacts within the British embassy in Tehran but kept them hidden from the Iranian government.[60] George McGhee informed the Foreign Office that Levy agreed to work for Iran only if the U.S. government approved, and that the U.S. government approved only if the British government did so. He added that the "Persians on no account should be privy to this scheme" and that Levy had "our interests much at heart." [61] The Foreign Office was assured that Levy was "100% with us," "appreciated the necessity of the British remaining in control of operations," and even advocated the seizure of any oil leaving ports "as stolen property." [62] When the Iranian government ignored Levy's advice against nationalization, he continued to collect his pay but privately told the British ambassador that Mossadeq's advisers were "a bunch of lunatics" and nothing could be done until they had been "got rid of." Iranians had good reason to take suggestions from such advisers with a pinch of salt.

Henry Grady, the American ambassador in Tehran at the very start of the crisis, minced no words in denouncing nationalization in private even though in public he displayed anti-British and pro-Iranian sentiments. He told Thornburg that Mossadeq's advisers were "gangsters and terrorists who would in due course have to be dealt with just as we did with [the ones] in Chicago." [63] In an article published in the *Saturday Evening Post* immediately upon his retirement in July 1951, he argued that "nationalization would not be in the country's interests" on the grounds that Iran could not run the industry and sell the oil. Instead he favored a scheme by which Iran would nominally take charge of the industry but actual management would remain in the hands of an AIOC subsidiary. He placed the blame for the "unnecessary tragedy" on the AIOC and Britain: the former for its refusal to include a 50/50 deal in the Supplementary Agreement, the latter for "fatuous" and "unrealistic" attitudes reminiscent of "Victorian colonialism" and failure to "take into account the rising tide on nationalistic-independence sentiment in formerly colonial or semi-colonial countries such as Iran."

The article continued by describing Mossadeq as having 95 percent of the country's support, and of being "a man of great intelligence, wit, and education—a cultured Persian gentleman." "He reminds me," Grady wrote, "of the late Mahatma Gandhi. He is a little old man in a frail body, but with a will of iron and passion for what he regards as the best interests of his people." The article ended by accusing the British of trying to rope the Americans into a scheme to bring down Mossadeq. "I have heard," Grady wrote, "the theme that beggars need money and economic pressures will bring them down so often that they sound like a phonograph record." He also blamed—in passing—his own government for sealing Razmara's fate by failing to give him a generous financial hand in time of need.[64]

The AIOC invited Bullard, the former British ambassador, to weigh in against Grady. Bullard responded that Grady's article, although highly important, misconstrued the situation in a number of ways. Mossadeq, Bullard argued, was seeking not a better deal, but—God forbid, the horror of all horrors—to make Iran "neutral" in the Cold War. The original AIOC offer had been very generous—more generous than a 50/50 deal, for it had guaranteed compensation in bad years when company profits could plummet. The AIOC had made significant steps toward Persianizing the staff. Negotiations with Mossadeq were a "waste of breath," since he was not interested in compromise. "What Iran needs," he argued, "was not money but to face realities and get down to work instead of sitting and complaining." After a long digression into nineteenth-century history, Bullard concluded that Iran should be grateful to Great Britain for having saved its independence from both Tsarist Russia and the Soviet Union.[65] Bullard was not inhibited in expressing Victorian prejudices. He often described Iranians as "inert," "dishonest," "cowardly," and "crooked." "The Persians," he wrote, "are pretty much like the Indians in character. They have incredibly twisted minds, which never accept the obvious explanation to any action however simple and straightforward." [66]

Such frappes between British and American diplomats left the false impression that the United States sympathized with the nationalization cause. The U.S. attitude toward Mossadeq and nationalization was best summed up by Loy Henderson, Henry Grady's successor as ambassador. Henderson, who helped engineer the 1953 coup, had served as ambassador to Iraq and thus came to Iran with considerable experience in oil issues. In reminiscences given two decades later, he admitted:

I found Mossadeq to be a charming person. By that I don't mean he was handsome. He was tall and gangling. His hawk-like face had the kind of tragic lines that are likely to win the sympathy of those with whom one talks. He had a high sense of humor which at times could be biting. He was a decent man to work with in spite of the fact that he was stubborn and opinionated. We desired to have good relations with him but not at the price of our approving the cancellation of the British oil concession. We did not believe that such an expropriation was in the basic interest of Iran, GB, or the US. Acts of this kind tend to undermine the mutual trust that was necessary if international trade was to flourish. . . . I finally came to the conclusion that no settlement of the oil problem was possible so long as Mossadeq was in control. [67]

Whereas "control" had been the operative term in confidential documents, the UK and U.S. governments, as well as the AIOC, scrupulously avoided the word in public. Professor Charles Issawi, an economist, years later reminisced how the oil companies were adamant that ivory-tower academics could not possibly understand the complexities and difficulties of their business. But when he produced a manuscript on the industry, their only objection was his use of the word "control."[68] They much preferred the word "own." They took strong objection to his statement "These companies controlled nearly 90 per cent of oil production outside the United states and the Soviet bloc and almost 80 per cent of refining capacity."[69] Throughout the twenty-eight-month crisis, Western spokesmen scrupulously avoided the taboo word. Instead, they stressed their willingness to "compromise," "settle," "strike a fair bargain," "come to an amiable settlement," "sign an equitable concession," and, of course, accept the "principle of nationalization."

To explain the failure of negotiations, the West readily resorted to "national characteristics"—especially with regard to Mossadeq's "personality." Iranians were deemed to be "irrational," "headstrong," "tiresome," "obstinate," "violent," "volatile," "unstable," "malcontented," "inefficient," "ignorant," "xenophobic," "childlike," "unwilling to recognize facts," "sentimentally mystical," "lacking common sense," "swayed by emotions," and "devoid of positive content." A *New York Times* editorial declared: "[The Iranian] is a man of infinite patience, of great charm and gentleness, but he is also—as we have been seeing—a volatile character, highly emotional, and violent when sufficiently aroused."[70] American and British diplomats liked to recommend *Alice in Wonderland* to each other as the best way to understand Iran.

Similarly, Mossadeq himself was deemed "impossible," "hopelessly irrational," "eccentric," "fanatical," "obsessive," "wild," "hysterical," "Messianical" [*sic*], "theatrical," "bizarre," "emotional," "sickly," "mentally unstable," "abnormal," "crazy," "demagogic," "inflammatory," "absurd," "single-mindedly obstinate," "old man of the sea," "a Robinson Crusoe," and, to boot, "effeminate" as well as "wily and

Oriental." Even before the crisis became full-blown, *Time* described Mossadeq as a "whirling dervish with a college degree" often wearing pajamas, sometimes pin-striped suits, "consumed by illness and by strange fires of faith," "bearing psychological scars" and "threatening" to deprive the Free World of essential oil. It quoted a British diplomat as saying, "We could deal with a reliable blackguard. But how can you deal with an honest fanatic?" [71]

Francis Shepherd—shunning diplomatic language—described Mossadeq as "Cunning, slippery, and completely unscrupulous. He does not make a pleasant impression on men. He is rather tall but has short and bandy legs so that he shambles like a bear. He looks rather like a cab horse and is slightly deaf." [72] George Middleton, Shepherd's charge d'affaires and later replacement, was somewhat more diplomatic. He described Mossadeq as "having a mind different from us" and being the "fanatical leader of the nationalist movement who can not distinguish between substance and shadow, and feverishly clutches at the latter thinking it is the former." [73] Middleton admitted—but only years later—that he had "great affection" for Mossadeq and respected him as "a highly civilized gentleman." He described him as "a charming conservative farmer," and "a good countryman, like a typical English Tory." [74] Shepherd, meanwhile, concluded his annual report for 1951 with the following explanation of why recent negotiations had failed:

The fault could be laid at the door of one man—Dr. Musaddiq. Himself an honest if misguided and often purblind patriot, his instinct for demagogy, his single-minded obstinacy, and his total lack of constructive ideas have rendered impossible the development into a genuine national revival of the upsurge of national sentiment on which he rode to power. Unwilling ever to recognise a mistake or concede a point, Dr. Musaddiq has fanned national pride into intolerance, religious revival into fanaticism and a desire for greater independence into stubborn isolationism and xenophobia. The Persian people, who are accustomed to poverty, may in future be called upon to suffer much more.[75]

To disseminate such views, the British press attaché in Tehran sent his counterpart in Washington "a steady supply of suitable poison too venomous for the BBC." The Washington attaché reported American columnists made "good use of this poison."[76] He boasted he even helped them write some of their pieces on Iran.[77] Drew Pearson—the venerable dean of American journalism and lead columnist for the *Washington Post*—circulated a completely fabricated story about how Fatemi, Mossadeq's right hand, had multiple convictions of embezzlement and jury tampering. "Do Americans," he asked rhetorically, "want such a crook to continue masterminding the whole Middle East oil crisis? . . . This man eventually will decide whether the US has oil rationing—or possibly whether the American people go into World War III."[78]

Stewart Alsop and his brother Joseph—both leading columnists for the *New York Herald Tribune*—warned that unless the United States took a firm stand, "all the little Musaddiqs elsewhere would be tempted to cause trouble."[79] After a conversation with Joseph Alsop, the Foreign Office noted he agreed that Mossadeq was "impervious to reason" and had "done nothing but listen to his own voice for forty years." He also agreed that "all educated and political elements in Persia lack realism and understanding."[80] *Time*, in a backhanded complement, named Mossadeq Man of the Year, but went on to describe him as "obstinate," "fanatical," "menacing," "weeping," "simple-tracked," "prone to tantrums," and "an appalling caricature of a statesman."

"The fact," it concluded, "that Iranians accept Mossadegh's suicidal policy is a measure of the hatred of the West—especially of Britain—in the Middle East . . . This old wizard in a mountainous land is, sad to relate, the Man of 1951." [81] The British press attaché in Washington was tempted to "horrify" the American public by spreading the rumor that Mossadeq reeked of opium and "indulged freely" in that drug. [82] He boasted that the U.S. press had been very cooperative in helping the British. [83]

The British ambassador in Washington seconded this boast. He wrote that the American press—naming *Life*, the *New York Times*, the *Washington Post*, and the *Wall Street Journal*—saw the situation much like the British did, and that American oil companies in their discussion with the State Department were warning that Iranian nationalism posed serious threats to their concessions throughout the world. [84] British officials in the United States also did their best to counter the "old-fashioned concept still prevalent that GB is an imperialist country with selfish designs on Persia." [85] They argued that Britain had helped the 1906 revolution; that the aborted 1919 Agreement had really been a Seven Year Plan thirty years before its time; that the 1933 Agreement had been freely negotiated; and that the Supplementary Agreement had been more than generous. They also stressed that Mossadeq in his long life had never bothered to visit Abadan. This tack was quickly dropped when it was pointed out that Fraser, in his long tenure as the AIOC chairman, had paid only one very brief visit to Iran. Meanwhile, the foreign minister assured his socialist colleagues in the cabinet that "AIOC is one of the most enlightened employees in the Middle East. The real trouble is the Persian government and the wealthy landowning class that has failed to use the very large royalties from oil for economic development." [86]

Of course, British papers—including the highbrows—
outdid the Americans in denigrating Mossadeq. The *Observer*
described him as "an incorruptible fanatic," a "confused but
passionate old man impervious to commonsense arguments
and expediency," and a "bewildered and desperately short-
sighted politician with only one political idea in that gigantic
head." [87] It labeled him in the same breath as a "tragic Fran-
kenstein," an "elderly Robespierre," and probably a "failed
Kerensky."

The London *Times* was no better: "He is not, in the ordinary sense, a brave man, perhaps a timid one. But he can be
brave when his emotions are sufficiently aroused and when
he can speak for Persia. He has a martyr's temerity, marred
by nervous instability and he can shed tears as a result of
it." [88] A series of unsigned articles—probably by Professor
Lambton—explained the whole crisis in terms of the "Persian character" and propensity to "blame others for their own
shortcomings." It claimed that internal contradictions—
between rich and poor, landlords and peasants, town and
country, the capital and the provinces—lead Iranians to project resentments onto "imaginary enemies," especially the
British and the oil company.[89] "The old order," the articles
claimed, "was on verge of collapse because of the stupidity,
greed, and lack of judgment on the part of the ruling class."
In short, the crisis had little to do with real grievances against
the oil company. Instead it had much to do with the desire
of the "ruling class" to find foreign "scapegoats" and "turn
internal discontent outwards and away from the exploitation to which they are often party and the maladministra-
tion from which they sometimes benefit." The conservative
Times was readily resorting to Marxist class analysis to explain the whole crisis. Its editors probably missed the irony.

Such explanations became mantras even though Britain's
main ally in Iran was precisely of the same "exploiting"

class. As soon as the crisis erupted, the British embassy in Tehran requested the BBC in London to double its Persian-language service and to replace an uncooperative reporter in Iran. It also requested the BBC to blacklist Professor Elwell-Sutton—the former press attaché now openly criticizing the AIOC.[90] He remained blacklisted for years to come for being "anti-British, anti-colonial, and anti-Shah."[91] His book *Persian Oil*—which remains to the present day one of the best studies on the crisis—had difficulty finding a publisher in Britain.[92] Launching a "propaganda" war, the BBC hammered away on how nationalization would inevitably impoverish the country by running to ground the refinery, giving power to incompetents, scaring off technicians, drying up needed royalties, and channeling revenues into pockets of corrupt government officials.[93] The Foreign Office forcefully complained whenever newspapers diverged from this official script—especially when they hinted that the "oil lobby" carried any weight within the State Department.[94]

In a long document entitled "A Comparison between Persian and Asian Nationalisms in General," Ambassador Shepherd tried to draw a sharp distinction between the two.[95] The former, he argued, lacked "authenticity" and "constructive ability," and, having missed out on being ruled by a colonial power, now "needed a firm hand. . . . perhaps a twenty-year foreign occupation like Haiti." This last point was clearly pitched for an American audience. He likened Iran to "a man who knows very well that he ought to go to the dentist but is afraid of doing so and is annoyed with anybody who says that there is anything wrong with his teeth." This document was printed and circulated widely in British embassies throughout the world. In other memos, Shepherd argued that Mossadeq was "clearly unbalanced" on the grounds he shunned the title Excellency, refused to use the ministerial motor-car, and, as a clincher, had a "daughter in a mental home in Switzerland." [96] Other Foreign Office documents readily resorted to such characterizations. One declared outright:

> Most Iranians are introverts. Their imagination is strong and they naturally turn to the agreeable side of things— they love poetry and discussion of abstract ideas. Their emotions are strong and easily aroused. But they continually fail to test their imaginations against reality and to subordinate their emotions to reason. They lack common sense and the ability to differentiate emotion from facts. Their well-known mendacity is rather a carelessness to the truth than deliberate choice of falsehood. This excess of imagination and distaste for facts leads to an inability to go conscientiously into detail. Often, not finding the world to their dreams, they relapse into indolence and do not persevere. This tendency is exaggerated by the fatalism of their religion. They are intensely individualist, more in the sense of pursuing their personal interest than in the noble one of wishing to do things on their own without help. Nearly all classes have a passion for personal gain and are ready to do most things for money. They lack social conscience and are unready to subordinate personal interests to communal ones. They are vain and conceited, and unwilling to admit to themselves that they can be in the wrong. They are always ready to blame other people.[97]

Another memorandum entitled "The Persian Character" declared:

> Although the Persians display a veneer of Western civilization, the character still derives from their long history of autocratic rule and from their Islamic background. Among those chief traits are an intense national pride, extending at times to overwhelming conceit; a keen in-

tellect, ready wit and broad sense of humour and zeal for
learned conversation; an unabashed dishonesty; a fatal-
istic outlook on life and indifference to suffering; and a
friendly and hospitable nature. The ordinary Persian is
vain, unprincipled, eager to promise what he is incapable
or had no intention of performing, wedded to procrastination, and lacking in perseverance and energy. Above all
he loves intrigue and readily employs prevarication and
dishonesty whenever there is even a remote possibility of
personal gain. Although in conversation, an accomplished
liar, he does not expect to be believed.[98]

Such cultural diatribes should not be taken as the root
cause for the failed negotiations—as some in cultural studies
would be tempted to believe. Rather, they should be taken as
byproducts of that failure. The root cause lay in the British
refusal to relinquish control over oil production, and, con-
comitantly, the Iranian determination to gain control over
the same production. In other words, the impasse came not
because of cultural or racial prejudices but because of the
economic clash between resurgent nationalism and old-
fashioned imperialism.

The British propaganda onslaught was so effective that
historians even today, sixty years later, continue to regurgi-
tate the claim that the UK was more than willing to come
to a fair settlement and that the United States offered many
such settlements. Daniel Yergin, the doyen of the oil business and author of *The Prize*, puts the blame squarely on
the Iranians—their "obsessions," "theatrics," and "phantas-
magories [*sic*]"; their "wild," "violent," and "exaggerated
emotions"; their "paranoid hatred" of the British; and their
Alice-in-Wonderland politics.[99] His long chapter on Iran has
much on "Old Mossy's" long nose and pajamas, but not a
single mention of the taboo word "control"—even though

the subtitle of his book is *The Epic Quest for Oil, Money, and Power.* This omission is doubly surprising since he claims that many turning points in recent history—such as the German invasion of Russia and the Japanese sweep into the South Pacific in World War II, as well as the dramatic emergence of OPEC in the 1970s—were all prompted by the desire to gain control over oil production. "OPEC members," he admits, "did not want to be mere tax collectors. It was not only a question of garnering more of the rents. For the exporters, the greater question was sovereignty over their own natural resources. Everything else would be measured against that objective." Yergin nevertheless scrupulously shies away from admitting that Mossadeq and Iran could have had that same objective—control over their natural resources.

Barry Rubin, a leading specialist on U.S.-Iran relations, claims that Britain and the United States "accepted nationalization," that the latter was "neutral" with a "pro-Iran tilt," and that negotiations failed because of Mossadeq's "inability to compromise." "He," Rubin insists, "found himself unable to make necessary compromises for fear that his supporters might, perhaps literally, tear him to pieces." [100] He entitles his book *Paved with Good Intentions: The American Experience in Iran.* Peter Avery, professor of Oriental Studies at Cambridge, depicts Mossadeq as a petulant child proud of having brought the world to the verge of a major international crisis. His chapter on the crisis is titled "What One Man Can Do." [101] Reza Sheikholeslami, professor of Iranian Studies at Oxford, mirrors the stock Western view that depicts British and American policymakers as rational, pragmatic, and coolheaded, but Mossadeq as spoiled, erratic, mendacious, unpredictable, ungrateful, and, to top it all, dictatorial.[102] But nothing can be more satisfactory for Occidentals than to have natives endorsing their own views. Sireen Hunter, in a recent book entitled *The Future of Islam and the West,* claims that

Mossadeq "failed" because of "his adamant refusal to accept a settlement." [103] Not surprisingly, the official BP historian, Ronald Ferrier, argues that negotiations failed because of Mossadeq's "insecurities" and "the genes in the Iranian political body." [104]

Even authors sympathetic to Mossadeq tend to buy this argument. Sam Falle, after admitting that Mossadeq had been popular, the oil company had been stingy, and the United States had been as fearful of real nationalization as the British, nevertheless ends up claiming that Mossadeq eventually fell because he, unlike Gandhi, was "irrational." [105] George McGhee—architect of a little-known deal accepted by Mossadeq but nixed by Prime Minister Eden—concludes his "Iran saga" by citing Dean Acheson on how Mossadeq "sowed the wind and reaped the whirlwind because he was a rich, reactionary, feudal-minded Persian inspired by a fanatical hatred for the British." [106] The *New York Times*, in leaking the CIA-Wilber document half a century later, wrote that Mossadeq "had become prisoner of his own nationalism and thus was unable to reach an oil agreement." [107] Mark Gasiorowski, who has interviewed many gumshoes involved in the coup, insists that Britain had accepted nationalization and America had presented reasonable compromises, but Mossadeq had rejected them all. [108] Finally, Stephen Kinzer, the author of a laudatory work on Mossadeq, underpins his flattering depictions with the claim that the oil negotiations eventually broke down because of his "Shi'i ideal of pursuing justice even to the point of martyrdom." [109] In other words, the fault really lay not with the West but with Iran.

Not surprisingly, post-revolutionary nostalgia for the "good old days" tends to reinforce such interpretations. For example, Farah Diba, the former queen, in her recent memoirs claims that ultimately negotiations failed because of Mossadeq's "intransigence" and "refusal to take up British offers." [110] Abbas Milani, author of a laudatory biography of the shah, insinuates Mossadeq was the main obstacle to any resolution on the grounds that Truman had concluded early on that "nationalization was a foregone conclusion." [111] Similarly, Gholam Reza Afkhami, author of another laudatory biography of the shah, claims in no uncertain terms that Churchill and Truman accepted nationalization but Iranian "xenophobia" prevented settlement. [112] The nitty-gritty details in the behind-the-scenes negotiations as illuminated throughout this chapter, however, reveal that neither the UK nor the United States was willing to back down over the hard issue of nationalization. They, rather than Iran, were the main stumbling blocks. The devil lies in the details.

The Hague (May–June)

The takeover of the oil installations prompted the British government to lodge a formal complaint against Iran with the Court of International Justice at the Hague—better known as the World Court. The court, established by the League of Nations soon after World War I, had become the main judicial organ of the United Nations immediately after World War II.

The British complaint was spelled out in a thirty-seven-page brief entitled "The Anglo-Iranian Oil Company Case." [113] It conceded that Iran, as a sovereign state, had the right to nationalize sectors of its own economy, but argued that in this case it had violated international norms on three major counts. First, it had unilaterally canceled a duly signed international contract—the 1933 Oil Agreement—stipulating that under no conditions could one party cancel the concession, and that, if one had complaints, it was obliged to seek arbitration and revision, not cancellation. Second, it had "discriminated" and "targeted" only British property.

Third, it had failed to offer "fair compensation." In other memos, the British government indicated that it considered "fair compensation" to mean the total profits expected for the duration of the contract. Since the 1933 contract had another forty-two years to run and the gross profits accruing to Britain in 1949–50 had been £48.3 million, this added up to the enormous sum of £2,028 million. The Foreign Office later admitted in private that it would demand an "astronomical" figure so that Iran would never be able to pay it and therefore would have to relinquish control over "operations" and "disposal of oil in the world market." [114] Historians of the crisis have tended to gloss over this not-so-insignificant issue.

The brief further argued that the British government had the right to represent the oil company, since it was the "diplomatic protector of its citizens," and, like the Iranian government, had been party to the 1933 Agreement. It furthermore argued that the Court of International Justice had jurisdiction over the case both because a rapporteur from the League of Nations had been present in the 1933 negotiations and because the 1933 agreement had involved the British government as well as the British oil company. A confidential note added: "We are unable to accept contention that [the] issue does not concern His Majesty's Government. . . . Oil industry is of vital importance to HMG not only as a main source of revenue, but also as providing funds for essential economic development. It is of great importance in the economy of the UK and the free world generally." [115]

In addition to legal arguments, the British government launched a major publicity campaign. The company, it proclaimed, had invested "enormous sums" to "turn deserts into towns." It had willingly offered "generous" supplements to the 1933 agreement—if these offers had been taken up, the country's financial problems would have been solved. It had "voluntarily" built major ports, installations, and towns;

laid miles of roads and pipelines; and constructed hundreds
of homes, clinics, bridges, schools, stadiums, and football
fields.[116] Of course, it did not forget the swimming pools. In
the years between 1934 and 1950, it had Persianized the staff,
increasing the number of senior Iranians from 25 to 941, junior from 702 to 4,549, and artisan from 1,759 to 17,380. It
insisted that it was only because of "violent nationalists" that
a fair Supplementary Agreement had not been signed.

The Iranian government countered that the World Court
had no jurisdiction over this case since the dispute was not
between two states but between a sovereign state and a private company. It argued that Iran, as a sovereign state, had
the right to nationalize its own resources without seeking
permission from an international body. It repeated the offer to pay "fair compensation." It also argued that the 1933
Agreement was invalid because it had been forced upon the
country, because the country had been dominated by a dictator, and because the company itself had failed to abide by the
same agreement. It had failed to promote Iranians to senior
positions. It had failed to open company accounts to Iranian
officials. It had failed to refrain from interfering in the internal affairs of Iran. The Iranian government also waged
its own propaganda campaign, accusing the company of exploiting the country, of double-bookkeeping, of mistreating
its labor force, and of behaving like a typical colonial power.

The Hague issued a quick temporary ruling. It proposed
that until a final ruling could be reached, the AIOC's operations in Iran should be supervised by a board of five—two
from each state and the fifth from a third. Britain promptly
accepted; Iran declined on grounds that the ruling violated
national sovereignty, contradicted nationalization law, and
would bring back the old AIOC in a "new form." In fact,
thirteen months later—in July 1952—when the World
Court issued its final verdict, it came down solidly on the

side of Iran. In a 9 to 5 ruling, with the British judge voting with the majority, the court determined that the case was not within its jurisdiction since it did not involve a dispute between two states. It agreed with Mossadeq that this was a domestic dispute between a private company and a sovereign state. The "lunatics" in Tehran had won their legal case at the Hague.

Just as the case was being argued at the Hague, the British were taking strong measures. The AIOC moved to "shut down" operations and instructed much of its staff to resign. To deter those tempted to work for the NIOC, it warned that salaries would not be convertible into sterling. Within six weeks of the Iranian flag going up over the AIOC offices, 2,094 Europeans—the entire British staff, together with 1,653 Pakistanis and Indians—had left with much fanfare, some on HMS *Mauritius*.[117] To deter others from filling these positions, the British exerted pressure on western European governments. For example, when some four hundred Germans applied to work for the NIOC, their government denied them permission, claiming they would not have proper protection in Iran since West Germany did not have official representation there.[118]

In addition, the British government froze Iranian assets in London—totaling £25 million; restricted the convertibility of other funds into dollars; stopped royalty payments; found bureaucratic problems to limit the export of iron, steel, lubricating oil, tin plates, sugar, and spare parts; drew up a detailed list of commodities traded between Britain and Iran; warned companies against doing business in Iran; and, most important of all, threatened to impound any tanker leaving Iranian ports with "stolen" petroleum. The Ministry of Fuel felt confident since it calculated that the Seven Sisters owned or controlled most of the world's 1,500 tankers.[119] The Soviets had only 10.

The ministry also felt confident that "special bonuses" could persuade independent tankers not to venture into Iranian ports. When a tanker commissioned by a Greek entrepreneur and flying the Honduran flag tried to break the embargo, it was seized entering the Red Sea and detained in Aden. The Foreign Office reported that AIOC officials, as well as many unnamed others, were keeping vigilant watch to prevent foreigners from "pirating" any oil. The British received assurances from a number of governments— including Italy, Japan, and Germany—that they would not issue licenses for the import of oil from Iran.[120] In a piece of Orwellian double-talk, the Foreign Office declared: "Our actions should not in any way be interpreted as an economic sanction or pressure."[121] After years of insisting that Iranians did not have the technical know-how to run the industry, the British soon had to admit, albeit privately, that the NIOC was able to keep the wells and refinery going but was unable to find export outlets precisely because of these actions.[122] Ambassador Grady warned Washington that the British were determined to destroy Mossadeq through these sanctions, that they wanted the United States to join in them, and that if the United States did so, it would end up absorbing much of the antagonism now directed at London.[123]

The British military, meanwhile, drew up a detailed plan for the occupation of Abadan.[124] Code named "Buccaneer," the contingency plan spelled out how six battalions would need only twenty-four hours to invade from Iraq and occupy the Abadan refinery. Prime Minister Attlee, however, never activated the plan. Neither did Churchill, his successor, even though he readily accused his predecessor of being "spineless." The operation "risked excessive dangers."[125] It could tempt the Soviets to invade Azerbaijan. It could spark another general strike. It could lead to acts of sabotage in the refinery and the oilfields. It would not guarantee control over the pipelines and oil wells. It could strain British military resources elsewhere. It could trigger a run on sterling—something that actually did happen later, during the Suez Crisis. A Defence Ministry official bemoaned, "The military difficulties of mounting an operation nowadays are almost entirely due to our having lost the use of the Indian army." [126] The former viceroy of India, Lord Admiral Mountbatten, stressed that an invasion could possibly prompt a Soviet response and would certainly be "disastrous" to the refinery. He advised accepting the principle of nationalization as a sap, but at the same time asking for so much compensation that Iran would have no choice but to cooperate in the future—especially in selling oil to the British Navy. [127]

The United States also objected to Buccaneer. Although they were as opposed to nationalization as the British, the Truman administration favored negotiations over military action. It presumed that Mossadeq could be persuaded to give up real control as long as he appeared to have won nominal nationalization. To bring about such a solution, Truman announced he was dispatching a personal emissary, Averell Harriman, to Tehran to act as an impartial broker between Britain and Iran. The British cabinet concluded it "could not afford to break with the United States on an issue of this kind." [128]

Harriman Mission (July)

Averell Harriman, a millionaire businessman and former secretary of commerce, had the reputation of being a successful trouble-shooter. He had been President Roosevelt's special envoy to Britain and the Soviet Union, and President Truman's personal spokesman with the Marshall Plan. The British foreign minister forewarned Ambassador Shepherd that although Harriman was "fundamentally well-disposed to us," he was "inarticulate," "reserved," and had a "strong sense of personal vanity." "Experience," he added, "has shown that playing this foible leads to best results." [129] Mossadeq, who liked to joke with negotiators, found Harriman humorless.

Harriman's avowed mission was to find a "compromise solution" acceptable to America's two "friends." His real task, however, was to persuade Mossadeq that nationalization did not necessarily mean outright "control" but "having authority over." He was to "educate" him on the complexities of the international oil business—the price of crude in the Mexican Gulf as opposed to the Persian Gulf, the technicalities of refining petroleum for different uses, the shortage of tankers, the differences between "upstream" and "downstream," the intricacies of calculating profits, and the relationships between the major producers and the independent producers.[130] He, together with Walter Levy, tried to overwhelm Mossadeq with facts and figures on prices, rates, market fluctuations, investment returns, and so on. Mossadeq, however, tried to redirect discussions toward the central question: who would control the production and sale of Iranian oil? What Harriman and Levy termed "education," Mossadeq saw as "obscuration" and "hoodwinking." They came away complaining that Mossadeq could only think in generalities. He came away suspecting they were trying to take him for a ride.

The British delegate at the UN later wrote that Harriman, before departing, had extensive meetings at the State Department with representatives of the American oil industry anxious to maintain a "tough policy" and pursue a "common front" on the Iranian crisis. They were concerned that "too many concessions in Persia" would have adverse "repercussions in other oil producing countries" including Venezuela. He added that Harriman and Levy left for Tehran "firmly supporting" the line that the AIOC must retain both "control" and the 50/50 principle.[131] The 50/50 deal had been elevated to the level of something sacred. The British embassy in Washington assured London that although Harriman was reticent in public, both he and Levy in private were 100 percent behind Britain.[132]

Harriman arrived in Tehran on July 15. This happened to coincide with the Tudeh Party's celebrations of the 1946 general strike. Just as Harriman landed in Tehran Airport, the Tudeh rally in Parliament Square was attacked by the Toilers Party and SUMKA (the Iranian National Socialist Party)—the main Nazi group. It was revealed years later that the attack had been encouraged by the CIA.[133] The authorities failed to take precautions, with the result that the street casualties were the worst in years—16 killed and more than 280 injured.[134] Tanks had to be used to restore order. An AIOC representative in Tehran informed Britannic House that the violence had been initiated not by the Tudeh but by Baqai's "hooligans"[135] Holding the police chief and the interior minister, General Zahedi, responsible for the bloodshed, Mossadeq replaced the latter with Amir-Alai from the Iran Party and tried to bring the former to account in a civilian court. The shah, however, protected the police chief in a military court, which gave him a suspended sentence totaling one month.[136]

Although the Tudeh rally had little to do with Harriman, American and British newspapers construed the whole incident to be a violent communist act designed to sabotage his mission. The British embassy, however, explained that Mossadeq had been reluctant to ban rallies and clamp down on the Tudeh because of his commitment to constitutional laws. "The Prime Minister," the ambassador reported, "is by mentality and background opposed to any form of repression. His advent to power coincided with May Day and his first action was to remove the ban on demonstrators for that day. . . . He has also transferred the trials [of Tudeh leaders accused of trying to assassinate the shah in 1949] to civilian courts." [137] There the original sentences meted out by military courts were overruled and new trials were ordered.

Harriman arrived with an entourage of five: his wife; Levy; an Air Force general to supervise his personal security; a State Department expert on the Middle East; and Col. Vernon Walters, a French-speaking Army intelligence officer, to act as his official interpreter with Mossadeq. Walters continued to serve this function for much of the next few months. The day after Harriman's arrival, Henry Grady, the American ambassador who had antagonized the British, announced his retirement. He felt that his position had been undercut by the presidential emissary. Ambassador Shepherd denigrated him as "vain," and, "like so many Americans ham-handed in his incursions into dangerous spheres." [138] Loy Henderson— Grady's replacement—had served as Harriman's right-hand man in wartime Moscow. He had also served as U.S. ambassador in Iraq and had the reputation of knowing how to "handle" Middle Eastern oil-producing countries. Instrumental in the 1953 coup, he remained in Tehran until 1956 when he took a seat on the board of the Suez Canal Company. Many years later, he confessed to an interviewer that he wanted good relations with Iran but not at the "price" of accepting the takeover of the oil industry: "We did not believe that such an expropriation was in the basic interest of Iran, GB or the US. Acts of this kind tend to undermine [the] mutual trust that was necessary if international trade was to flourish." [139]

Harriman's mission lasted a full forty days. In a report on the mission, he wrote that in discussions with Mossadeq he had made it clear the United States accepted "nationalization" but insisted on having "a foreign-owned company to

act as an agent of NIOC in conducting operations in Iran."
He went on to say, "We have made it plain that operations in
Iran must be run on an efficient basis and this could only be
accomplished through [a] foreign-owned company operating
with freedom in day to day management though acting under [a] policy principle established by the government or the
National Oil Company." [140] He complained that Mossadeq
had retorted that such a scheme would merely "disguise" a
new concession given to British and other foreign companies.
Making no headway, Harriman rushed to London, together
with Shepherd, in a desperate attempt to personally persuade
the British cabinet to restart direct negotiations with Mossadeq. He told Colonel Walters, "I am simply not used to
failure." [141]

Norman Seddon, the remaining AIOC manager, was skeptical of the London venture. He reported back to Britannic
House that the Iranians "think they can bring us down to our
knees," that toughness was the best way to deal with them,
that there was no possibility of reaching a "satisfactory settlement," and that both Sayyed Ziya and Qavam had assured
him that Mossadeq would not last long. He added that Harriman and Levy had done an "excellent job in bringing home
to the Persians the facts of life." He concluded, "I remain
very doubtful, as to whether it will be possible to reach any
agreement as long as the present Government exists." [142]

Stokes Mission (August)

The British cabinet—after some prodding—sent Sir Richard
Stokes, the Lord Privy Seal, to Tehran to negotiate directly
with the Iranian government. A millionaire entrepreneur
with socialist convictions, Stokes was reputed to know
how to deal with large business corporations. Before leaving, the cabinet issued him strict guidelines. "The ultimate

objectives," the guidelines stipulated, "are to maintain the
flow of oil through control by a British company," "safeguard the UK balance of payments," "not injure UK interests in other countries," and "prevent Persian interference
with the running of the AIOC machine." He was told that
Mossadeq was "unintelligent," "obstinate," and, therefore,
"unlikely to recede from his original position." He was also
told that he was not likely to last long because of increasing
opposition—especially from the shah and "moderate public
opinion." [143]

Stokes brought with him an MI6 colonel as his Persian
interpreter, and a colleague who had supervised recent na-
tionalizations in Britain to "educate" Iranians on the intricacies of such operations. Accompanied by Harriman, they
arrived on August 3 and remained there until August 22.
The delegation, joined by Sir Francis Shepherd and his embassy advisers, had eight long meetings with their Iranian
counterparts. The Iranian delegation was headed by Matin-
Daftari and members of his Mixed Commission—especially
Shayegan, Sanjabi, Saleh, and Hassebi. The two sides invited
Harriman and Levy to participate in one key session. An unnamed AIOC informant reported to William Fraser that the
British delegation tried to "cook up a broth" palatable to all.
He advised the company to keep a "low profile" since it was
a "pariah" in Iran. But he reassured Fraser that Stokes and
the "Americans were working hard to help us." He stressed
they were determined to "arrive at a settlement which would
not upset the rest of the Middle East." [144]

Stokes was no more successful than Harriman—simply
because his aim was no different. He was willing to concede
"authority," but, following instructions, refused to relinquish "control." Mossadeq, on the other hand, was willing
to discuss compensation, sale of oil to the AIOC, and rehir-
ing of British technicians, but refused to give ground on the

vital issue of control. Stokes's proposals conceded "general authority" to Iran, but delegated "executive management" to an operating organization to be registered in Britain as a British company. This organization would retain full power to explore, drill, refine, and sell oil in international markets. It would hire the technicians and the tankers needed for its operations. It would retain full executive powers for another twenty-five years but promised to pace up the process of Iranianizing the staff.

Stokes and his nationalization expert, however, were evasive when asked such pertinent questions as: How had Britain determined "fair compensation" for the recently nationalized coal, steel, and electrical industries in Britain? Who appointed the directors of these nationalized industries? Why could not previous AIOC technicians work for the NIOC? All they could reply was that AIOC employees were adamant they would not work for Iran. "He wished to make clear," Stokes stated, "that neither he nor anyone else could make the staff do what it did not want to do. As he had said in the first meeting the staff would not work for any management which they themselves did not consider proved and experienced both technically and administratively. The day to day management of the industry must be in British hands. . . . In brief, Persia had the oil and the UK had the knowledge of running the industry and distributing and selling its products." [145]

Stokes did not limit his meetings to the official delegation. He met Mossadeq and the shah each twice. The shah, too, asked why AIOC technicians could not work for the NIOC. "I replied," wrote Stokes, "that the staff was insistent it must have British control and administration in charge of their day to day affairs." [146] The first meeting with Mossadeq did not go well. The MI6 interpreter was caught taking notes in violation of Mossadeq's instructions. Walters had to fill in.

The second meeting was equally unproductive. Stokes tried to "educate" Mossadeq on complexities; Mossadeq tried to bring the conversation back to the issue of control. Mossadeq rejected outright the "operating organization" on the grounds that such a scheme would not only diminish Iran's "power of management" but would also "revive the former AIOC in a new form." [147] Stokes also found time to meet Kashani, Sayyed Ziya, the latter's main financial backer, the presidents of the Majles and Senate, twenty other senators, the assistant court minister, the editor of *Kayhan*, and the head of the main anti-Tudeh trade union. These meetings reinforced Iranian suspicions that the British were incessantly meddling in their internal politics.

While Stokes was doing his rounds, Henderson—in a long, private conversation—sounded out the shah on the possibility of "replacing" Mossadeq. The shah responded that however much he would like to get rid of him and however much he realized Mossadeq's policies were "leading Iran to ruin," he could not go against overwhelming national sentiments. Henderson's note on the conversation sums up the shah's tragic role in the whole crisis—and well beyond:

> I told him that Iran's position was growing daily more desperate and in the end it might be necessary to resort to desperate measures. The Shah replied the "Brits tell me there should be [a] strong man and take resolute action, but these so-called strong men like my father, Hitler, Stalin, etc, took resolute and bold action when they knew that national sentiment was behind them. They never moved against basic feelings [of] their peoples. In this case national feelings are against Britain and these have been inflamed by demagogues: no matter how strong and resolute I may wish to be, I cannot take [an] unconstitutional move against strong current of national feelings. . . . I

am convinced that [any] attempt on my part to remove
Musaddiq just now would give his friends and my enemies opportunity to convince the public that [the] Crown
has degenerated to [a] mere British tool and such prestige
as [the] Crown has would disappear. [The] only hope as I
can see it is for Musaddiq either to become more sober and
reasonable or for him to make so many mistakes that responsible leaders of Iran will overthrow him in Majlis.[148]

If the definition of tragedy is drama in which the protagonist is cognizant of the dangers looming ahead and knows
how to avoid them yet cannot do so because of forces beyond
his control, then the shah's fate in the whole crisis can be
seen as one of high tragedy.

While Stokes was in Iran, Tehran was shaken by revela-
tions of the so-called Seddon Files. Claiming that Seddon was
meddling in politics, the police raided his house and found
reams of AIOC correspondence. These letters dealt mostly
with routine matters, but the press construed them evidence of oil-company interference in internal politics. What
is more, someone—probably Baqai's Toilers Party—added
doctored correspondence to the files supposedly between
the AIOC and the Tudeh Party.[149] This reinforced the notion that the British and the Soviets had common interests
against Iran and that the AIOC and the Tudeh had worked
together to bring about the 1951 general strike. This provided propagandistic ammunition for the right—both inside
and outside the National Front.

In his autopsy on the Stokes mission, Ambassador Shepherd wrote:

The missions of Harriman and Stokes were unproductive.
The Persians had indeed throughout shown their inability to understand the fundamental requirements for the

conduct of the oil industry and have been unwilling to recognize the facts which have been presented to them in many ways and from many different sources. It does not seem in retrospect that the Persians have been prepared to listen to the guidance of reason and common sense, but have been swayed to a large extent by emotion and by fear that in acknowledging the cogency of the arguments and explanations put forward to them they would in some way have been betraying the interests of their country. They have succeeded by obstinacy and a series of almost incredible blunders in destroying for the time being in a period of five months an industry it has taken fifty years to build up.[150]

In separate telegrams to the Foreign Office, Shepherd added, "My personal view is that there is now no more chance of reaching a reasonable agreement with Musaddiq than ever there was and that the moment has come for us to try and get him out. . . . What the breakdown of negotiations means is that we have no (repeat no) future hope of reaching a reasonable settlement with the present Persian Government. The departure of Mr. Harriman from Tehran shows there is no further hope from mediation." [151] Officials at the Ministry of Fuel were equally blunt but far more honest:

If Dr. Mussadiq resigns or is replaced, it is just possible that we shall be able to get away from outright nationalization . . . It would certainly be dangerous to offer greater real control of oil operations in Persia. Although something might be done to put more of a Persian facade on the setup, we must not forget that the Persians are not so far wrong when they say that all our proposals are, in fact, merely dressing up AIOC control in other clothing. . . . Any real concession on this point is impossible. If we reached settlement on Mussadiq's terms, we would jeopardise not only British but also American oil interests throughout the world. We would destroy prospects of the investments of foreign capital in backward countries. We would strike a fatal blow to international law. We have a duty to stay and use force to protect our interest . . . We must force the Shah to bring down Mussadiq.[152]

The British government responded to the failure of the Stokes mission by submitting a formal complaint to the Security Council in the UN claiming that Iran was jeopardizing world peace by rejecting outright the temporary ruling issued earlier by the Hague.

Mission to the UN and the United States (October–November)

The British complaint to the UN prompted Mossadeq to personally present the Iranian case before the Security Council. He arrived in New York on October 8 with a delegation that included Matin-Daftari, his main adviser on international law; Shayegan, his personal adviser; Fatemi, his vice premier; Hassebi, his oil expert; Sanjabi of the Iran Party; Baqai of the Toilers Party; and Saleh, his ambassador to the United States. The visit had also been prompted by a diplomatic faux pas. President Truman had sent a telegram to Prime Minister Attlee inviting him to visit Washington. A copy of the invitation, addressed simply to the prime minister, had been sent to the Tehran embassy, and the staff there, thinking it was intended for the Iranian prime minister, had delivered it to Mossadeq. To cover up the embarrassment, the State Department promptly announced that the invitations had been intended for both prime ministers. Mossadeq found the mistake funny but took up the unintended invitation nevertheless.

At the UN, Mossadeq repeated the arguments presented at the Hague, giving greater emphasis to political ones and lesser to legalistic ones.[153] He spoke in French. When he grew faint in the midst of his long speech, he handed the text to Saleh for completion. He argued that the World Court and the Security Council had no jurisdiction, since it was an internal dispute between a sovereign state and a private company. He accused Britain of dangerously escalating the issue into an international crisis by threatening invasion, massing warships, and imposing sanctions. He said he would readily plead guilty to endangering world peace if he had placed Iranian warships on the Thames. He accused Britain of old fashioned "imperialism"—of imposing unfair restrictions on his country, interfering in its politics, and rapaciously exploiting its natural resources. He argued that whereas India, Pakistan, Indonesia, and many other countries were gaining their independence and legitimate rights, Britain continued to treat Iran in a typical colonial fashion reminiscent of the old East India Company. "[The] AIOC," he noted, "is notorious in Iran as the Colonial Exploiting Company." It kept its accounts secret; forced workers to live in abject misery; refused to train nationals for responsible positions; and out of annual profits of more than £62 million gave Iran a measly £9 million. He stressed yet again that Iran was willing to offer "fair compensation," rehire British technicians, and sell oil to regular customers. "We have no desire," he concluded, "to commit economic suicide or kill the goose that laid the golden eggs." The British UN ambassador asked London for data to rebut Mossadeq's profit statistics. London responded but instructed him to keep them secret—especially from Mossadeq and the American oil companies.[154]

Unable to gain enough votes on the Security Council, Britain "made virtue out of necessity" and accepted a face-saving "compromise" resolution introduced by France. The resolution postponed further discussion until the Hague issued its final verdict. This was taken in Iran as a major victory for Mossadeq. The Soviet Union, of course, had opposed the British resolution from the very start. And nonpermanent members, led by India and Ecuador, had also refused to go along with the British.[155] James Goode, a U.S. diplomatic historian, writes, "Musaddiq's arguments touched third world delegates whose nations had experienced colonialism or other forms of imperialism. . . . Postponement represented a victory for Musaddiq whose prestige at home soared."[156] The British complained that the UN had failed to meet its responsibilities but claimed that at least the issue had remained alive. While in New York, Mossadeq had a full medical checkup. It was administered by the very same doctor who had operated on the shah and happened to be a close acquaintance of Allen Dulles, the future head of the CIA.

Immediately after the UN presentation, Mossadeq traveled to Washington, where Colonel Walters continued to serve as his main interpreter. He had lengthy discussions with McGhee, Acheson, and Truman. The State Department briefed Truman that Mossadeq was "well informed," "honest and idealistic," "alert, witty, and affable," yet "voluble, emotional, impractical, and unrealistic." He was also told that "the majority of the population supported his opposition to foreign interference." He was advised to steer the conversation away from specifics and toward vague generalities about the "dangers of communism," "America's friendship for Iran," and "our disinterested concern about the oil crisis."[157]

These discussions in Washington, unlike the previous ones, surprisingly made some headway. Thirty years later,

McGhee revealed that he had put together a complex package that seemed to be acceptable to Mossadeq. The NIOC
would own the Kermanshah refinery and administer all the
oilfields—that is, it would control the exploration, production, and transportation of crude. But the Abadan refinery would be sold to a non-British company—preferably a
Dutch one—which would train Iranians and hire its own
technicians. The sum accrued from the sale of the Abadan refinery would go to the AIOC as "compensation." The NIOC
would sell annually to the AIOC at least 30 million tons of
crude for the next fifteen years. The NIOC board would
consist of three Iranians and four non-Iranians. Its transactions would remain in sterling, although Swiss and Dutch
currencies would be acceptable. While McGhee was ham-
mering out this proposal with Mossadeq, Acheson was reas-
suring the British that he continued to fully support their
two fundamental principles: "oil produced in Persia must
be subject to British control and distribution" and "no arrangement can be made which would upset the world oil
market." [158]

At the urging of the United States, Mossadeq prolonged
his visit while waiting first for the general elections in Britain and then for the replacement of Attlee by Churchill
in 10 Downing Street. He toured Philadelphia, had a full
checkup at Walter Reed Hospital, and visited George Mc-
Ghee's gentleman's ranch outside Washington, where he
exchanged crop tips with local farmers. The U.S. administration, McGhee admits, was under the false impression that the
incoming Conservative government would be more flexible.
In fact, Churchill and Eden, the new foreign secretary, had
during their electoral campaign mercilessly tormented Labour for being spineless and weak-kneed "appeasers." Eden,
who had studied Persian as an undergraduate and flattered
himself as an expert on the "Oriental mind," quickly took

personal charge of the "oil problem," replacing the "inadequate" Working Party with his own Ministerial Committee.

Not surprisingly, Eden rejected outright McGhee's package as "totally unacceptable." He insisted it was far better to have "no agreement than to have a bad one." [159] Although surprised by Mossadeq's willingness to relinquish the Abadan refinery, he insisted that the AIOC should not only return to Iran but also regain full control over the oilfields. His colleagues echoed him, claiming that the package was "impractical" and a "blow to our investments elsewhere." They also claimed that Shell would refuse the Abadan refinery unless it controlled the oilfields; and Western technicians would not work for the NIOC because Iranians were "unreliable, incompetent, and unwilling to listen to consultants." [160]

The rejection was subsequently backed up by the major oil companies. Separate delegations from Shell, Standard Oil, Socony-Vacuum, and other companies reinforced the British view that "it was not in their interest to come to an agreement" with Mossadeq, and that if nationalization "paid off" in Iran, it would have disastrous effects on other countries.[161] Goode, the diplomatic historian, writes, "The British government would accept no settlement that would threaten their overseas investments even if it meant Iran went communist. Musaddiq could not be allowed to profit from the takeover of AIOC properties, nor humiliate them or discriminate against them." [162]

The British put negotiations on hold and continued to wait for what they were convinced would be the imminent and inevitable removal of Mossadeq—either by the shah or by the Majles. Their policy was blunt: "We will negotiate with a successor Government and not with Musaddiq." [163] Eden's advice to Churchill was, "I think we should be stubborn even if the temperature rises somewhat." [164] His public stance was more pious: "Patience is from God. Haste is from

the devil."[165] Shepherd detected two nuanced "differences"
between the UK and the United States: the former was convinced if the "oil issue simmered a while," there would soon
be a change of government in Tehran; the latter was willing to sacrifice the AIOC as long as the 50/50 principle was
upheld and the international oil business was not overly dis-
rupted.[166] McGhee writes:

> I, and several others who had been closely involved in
> the negotiations—were waiting in the Department com-
> munications room when Acheson returned to our Paris
> Embassy from his fateful luncheon with Anthony Eden.
> Acheson said over the Paris line that Eden wouldn't buy
> it, that he thanked us for our efforts but that he couldn't
> accept our proposal and didn't want to negotiate any fur-
> ther. He asked us to tell Musaddiq that it's all off. There
> was silence as we grasped the fact that we had failed. To
> me it was almost the end of the world—I attached so
> much importance to an agreement and honestly thought
> we had provided the British a basis for one.
>
> I asked for an appointment with Musaddiq, and when
> I entered his bedroom at the Shoreham he merely said,
> "You've come to send me home."
>
> "Yes," I said, "I am sorry to have to tell you that we
> can't bridge the gap between you and the British. It's a
> great disappointment to us as it must be to you." It was
> a moment I will never forget. He accepted the result qui-
> etly, with no recriminations.[167]

This little-known incident—which conventional histories
tend to overlook entirely—belies the conventional notion
that Britain, unlike Iran, was always willing to compromise.
Despite the British nixing of the deal, Col. Vernon Walters
in his memoirs claims the Washington negotiations failed

simply because Mossadeq "did not feel himself in a position to accept any agreement." [168] Similarly, Dean Acheson claims in his memoirs that Mossadeq could not compromise because he had "truly sowed the wind and reaped the whirlwind":

> Mossadeq's self-defeating quality was that he never paused to see that the passion he excited to support him restricted his freedom of choice and left only extreme solutions possible. We were, perhaps, slow in realizing that he was essentially a rich, reactionary, feudal minded Persian inspired by a fanatical hatred of the British and a desire to expel them and all their works from the country regardless of the cost. He was a great actor and gambler.[169]

Acheson was less disingenuous in confidential memoranda. He wrote how telling Churchill, "the wounded lion," that the AIOC could not return to Iran and that the Abadan refinery had to be handed over to the Dutch was tantamount to asking the United States to "step aside in favor of Guatemala." [170]

As a parting gift to Mossadeq, President Truman offered a $23 million loan to be channeled through the U.S. development program known as Point IV. Mossadeq left Washington on November 18, and, on his way back home, stopped over in Cairo, where he received a tumultuous welcome. Enthusiastic crowds literally carried his car down an avenue, which they named after him. Egypt was in the midst of its own campaign to nationalize the British- and French-owned Suez Canal Company. Mossadeq received an even more tumultuous welcome in Tehran. In his report to Parliament, he explained the British strategy was to regain control over the oil industry, pretend to accept the principle of nationalization, and bide their time until they could overthrow his government.[171] Using the opportunity, he shuffled his cabinet, obtained a unanimous vote of confidence, and set the date for the forthcoming seventeenth Majles elections.

In the cabinet shuffle, Mossadeq gave the justice ministry to Amir-Alai; the education ministry to Saleh; the communications ministry to Dr. Ghulam-Hussein Sadiqi, a French-educated sociologist at Tehran University; the agricultural ministry to Khalel Taleqani, a young French-educated agronomist; the labor ministry to Ibrahim Alemi, a French-educated lawyer whom the British deemed "completely subservient" to Mossadeq; the war ministry to Gen. Morteza Yazdanpanha, an old career officer; and the economics ministry to Ali Amini (Amin al-Dawleh), a French-educated aristocrat and former head of the Industrial Bank. Amini also happened to be his distant relative and a longtime critic of the shah.

Mossadeq's first cabinet had been "right-leaning"; the second was clearly left-leaning, since four of the ministers— Amir-Alai, Saleh, Sadiqi, and Taleqani—came from the Iran Party. In a long address to Parliament, Mossadeq promised free elections, reminded the audience he had always advocated electoral reform, and vowed to remain in office until the oil problem was solved.[172] Loy Henderson confided to Francis Shepherd that Mossadeq had reached a new level of popularity and that the shah "feared more having him in opposition than in power."[173] Henderson was instructed to read Mossadeq the "Battle Act" about selling oil to countries behind the Iron Curtain.[174]

Shepherd, in one of his long, opinionated memos, admitted that Mossadeq still enjoyed popularity but added it would be best to persist with procrastination, since "there is now a good prospect that the opposition will shortly overturn him":

It seems clear that Mr. Musaddiq himself, aided by clever propaganda, has captured the imagination of the Persian people to a considerable extent. There are very good reasons for this which can only be understood in light of a knowledge of Persian history and the Persian character. To begin with, unlike all other Prime Ministers since 1923, Musaddiq is not an obvious nominee of the Shah or of one or another great power. Secondly, he had done something which is always dear to Persian hearts: he had flouted the authority of a great power and a great foreign interest and he has gone a long way towards damaging the prestige of the first and the prosperity of the second. . . .

But while the initial popularity of Mussadiq's negative achievements coupled with the effect of his frail and ailing figure on those many Persians in whom a strain of sentimental mysticism still runs, must be accepted, I believe that as a movement the National Front is largely devoid of positive content. It has taken firm hold only on a small minority.[175]

George Middleton, Shepherd's charge d'affaires, reaffirmed these views. He predicted that Mossadeq's position would inevitably weaken because of hostility from the armed forces, difficulties in the economy—especially in the bazaar—the American ambassador favoring a "clean break," and, most important of all, the expected increasing opposition in both the Senate and the forthcoming Majles.[176] In February 1952, a top level Anglo-American meeting was convened in London to discuss the Iranian crisis. Its records have been destroyed.[177]

The Seventeenth Majles

Most constituencies in Iran were "rotten boroughs." Elections in small towns and rural constituencies were determined partly by local magnates—especially big landlords and tribal chiefs, herding their peasants and tenants to the polls—and partly by provincial officials, including military commanders, packing the electoral boards, supervising the balloting, and announcing the results. Over the years, Mossadeq had introduced bills to increase urban representation, create university seats, and make the electoral boards more independent. Since his reform bills had been shelved, he had no choice but to enter the new elections with the existing system.

The results in rural constituencies and small towns were predictable. Landlords and businessmen linked to Britain—such as Sheikh Hadi Taheri and Hashem Malek-Madani—were reelected from their hometowns. The two were generous supporters of Sayyed Ziya. The British profiles described Taheri as "very friendly to us," "one of the most solid and reliable deputies," and a "patriot who would not allow his patriotism to interfere unduly with his personal interests." Jamal al-Din Imami, the Majles president who had made the mistake of offering the premiership to Mossadeq, was elected from Khoi. Realizing he would not be reelected from Tehran, he ran for this constituency in Azerbaijan, which had been under martial law ever since 1946. Sayyed Hassan Imami, the Imam Jum'eh of Tehran and a high court judge with a long career protecting royal estates from their dispossessed previous owners, won a seat from Mahabad, which also had been under martial law since 1946. Abdul-Rahim Faramarzi, editor of *Kayhan*, was elected from Veramin near Tehran, where the royal family and Sayyed Ziya owned large estates. Morad Ibrahim Rigi, a Baluchi chief, was reelected from Baluchestan. Similarly, four Zolfaqaris, leaders of their tribes in eastern Azerbaijan, were all elected from their home province.

The elections in the cities were far more competitive. But the competition was not so much between royalists and the National Front as between two wings of the National Front. On one side were the Iran Party and Mossadeq's secular followers. On the other side were Ayatollah Kashani's Mujaheden-e Islam and Baqai's Toilers Party, with tenuous support of the Fedayan-e Islam. The two jockeyed to field their candidates and gain influence inside the interior ministry, whose head changed a number of times during the elections. In Tehran the two wings managed to put together a winning joint slate that included Makki, Kashani, Hassebi, Haerizadeh, Baqai, Nariman, and Shayegan.

In provincial cities, however, the two fielded separate candidates. Iran Party leaders, such as Razavi, Sanjabi, and Moazemi, won in their hometowns—in Kerman, Kermanshah, and Golpayegan respectively. Meanwhile, Kashani's candidates did the same in such towns as Shahrud and Tabriz. The campaign in Qom turned into a three-way race with Kashani, the National Front, and the local clerical establishment fielding separate candidates.

In the midst of the campaign, a sixteen-year-old member of the Fedayan shot and wounded Fatemi, denouncing him as a *kafer* (unbeliever). The would-be assassin lived to become a venerable Majles deputy in the Islamic Republic. Watching the elections closely, the British embassy commented, "The dissension between Kashani and Musaddiq was brought into the open this week. Kashani has been increasingly dissatisfied with Musaddiq and the Interior Minister because they will not help him in getting his candidates elected to the Majles; he is also aware that the scandalous 'recommendations' for elections by his sons has seriously damaged his own prestige."[178] Fearing the urban races could spiral out of control and the rural vote might produce a conservative bloc, Mossadeq suspended the elections when 79 deputies—out of a possible 136—had been elected. This was just enough to provide the new Majles with a quorum.

The convening of the Majles in April 1952 gave the UK and the United States the opportunity to bring down the government. Mossadeq could rely on twenty-five votes; Kashani on ten; the shah on twenty; others, such as the two Qashqayi brothers, Khosrow and Mohammad-Hussein, declared themselves independent. In other words, Mossadeq could carry the day as long as he retained the support of Kashani and some independents. Sayyed Ziya boasted—with a great deal of exaggeration—that he had the secret support of at least twenty-five deputies.[179] The British embassy reported there were clear indications the shah was trying to come to some kind of understanding with Kashani, and the latter had instructed his followers to cease criticizing the royal family.[180] Gen. Abdul-Hussein Hajazi, a former governor of Khuzestan who enjoyed the confidence of both the court and the British, assured the latter that the former intended to "overthrow" Mossadeq as soon as the Majles convened.

The British retorted that they were tired of such promises, having heard them after the Harriman mission, after the Stokes mission, and after Mossadeq's trip to America.[181] They wanted something more substantial. Middleton assured London the shah wanted Mossadeq to go but preferred that he should go quietly after having lost the "people's" support.[182] A Foreign Office diplomat in London wrote in the margins of a Tehran report: "I tend to the view that Musaddiq still enjoys some public support, more than some of our close friends would have us believe. . . . Coup d'état may well be the only answer." [183]

The Majles began ominously for Mossadeq. It elected Hassan Imami over Moazemi by a vote of 39 to 35 to be house president. The British reported the palace had lobbied against Moazemi, whom it claimed to be a "crafty, unreliable, pseudo-socialist and reputed to be the richest man in the majles." [184] The House also delayed discussing Mossadeq's request for a bill to give him special powers lasting six months to deal with the economic embargo. At the same time, the Senate procrastinated in giving a vote of confidence to the new cabinet. The British embassy commented: "The Senate opposition has probably strengthened Musaddiq's position in the eyes of the mass of the people. It is relatively easy for government propaganda to represent the Senate as a reactionary, blood-sucking body totally subservient to foreign interests." [185]

More ominously, Hassan Imami and Malek-Madani lobbied behind the scenes on behalf of Qavam, billing him as the only politician capable of solving the oil crisis. This idea was eagerly pushed by both Shepherd and Henderson—especially after the latter had a long private meeting with Qavam. Henderson fully agreed with Shepherd that "it was hopeless to try to do business with Musaddiq" [186] He told Washington, "Iran is a sick country and [the] Prime Minister is one of the sickest leaders. We cannot consider therefore either Iran or him as normal." [187] Speaking in favor of Qavam, he argued that Mossadeq's "retirement" was an absolute prerequisite for a settlement, since neither he nor the British were willing to yield any ground. [188] The British embassy reported that Henderson had come away from a three-hour secret meeting with Qavam "impressed by the old man" and convinced he was the "best person to succeed" Mossadeq. [189] Foreign Minister Eden instructed his ambassador to back the American ambassador in urging the shah not to waste time in replacing Mossadeq with Qavam. [190] But the precise role played by the United States in this saga remains hard to document. The volume in *The Foreign Relations of the US* relevant for these weeks has long gaps. [191]

The British embassy heard rumors that Baqai, Makki, and

Haerizadeh were tempted by this solution—especially since they had worked with Qavam in the 1940s. It also reported that Baqai was receiving funds from the Americans to renew his support for Qavam.[192] It later reported that Qavam had in his possession an embarrassing letter from Baqai promising him support.[193] Some rank-and-file members of the Toilers Party were later outraged to discover that their leader, while outdoing others in radical rhetoric, had been holding secret meetings with Qavam as well as with the shah.[194] Kashani, who bore a personal grudge against Qavam because of his arrest in 1946, recommended to Ala, the court minister, other candidates to replace Mossadeq.[195] The shah himself was reluctant to help Qavam because of their past differences. As he told Hassan Imami, "It is all very well bringing Qavam to power, but how are we going to get rid of him when we want to do so?"[196] The same Imami, meanwhile, approached the British for money to win over some clerical deputies. The Foreign Office cryptically commented, "Apparently, the wheels of Islam need more lubricating than those of other faiths."[197] The embassy reported that the shah was quietly subsidizing Hassan Imami to weaken Mossadeq.[198] It also reported that the chief of court protocol was "working like a beaver among the deputies with a view of getting rid of Musaddiq" but without a clear candidate in mind.[199] Despite these reports, the British remained convinced that the shah could dismiss Mossadeq at will and even dissolve the Majles:

> Without the Shah's support, Musaddiq could have been overthrown easily. . . . It is possible that Musaddiq has a curious hold over him and is able to blackmail him every time he sees danger of his government being overthrown. Another possibility—with some, but not all, of my Persian acquaintances—is that the Shah has never forgiven us for deposing his father. All his recent behaviour can be

traced to an almost insane desire for revenge. As a long term policy it seems that we should try to work towards divesting the Shah of all his power and if necessary, even to send him the way of his illustrious father. . . . It is difficult for the Western mind to understand the motives that have actuated the Shah.[200]

The British still could not admit to themselves that the shah did not dare to sacrifice all patriotic credentials by openly coming out against Mossadeq and the nationalist movement.

Getting wind of these intrigues, Mossadeq engineered a constitutional crisis. He demanded the right to name his war minister, citing the clauses in the constitution that stipulated the monarch should reign and not rule, and that members of the cabinet, including the war minister, should be accountable to the nation, not to the monarch. He also stressed that the armed forces should be accountable to civilians—the cabinet accountable to the Majles, which, in turn, was accountable only to the nation. The shah, however, was used to treating the military as his private possession and keeping out all politicians—including Qavam. Control over the war ministry can be described as the county's longstanding constitutional problem ever since Reza Shah's abdication in 1941. Middleton reported that the shah did not hesitate in refusing Mossadeq's demand for the war ministry, since "virtual control of the armed forces was his principal source of influence in the country." [201]

By raising the issue, Mossadeq made a direct pitch to the public, bypassing not only the shah but also the Majles and Senate. He was calling on the public to choose between himself and the shah, between himself and the parliamentary opposition, and between himself as the national spokesman and the British-owned oil company. For the first time he was openly criticizing the shah for violating the constitution and standing in the way of the national struggle. He emphasized that the country would not enjoy real freedom as long as the armed forces and the war ministry continued to tamper with elections. His resignation speech to the nation included these explosive words: "In the course of recent events, I have come to the realization that I need a trustworthy war minister to be able to bring to a successful conclusion the national struggle launched by the Iranian people. Since His Majesty has refused my request, I will resign to permit someone who enjoys royal confidence to form a new government and implement His Majesty's policies. In the present situation, the struggle started by the Iranian people cannot be brought to a victorious conclusion."[202] The pitch proved to be a resounding success. It produced what has gone down in Iranian history as Siyeh-e Tir (30th Tir)(21st July)—or simply the July Uprising.

July Uprising

Mossadeq handed in his resignation on July 16. A closed session of the Majles—with Mossadeq supporters boycotting the meeting—immediately offered the premiership to Qavam. The vote was 40, with 2 abstentions. The 40 probably included Baqai, Makki, and Haerizadeh. Qavam wasted no time accepting the offer and consulting the British embassy on the composition of his cabinet. He also offered to reopen oil negotiations.[203] In a radio address to the nation, he began by boasting that he had initiated the oil nationalization campaign in 1947. He went on to promise to settle the problem as soon as possible by being "more flexible and prudent." He ended by denouncing troublemakers, demagogues, street politicians, and "hypocrites who under the guise of fighting red extremism undermine the constitution and instead strengthen black reaction and outdated superstitions." It was rumored that he had been offered American aid. It was also rumored that he had issued an arrest warrant for Kashani. Hassan Arsanjani, Qavam's adviser, admitted that the speech had been a major blunder, forcing Kashani back into Mossadeq's fold.[204] Not surprisingly, Kashani joined the National Front and the bazaar guilds in calling for mass protests. He proclaimed "foreign powers were using Qavam to undermine the nation's religion, freedom, and independence."[205]

The call for mass protests was seconded by the Tudeh Party. This was the first time the Tudeh had come out in full support of Mossadeq. The party called for a nationwide general strike and urged supporters to pour into the streets. The British embassy estimated more than 90 percent of organized labor in Tehran, especially in industry, heeded the Tudeh call.[206] Immediately after the uprising, Kashani thanked the Tudeh for helping bring "victory against British imperialism."[207] Both Fateh and Arsanjani—neither of whom by any stretch of the imagination could be described as pro-Tudeh—credited the party for playing the crucial role in the whole uprising.[208] This reflected major change in Tudeh policy. Until then, ultra-leftists had dominated the leadership and had tended to label Mossadeq as a pro-American "lackey." From that point on, more pragmatic leaders, notably Nuraldin Kianuri, held the majority in the central committee and tended to see Mossadeq as "an anti-imperialist patriot."[209]

The crisis came to a head on July 21. After three days of intermittent protests and work stoppages, especially in the bazaars, most cities were shaken on that day by general strikes and massive demonstrations. Tehran began the day ominously quiet—almost all offices, shops, markets, factories, buses, and taxis were at a standstill. Even shops in the wealthier northern neighborhoods were shuttered. By late morning, demonstrators from the southern working-class districts as well as the central bazaar converged on Parliament Square. They were surrounded there by troops, trucks, and tanks. For five hours, the capital was in complete turmoil. One of the shah's brothers was nearly lynched when his chauffeur took a wrong turn into an angry crowd. A statue of Reza Shah was toppled. A deputy was pelted with stones when he tried to persuade the crowd that the problem could be solved peacefully. A tank officer declared he would never obey orders to shoot into the crowd. An Army jeep was torched. Hundreds of detainees from previous demonstrations broke out of jail when their guards took off their uniforms and went into hiding. A number of officers were attacked and injured. Qavam's home was ransacked. A middle-aged woman sitting on a demonstrator's shoulders addressed the large crowd outside Parliament. The main slogans were: "Long Live Mossadeq," "Down with Qavam," "Down with the Shah," and "Down with the Anglo-American Imperialists." The British embassy was surprised that during the whole upheaval there was "little looting or damage to property." [210]

By two p.m., the shah, fearful of over straining the loyalty of the rank-and-file, ordered the Army back into their barracks. He had refused Qavam's request to dissolve the Majles and declare martial law. Middleton complained that throughout the crisis Ala had given the shah "bad advice" and that the shah himself had "lacked moral courage." [211] Qavam handed in his resignation at five p.m. and went into hiding. Middleton reported he and Henderson had done their very best to "stiffen the shah's will" but had failed because the "rioting had destroyed the last shred of his courage." [212] He added, "The Shah and indeed the whole Court appear to be paralysed with fear. Ala insisted that only [the] resignation of Qavam would satisfy public opinion. I replied if the mob were allowed to dictate terms the whole authority of the State including the position of the monarchy would be fatally impaired." [213] Middleton, however, admitted the "crowd was jubilant at the victory and the town was in a very excited state." In his end-of-year summary, Middleton reported that Mossadeq became the "idol of the mobs and was able to use this popularity to cow all the politicians opposed to him. . . . The Shah's fatal weakness of character once more ensured a victory for the forces of disorder. Persia suffered the consequences of this weakness and of Musaddiq's extraordinary buoyancy. . . . There now seemed no chance of replacing Musaddiq by constitutional means." [214] Years later, Middleton admitted that if the Army had continued to shoot into the crowds, the crisis could have easily turned into "another 1917." He also admitted—inexplicably—that he thought Qavam was "quite mad" in thinking he could take charge. [215]

The day after Qavam's resignation, the Majles voted overwhelmingly to give the premiership back to Mossadeq. It also voted to give him the portfolio for the war ministry with the authority to appoint the chief of staff—who, in turn, would have the authority to make the top military appointments. This was the first time the link between the Pahlavi dynasty and the armed forces had been broken. A huge rally gathered outside Parliament to celebrate the uprising. The rally was cosponsored by the Tudeh Party, the National Front, and Kashani—belying the latter's later claim he was fearful of a communist takeover. Coincidently, the Hague issued its final verdict favoring Iran and ruling that it had no jurisdiction in the oil dispute. Mossadeq had scored a double victory. Middleton, in his end-of-year report, wrote:

On the following day [the day after the riots] the Majles inevitably voted for Dr. Mussadiq. At the same time the verdict of the International Court, which had been announced on July 21, became known in Tehran. Its decision that it was incompetent to consider the oil dispute was naturally interpreted as a complete endorsement of Persia's case and crowned Dr. Mussadiq's triumph. The Shah capitulated to his demand, confirmed him as Prime Minister, appointed him Minister of War, and accepted his nominee as Chief of Staff. The Majles now voted Mussadiq full powers for six months to enact a "programme of reform."[216]

Middleton added that "Musaddiq has so flattered the mob as the source of his power that he has, I fear, made it impossible for a successor to oust him by normal constitutional methods."[217] Sam Falle writes that the day after the uprising, Middleton began to think of "fair or foul means" to remove Mossadeq.[218] A week later, Henderson had an "exhausting and depressing" two-hour session with Mossadeq. He tried to convince him that the United States had absolutely nothing to do with Qavam's election. When Mossadeq expressed skepticism, Henderson concluded that he was "not quite sane and therefore should be humored like a child rather than reasoned with."[219] The session ended with Mossadeq laughing at Henderson's claim that the United States was in many ways trying to help Iran." According to Henderson, "Musaddiq said if we were really trying to help by [means] other than words, we were certainly succeeding in hiding our helpful activities."

A parliamentary committee appointed to investigate the uprising reported that the bloodiest incidents had taken place in the bazaar, especially among drapers, grocers, and metalworkers; in the working-class districts near the railway station; and, of course, in Parliament Square. The report listed twenty-nine as dead in Tehran, including four workers, three car drivers, two craftsmen, two shopkeepers' assistants, one peddler, one tailor, one student, and one barber.[220] Others, however, claimed the real figures were as high as thirty-two dead, thirty-six injured, and ninety-six missing.[221] Ala, the court minister who had advised caution, told the shah that "blood was rolling in the streets," that more than five hundred had been killed, and that the "whole city was on verge of revolution." [222] *Ettela'at* reported more than one hundred had been injured and more than six hundred arrested.[223] Similar protests had shaken other cities—especially Isfahan, Abadan, Shiraz, Kermanshah, Ahwaz, Rasht, and Hamadan. The Majles hailed the dead as "national martyrs" and Siyeh-e Tir as Qiyam-e Melli (National Uprising). The Western press, however, denounced the protestors as a "violent rabble." [224] For example, the *Washington Star* published an editorial—written with the help of the British press attaché—entitled "The Mob in Iran":

> One of the more depressing aspects of Mossadegh's quick return to power is that the return has been made possible by the mob spirit. Although his policies have brought Iran to the brink of ruin—to the point when a coup by the Communist Tudeh is quite conceivable, he seems at least in Tehran to have most of the people behind him, and they are people who have acted in the past few days as if they were psychoneurotic hysterics intent upon promoting the destruction of both themselves and their country. Never has a majority looked less wise, never have popular passions looked uglier. This mob—for it must be called that—does not appear to have been motivated by the slightest semblance of common sense. Led by homicidal fanatics of every type. . . . Iran has become a place of gravest uncertainties.[225]

Mossadeq followed up his victory with a series of hammer blows at the shah. In addition to retaining the portfolio of the War Ministry for himself, he renamed it the Defense

Ministry; cut the military budget by 15 percent; appointed investigatory committees to look into past arms deals; retired 135 senior officers—by early 1953 the Retired Officers Club contained more than four hundred members; and, most important, named Gen. Muhammad Taqi Riyahi to be the chief of general staff. Riyahi, a graduate of St. Cyr, had strong ties to the Iran Party. Mossadeq and Riyahi then named their own men to head the police, the gendarmerie, and the customs guards. They also instructed these heads to communicate directly with the ministry and the general staff—not with the shah. The long-standing practice had been for these heads of the armed services to have weekly face-to-face meetings with the shah—bypassing both the ministry and the chief of general staff.[226]

Mossadeq, moreover, trimmed the court budget and the special stipends allocated to the royal family; restricted the monarch's access to foreign ambassadors; forced the shah's mother and twin sister, both of whom had conspired with the opposition, to leave the country; replaced Ala with Abdul-Qassem Amini as court minister (Amini was critical of the court); and, most serious of all, transferred the vast royal estates inherited from Reza Shah back to the state where they had been between 1941 and 1949. Thus in one blow he drastically cut the patronage system enjoyed by the shah. Furthermore, he ousted Hassan Imami, the royalist Majles president, and obtained from Parliament special six-month powers to carry out not only financial but also economic, legal, educational, and electoral reforms. These reforms would need to obtain parliamentary approval at the end of the six months.

What is more, Mossadeq shuffled the cabinet, bringing in more trustworthy ministers. Jahanger Haqshenas, Sheifullah Moazemi, Baqer Kazemi, and Khalel Taleqani—all Iran Party technocrats—became respectively ministers of roads, communication, finance, and agriculture. Sadiqi, the French-educated sociologist and Iran Party member, became minister of interior. Fatemi was made foreign minister. Ali-Akbar Akhavi, a French-educated lawyer and former New York businessman, was given the ministry of economy. Dr. Mehdi Azar, a French-educated doctor teaching at the medical school, was made minister of education. Abdul-Ali Lutfi, a veteran of the constitutional revolution, became minister of justice. Lutfi had a traditional education but was a strict constitutionalist, favoring civilian over military courts. Ibrahim Alemi, another Iran Party member and French-educated lawyer with a reputation of impeccable honesty, was made minister of labor. And Dr. Saba Farmanfarmayan, a French-educated doctor and a relative of Mossadeq, was made health minister. For the first time ever, the cabinet contained no court placemen. For the first time, so many of the ministers were novices without ceremonial attire, and they had to appear before the shah for their inauguration in ordinary civilian clothes. Middleton found the shah to be so depressed that he was contemplating abdication.[227] Acheson concluded that Mossadeq was "clearly now in a much stronger position vis-à-vis the Shah, the Majles, and the public than any other time since the nationalization of oil in April 1951."[228]

Armed with its six month powers, the administration drafted an impressive array of reform bills—extending suffrage to women, increasing urban representation, and restricting the vote to literates in council elections; providing greater protection to the press; strengthening the independence of the Supreme Court; placing a 2 percent levy on large amounts of property (this was the first real tax on wealth); providing health coverage for factory workers; and, most significant of all, increasing the peasants' share of the harvest by 15 percent. Middleton remarked that landlords naturally objected that peasants would waste the money on drink and opium.[229] To overcome Senate opposition, Mossadeq, who had never accepted its creation in 1949, persuaded the Majles to cut the upper house's term from six years to two—thus, in effect, promptly dissolving it. Kashani, not wishing to be identified with the establishment, went along with the dissolution.

In an autopsy on the July Uprising, Middleton claimed the protests could have been contained if the shah had not been "gripped by fear"—fear of Qavam, fear of Kashani, and, most important of all, "fear of exposing himself to the fury of the populace." He argued, "I can only repeat what I have previously written about the Shah's character. He hates taking decisions, and cannot be relied upon to stick to them when taken; he has no moral courage and succumbs to fear. . . . This attitude is one of the central features of the crisis. We had long known he was indecisive and timid, but we had not thought that this fear would so overcome his reason as to make him blind to the consequences of not supporting Qavam.[230]

But Middleton's claim that the storm could have been weathered is belied by other reports—many of them from Middleton himself. On the same day the embassy insisted the shah should have held firm, it admitted that reports from other cities indicated that "disorders in the provinces were more severe than suspected" and that Isfahan had been taken over by demonstrators "with casualties reaching into the hundreds." Middleton admitted as much when he described the uprising as "a turning point in Persian history." "The old system has always been, with certain variations, that the small ruling class in fact nominates successive Prime Ministers with the throne acting more or less as umpire. Since yesterday I doubt whether this pattern can ever be repeated. The mob successfully defied the security forces and from now on the mob will be the decisive factor in judging the acceptability of any future government."[231]

Even more significant, Middleton reported that he and Henderson were now both convinced that the only solution to the crisis was a military "coup d'état." [232] Henderson told his secretary of state that further oil negotiations had "no chance," since Mossadeq continued to insist on "control" and the British adamantly refused to contemplate any solution based on such premises. [233] In a top-secret telegram, the Foreign Office informed the British embassy in Washington that American policymakers now wished that Iran had a Muhammad Neguib—the general who had headed the recent coup in Egypt. [234] The War Office, meanwhile, asked its military attaché to undertake an urgent report on the loyalty of the armed forces, on their ability to carry out a coup, and who could feasibly fill the role of General Neguib. [235] The military attaché promptly supplied the names of four generals, but added that since none of them had much prestige in the armed forces, the "coup would have to be in the name of the Shah." [236]

3

The Coup

> I refused any aid until the oil issue was settled. Matters came
> to a head in August when Mossadeq for three days, backed
> by the Communist Party, seemed the irresistible dictator of
> Iran. . . . But fortunately the loyalty of the Army and fear of
> communism saved the day.
>
> —President Dwight D. Eisenhower, in a speech entitled
> "Peace with Justice"

Preparations

It is easier for a camel to pass through the eye of a needle
than for a historian to gain access to the CIA and MI6 files
on the coup. Despite this difficulty, the outline of the coup
can be pieced together from a number of sources: from Foreign Office and State Department documents—some classified American documents appear inadvertently in the British
archives because after the break in Anglo-Iranian relations
in October 1952, Washington shared with London important reports sent from Tehran; from routine correspondence
published by the State Department in its annual *Foreign Relations of the United States*; from a close reading of contemporary newspapers—especially those with reporters in Tehran;
from interviews and memoirs published in Iran as well as
in the West—especially after the 1979 revolution; and from
accounts written by MI6 and CIA operatives such as Kermit
Roosevelt and Donald Wilber. The latter has left us by far

the most important document—his in-depth analysis primarily for the CIA itself, laying out the plan of operations, summarizing the coup, and concluding with a postmortem. Of course, all these sources need to be read against the grain, taken with a pinch of salt, and the gaps filled in with common sense and circumstantial evidence.

The United States, as well as the UK, had long relied on political means—notably the shah and the Majles—to oust Mossadeq. But after the July Uprising, they concluded that his permanent ouster could be attained only through an outright coup. Although the finishing touches did not come until early 1953, they began to think in terms of a coup immediately after Mossadeq's triumphant return to power in mid-1952. The two nations brought to the table their particular assets—not all of which they divulged to each other.

The British came with five major assets. First, they had experts who had much experience working in the country, knew the language well, and had cultivated close personal ties with members of the old elite. These experts included Lancelot Pyman, a recluse in charge of the Iran desk at the Foreign Office ever since the late 1930s (the shah was convinced Pyman was primarily responsible for his father's forced abdication); Norman Darbyshire, an MI6 officer who had been stationed in Iran for much of World War II; Col. Geoffrey Wheeler, another MI6 hand who had been in and out of the country since the 1920s; Robin Zaehner, the press attaché, an expert on mysticism and soon professor of Eastern religions and ethics at Oxford (in a strange turn of events Zaehner was later rumored to be a KGB "mole"); Sam Falle, Zaehner's assistant, in charge of dealing mostly with younger politicians; and Professor Ann Lambton, the former press attaché who had consistently since April 1951 advised the Foreign Office not to concede any ground to Mossadeq and instead to work for his removal.[1] The actual chief of MI6 operations in Tehran, Christopher Montague ("Monty") Woodhouse, was not himself an Iran expert but had much cloak-and-dagger experience from the recent Greek Civil War. He has left us a much self-censored but nevertheless useful memoir entitled *Something Ventured.*

Second, the British had an informal network within the Iranian armed forces. Dating from World War II, this network was formed of conservative officers coming mostly from aristocratic families: Gen. Hassan Arfa, a former chief of staff, who, after being forced out by his rival, Razmara, had retired to his estates in Veramin outside Tehran; Col. Teymour Bakhtiyar—Queen Soraya's cousin; Col. Hedayat Gilanshah—a UK-trained pilot and adjutant to the shah; Col. Hussein-Ghuli Ashrafi, a brigade commander in the Tehran garrison; and, most important of all, Col. Hassan Akhavi, who for years had headed G2—the intelligence service in the Army. Hussein Fardoust, a member of the shah's inner circle, later described Akhavi as the "real brains" behind the Iranian side of the coup.[2] Colonel Akhavi's brother, Ali-Akbar, was minister of economy and remained faithful to Mossadeq to the very last.

This pro-British military network—led by Akhavi and Arfa—had promoted its own members, sidelined others, and done its best to keep leftists out of the crucial Tehran garrison.[3] The British military attaché at one point described Arfa as "wholeheartedly cooperating with us" but "suffering from spy mania."[4] Thanks to this network, MI6 had an impressive military Who's Who—something the CIA sorely lacked.[5] According to Donald Wilber, much of the coup preparations in London involved studying these personality files. The one clear lesson the CIA drew from the whole Iran experience was the need to compile similar files for other countries. In Wilber's own words, the agency had the urgent need to collect personal information, "however, trivial," to know exactly "who the officer is, what makes him tick, who his friends are, etc. . . . It is vital to have as detailed biographical information as possible on all military personnel whose presence might bear upon the problem including possible enemies as well as friends."[6]

Third, MI6 had a long-standing local civilian network, headed by three merchant brothers—Assadullah, Saifullah, and Qadratullah Rashidian. Their father had been imprisoned by Reza Shah for having close ties to the British. They had an import business ostensibly for bringing in British films but which they used as a conduit for channeling MI6 money to local supporters, including Sayyed Ziya and his National Will Party. Mossadeq's liberal attitude gave them the opportunity to take frequent trips to London and to recruit clients in Tehran. Woodhouse estimated that the Rashidians funneled more than £10,000 every month to unnamed clerics, journalists, and politicians—especially Majles deputies. Sam Falle mentions in passing he had regular breakfast meetings with one or the other of the Rashidians.[7] After the coup, the Foreign Office euphemistically praised the brothers as "our true and loyal friends" with a "hand in organizing the recent overthrow." It described them as having "friends" in high places—especially Princess Ashraf; Colonel Bakhtiyar; and Soleiman Behdudi, chief of court protocol.[8] They had also probably recruited Ehsam Lankarani, a mid-level Tudeh organizer who was assassinated once his cover was blown.

The Rashidians' main strength lay in the Tehran bazaar: among the guilds of butchers, bakers, and confectioners; among the wholesale vegetable dealers; among the wrestlers in the local *zurkhanehs* (houses of strength); and among lower-level preachers sympathetic to the Fedayan-e Islam, such as Hojjat al-Islam Muhammad Taqi Falsafi.[9] In a long analysis of the Fedayan written soon after the group had tried to assassinate Fatemi, Robin Zaehner cryptically wrote there was no reason why Britain and the Fedayan could not "continue" to work together against the National Front.[10] He added that the Fedayan had working relations with Sayyed Ziya despite the latter's open ties to Britain. After all, Zaehner explained, Ziya was a *sayyed*, was religious, and promised to enforce the *shari'a*. He further explained that since the Fedayan's main concern was the implementation of the strict laws on alcohol, prostitution, and the veil, and since none of these really concerned Britain, there was no reason why the two could not work together. This, he admitted, may have sounded "incredible," but was feasible. The U.S. embassy reported that immediately after the assassination attempt on Fatemi, "opposition" newspapers led by *Ettela'at, Kayhan, Dad, Atesh,* and *Tolu* "adopted" the Fedayan, used it as a "weapon against the government," and gave it "sympathetic coverage."[11] At one point, General Glubb, the British commander of the Arab Legion in Jordan, conveyed a message from the Muslim Brotherhood in Egypt offering to use its influence to help the British in Iran.[12] Politics clearly makes strange bedfellows.

The Rashidian connection with *zurkhanehs* lay through two famous *lutis*: Sha'aban Bemorkh (Brainless Sha'aban) and Tayeb Haj Rezayi. For many, the term *luti* was synonymous with *chaqukesh* (knife-wielder), thug, and racketeer. Brainless Sha'aban "protected" the wholesale vegetable market at Shahpour Square; Tayeb the wholesale fruit market in nearby Sultan Mosque Square. The two respected each other's turf. They had their own bodybuilding groups and religious gatherings—especially *rouzehkanehs* (prayer meetings) and *dastehs* (Muharram flagellation processions). They—like most *lutis*—were in and out of prison. In his old age, in exile in Beverly Hills, Brainless Sha'aban claimed he "had never in his whole life carried a knife."[13] Although both *lutis* played important roles in the forthcoming coup, their paths later parted. Tayeb led protest demonstrations in 1963 and was promptly executed. Brainless Sha'aban continued to run a well-financed athletic club in his neighborhood until the 1979 revolution. Because of his role in 1953, he was dubbed Sha'aban the King Maker.

Fourth, the British embassy had regular meetings with a long array of influential politicians. They included: Ernest Perron, the shah's childhood friend from Switzerland (Perron lived permanently in the palace despite Queen Soraya's objections); Ahmad Human, the deputy chief of court protocol; Shahpour Reporter, a Zoroastrian from Delhi working in Tehran as a special correspondent for the London *Times* (he was knighted immediately after the coup); Sheikh Hadi Taheri and Hashem Malek-Madani—the veteran Majles deputies; and, of course, Sayyed Ziya, who reported in his regular visits on his weekly meetings with the shah. He also reported on his occasional visits with Ayatollah Kashani, whom he encouraged to stand up against Mossadeq "especially when the time came to overthrow him." [14]

The embassy also had frequent meetings with the two sons of the clerics who had been prominent in the 1906 constitutional revolution: Ayatollah Muhammad Reza Behbehani and Sayyed Muhammad Sadeq Tabatabai. The former presented himself as the ideal conduit for channeling money against Mossadeq.[15] The British embassy later credited him for playing "an important part in the coup" and remarked that he received "regular payments for his services, in particular from the Shah." [16] The latter billed himself as a "courageous politician" capable of heading a new government and claimed that Mossadeq was an "epileptic suffering from syphilitic deterioration of the brain." [17] These regular meetings, however, ended abruptly in October 1952 when Mossadeq closed down the British embassy, accusing it of meddling in internal affairs and even of plotting a military coup. Sam Falle, one of the last diplomats to leave, years later wrote that he and his colleagues had never felt personally harassed or threatened, even in the worst days of the crisis.[18]

Finally, the British had established contact with Gen. Fazlullah Zahedi as early as October 1951 when Zahedi, after being dismissed as interior minister for mishandling the Harriman riots, had presented himself as the ideal coup leader and had boasted a large following in the armed forces. Although the boast proved hollow, he did have some following among older officers. Some—like Gen. Nader Batqama-lich and General Baqai—had been interned with him and Ayatollah Kashani during World War II. This was now an asset, since they could not be tarred with the British brush. Zahedi also had some support in the Association of Retired Officers—especially among the 135 purged by Razmara and Mossadeq. Only a few days after the July Uprising and after the Foreign Office request for possible candidates to lead a coup, the British military attaché had sent in Zahedi's name together with the names of three other generals: Arfa; Mu-hammad Shahbakht, a seventy-year-old veteran of the dis-banded Cossack Brigade; and Abdul-Hussein Hajazi, who had won AIOC favor during the 1946 oil strike.[19] The Brit-ish choice immediately fell on Zahedi. He soon drew up a "shadow cabinet," formed of technocrats, journalists, and politicians amiable to both the UK and the United States.[20]

Zahedi's main strength, however, lay in the religious wing of the National Front: with Kashani; Qonatabadi, the leader of the Mujaheden-e Islam; and Baqai, Makki, and Haerizadeh—the three vocal Majles deputies. The British military attaché reported that Zahedi, in drawing up his shadow cabinet, promised Kashani a "say" in the future gov-ernment.[21] After one of his routine meetings with the court go-between, Robin Zaehner reported cryptically: "Perron gave an impassioned defence of the Shah's 'astute' policy. He claimed that the Shah had succeeded in detaching Kashani, Makki and Baqai from Musaddiq and that thanks to the Shah the National Front had practically ceased to exist. I did not dispute this but would put on record that the detaching of Kashani and Makki was due to quite other factors, and that these were created and directed by the Rashidian brothers." [22] In a separate report, he added that the "two rascally sons of Kashani"—Mustafa and Abul Maali—had opened an office with the ostensible purpose of facilitating commercial transactions but with the real aim of smuggling in contraband. He estimated their illegal transactions had within a few weeks cleared more than two million rials. [23] He also reported that Kashani was privately looking around for further funds. [24]

Two weeks after the July Uprising, Sam Falle reported: "I saw Zahedi yesterday. He was in surprisingly good spirits and seemed hopeful about his chances. Discontented members of the National Front, namely Makki, Haerizadeh and Baqai, as well as direct emissaries from Kashani, had been to see him secretly. These visitors opposed Dr. Musaddiq mainly, it would appear, because they had not sufficient say in the government. I understand he also has contacts with the Americans." [25] The British embassy later added, "General Zahedi, whose supporters number such diverse elements as Haerizadeh, Baqai, and the old right-wing opposition, has established himself as the only alternative prime minister in sight. His chance of success depends largely on the progress he makes in further wooing Kashani." [26] At precisely the same time the British embassy was trying to woo Kashani it was also arguing that "there was no hope of coming to an agreement" on oil with Mossadeq because the latter was "completely under the influence of Kashani whose avowed object is to drive all foreigners and foreign influence from

Persia." [27] Alice in Wonderland would have felt quite at home inside the British embassy.

The Americans, for their part, brought to the table their assets—the most important being the embassy compound itself. The importance of the embassy grew after December 1951, when British consulates in Shiraz, Isfahan, Mashed, Ahwaz, Khorramshahr, and Kermanshah were shut down. It grew even more after October 1952, when diplomatic relations with the UK were broken and the British embassy in Tehran was closed down. The Foreign Office calculated that the U.S. embassy contained a staff of fifty-eight, all with full diplomatic status. The Soviet embassy had only twenty-one; the French nine; and the British before its closure twenty-one. [28]

The American diplomatic presence was augmented both by Point IV and by three separate military missions. Point IV, mainly an agricultural program, employed 138 Americans—more than in the whole of the Arab world combined. [29] It set up headquarters right across from Mossadeq's home. A foreign journalist reported that Point IV initially gave only "token aid," but this was suddenly increased in 1953 to more than $44 million. He added that there was general suspicion the program was "a cover for spies." [30] Ardasher Zahedi, the general's son, worked for Point IV and carried messages back and forth from the Americans to his father in hiding.

The three military missions—for the Army, Gendarmerie, and Air Force—had 123 American advisers. Launched in 1942, these missions were led in 1952–53 by Gen. Robert McClure, a "psychological warfare" expert rushed in from Korea. The advisers were in daily contact with field officers, especially tank commanders. Ever since 1946, the Pentagon had been delivering to Iran a modest but steady stream of light M3 (Lee) and heavy M4 (Sherman) tanks. In 1952 alone, it delivered forty-two Shermans, and took to America for training as many as three hundred officers.[31] The U.S. embassy was pleased to report in 1952 that even officers handpicked by Mossadeq remained "amiable to the American advisers."[32] McClure and his colleagues had the audacity on the eve of the coup to sound out even Gen. Muhammad Riyahi, Mossadeq's trusted and faithful chief of staff.[33] An Indian visitor in early 1953 reported that "the first thing that strikes one in Tehran is the large number of Americans. Their exact number is not revealed but more Americans are in Iran than in any other Middle Eastern country. There must be at least one thousand in Tehran alone."[34]

The CIA had two main academic experts on Iran: Donald Wilber and Richard Cottam. Wilber, often described as a "gentleman spy," was a professional intelligence officer. He had traveled in and out of the Middle East since the 1930s under the guise of being an archaeologist and art historian. His previous feat had been the near liquidation of the famous Persian poet Lahuti living in exile in the Soviet Union. Wilber had forged Lahuti's "memoirs" and published them, claiming they had been smuggled out of the Soviet Union. The poet had been lucky to survive Stalin's paranoia. After leaving the CIA, Wilber identified forged manuscripts for antiques dealers and wrote books on Iranian art, architecture, and modern history. Immediately after the Islamic Revolution, when Roosevelt published his account of the coup, Wilber tried to publish his own version, but the CIA redacted it to four brief pages.[35] To rectify this, he left a copy of the official account he had written for the agency in 1954 with friends to publish at some appropriate time after his death.

Cottam, the other academic, was a former Mormon and a Fulbright scholar at Tehran University. He later became professor of political science at the University of Pittsburgh. In Tehran, he gathered information not only on the

Tudeh—which he generously shared with the British—but also on Baqai's Toilers Party, as well as on the Arya (Aryan) Party and SUMKA. These latter two groups—wearing black and gray shirts respectively—outdid each other in mimicking the German Nazis and denouncing both Jews and communists. Arya had been formed in 1946 by Hadi Sepehr, a racial theorist who had been interned during World War II. Arya had some help from General Arfa and his entourage of army officers. SUMKA had been formed in 1951 by Dr. Davoud Munshizadeh, a German-educated philologist of ancient Iranian. He had lost a leg in an air raid while working as a radio propagandist for the Third Reich. He deemed Sepehr a "half-illiterate simpleton." Munshizadeh's dream was to rebuild the Third Reich on the pure Aryan land of Iran. SUMKA, the largest of the two fringe groups, had no more than three hundred members at its height.[36] The British suspected the CIA as well as the shah of bankrolling SUMKA as well as the Toilers and Arya Parties.[37] The British embassy reported that Hussein Ala, the court minister, regularly met Sepehr, and that Baqai worked closely with both Arya and SUMKA. The British embassy further reported that Cottam shared with them information on the political attitudes of his colleagues at Tehran University.[38] If Iranian politicians seemed to be from *Alice in Wonderland*, Anglo-American diplomats were straight out of Brecht and Weill's *Threepenny Opera* and *Rise and Fall of the City of Mahagonny*.

The CIA had three local "operatives": Col. Abbas Farzandegan; and two experienced agents "Cilley" and "Nerren," whom Roosevelt nicknamed the "Boscoe Brothers" after the popular chocolate-milk drink of the day. Farzandegan, a staff officer, had gotten to know many of the field commanders in the Tehran garrison over the years. He had also befriended Col. Valiallah Qarani, the commander of the Qazvin garrison.

In 1952, Farzandegan was rushed off to the United States to get special training in covert communications. In later years, he was rewarded by being placed on the board of ITT (International Telephone and Telecommunications).

The Boscoe Brothers, whose true identities were kept secret even from MI6, were Farrokh Keyvani and Ali Jalali.[39] They were not, in fact, brothers. The former was a lawyer with business connections in Hamburg. The latter was a journalist who worked intermittently for the Associated Press, the *Daily Telegraph, Ettela'at-e Haftegi, Mehan Parestan,* and *Tehran Mosavar.* Roosevelt wrote that they had been recruited in 1950, brought to the United States for vetting, and turned out to have had "mysterious" espionage experience from earlier years.[40] This previous experience was probably from Nazi Germany. The two funneled money to downtown *lutis* and the *zurkhanehs*—especially Taj Sports Club. They also funneled money to such newspapers as *Mellat-e Iran* (Nation of Iran), *Mellat-e Ma* (Our Nation), *Atesh* (Fire), *Dad* (Justice), *Setareh-e Islam* (Star of Islam), *Asiya-e Javanan* (Youth's Asia), *Neday-e Sepehr* (Sepehr's Voice), and *Aram* (named after the Zoroastrian God). Roosevelt mentions in passing the Boscoe Brothers had engineered the attack on the day of Harriman's visit. He fails to mention that the attack resulted in heavy casualties and was instigated through SUMKA, the Arya Party, and the Toilers Party. Wilber also tends to gloss over any such details that could be embarrassing if revealed to the American public and the U.S. Senate.

Finally, the Americans intensified their courting of Ayatollah Kashani—especially after the July Uprising. He was interviewed by a long relay of U.S. visitors—reporters from the *Herald Tribune* and the *New York Times*; delegates from the U.S. Congress; and academics supposedly interested in religion and Muslim-Christian relations. They flattered him as being the real spokesman for the whole Muslim world. He

also met on three separate occasions—all in closed sessions—
with Loy Henderson. One session lasted one and half hours;
its transcripts remain classified. The British reported that
Kashani had privately confided in the Americans that he
favored Zahedi as Mossadeq's successor.[41] The U.S. ambassador got the distinct message that Kashani had concluded
that "Iran could be saved only by a coup."[42] By early 1953,
the CIA was informing the president that Kashani was a
"key figure promoting pro-Shah street demonstrations in
Tehran."[43]

Economic Pressures

While the CIA and MI6 laid the ground for a coup, their
governments worked together behind the scenes to intensify economic pressures on Iran. They presented through the
International Bank a much-heralded final "compromise"
offer—which they knew would be unacceptable. Throughout these negotiations, the State Department and Foreign
Office vetted all statements issued by the International
Bank.[44] According to the "compromise," the United States
would offer Iran a loan of $10 million; and the UK would
"accept" nationalization and lift economic sanctions. In return, Iran would agree to have an international panel determine the "fair compensation" to be paid to the AIOC. When
Mossadeq insisted the agreement should specify that "fair
compensation" would be based on the current value of the oil
installations, the negotiations stalled. He suspected that compensation would be set at such a high level that Iran would
placed "under bondage for the next twenty-five years"—in
which case the whole purpose of nationalization would have
been undone.[45]

His suspicions were well grounded. The AIOC's notion
of "fair compensation" was based not on current value but

on projected profits to the very end of the concessions—into 1993. The company was thinking more in terms of £100 million and projecting annual earnings of £46.5 million for the next 42.5 years.[46] Even Dean Acheson suspected the British were thinking in "astronomical" figures.[47] Mossadeq suspected the British were "marking time to undermine him."[48]

In confidential joint meetings, the Foreign Office and the State Department agreed that the International Bank should not undermine the "50/50 principle"—to do so "would cause substantial damage elsewhere."[49] George Middleton, the British charge d'affaires who participated in the International Bank negotiations, years later admitted there was an Anglo-American consensus that nationalization should under no circumstances succeed: "There was considerable fear that a bad example would have repercussions elsewhere. We already had Mexico. We didn't want to see it happen ten more times."[50]

One oil expert admitted after the coup that the International Bank negotiations had broken down because the British insisted on compensation for projected long-term future profits. "If the idea got around," he wrote, "that oil concessions could be broken without compensation, the monarchs and politicos of the Middle East would lose no time proving that they too were sovereign."[51] The American president himself told the National Security Council that they could not contemplate any deal that "might have very grave effects on United States oil concessions in other parts of the world."[52] The chief MI6 man in Tehran later admitted these negotiations were not serious, since the British government had absolutely no interest in coming to a settlement with Mossadeq.[53] The American rejection of Mossadeq's definition of "fair compensation" became part and parcel of the destabilization strategy. On July 11, the very same day Eisenhower signed off on the CIA coup plan, the State Department gave a "psychological blow" by publicly stating that "compensation should not be calculated on the present value of the installations alone." [54] In other words, the United States accepted the UK definition of fair compensation.

This "final offer" was designed to mislead the public into thinking that Tehran, not London, was the main obstacle. This conclusion was readily accepted by politicians out to destroy Mossadeq. It was even accepted by some Mossadeq supporters. One prominent pro-Mossadeq academic claims "his decision to turn down the Bank's mediation was the greatest mistake during his premiership, if not in the whole of his political career." [55] Such misconceptions have continued into the present day.

While making this unacceptable offer, the UK and the United States increased economic pressures. The Americans further trimmed economic aid, restricting it to Point IV and the three military missions. In renewing the latter, Mossadeq quipped to an American colonel that he hoped they would not strengthen the military to the point it could overthrow him. [56] The president made it clear in a private letter he would not extend aid until the oil issue was resolved. Loy Henderson warned Mossadeq that an oil-rich country could not expect aid from American taxpayers. The secretary of state even forbade the Import-Export Bank from meeting with an Iranian delegation to discuss an emergency loan. What is more, the State Department warned that any American company buying oil from Iran ran the serious risk of "legal action by AIOC."

The British, for their part, tightened their embargo. They closed down their Imperial Bank; increased restrictions on exports and sterling transfers; lobbied aggressively and successfully to deter independent companies from buying

Iranian oil; and threatened to impound all tankers leaving
Iran. They also warned others of the long-term implications
if Iran succeeded in breaking the embargo:

> If foreign governments intervene to permit import oil
> Persian oil . . . this will force major oil companies to re-
> duce their prices to the level of those of the stolen oil . . .
> The reduced returns to the Middle Eastern countries in
> form of royalties and taxes would produce *havoc* [em-
> phasis in the original] in the relationships between the
> companies and the Middle Eastern government—havoc
> to such a degree that the availability of Middle East sup-
> plies for world trade would be disastrously affected and
> other equally serious situations could arise internally in
> the Middle Eastern countries themselves.[57]

In June 1952, the Royal Navy impounded on the high
seas—some would say pirated—a Panamanian tanker commissioned by a small Italian oil company carrying oil from
Abadan. In the eighteen months from January 1952 until
the coup, Iran exported only 118,000 tons—equivalent to
just one day's production. When, a few years later, Enrico
Mattei, who, as head of the Italian oil ministry had taken
much interest in helping the NIOC, died in an air crash, it
was rumored that he had paid the price for daring to challenge the Seven Sisters—a term he himself had coined. By
early 1953, the NIOC was losing considerable sums every
month paying employees even though the refinery was not
working at full capacity. "The blockade," a foreign journalist remarked, "has smitten Iran badly, but not crippled it." [58]
The CIA came to a similar conclusion:

> Even in the absence of substantial oil revenues and of
> foreign economic aid, Iran can probably export enough

[non-oil products] to pay for essential imports through
1953, unless there is a serious crop failure or an unfavorable export market. The government probably will be
able to obtain funds for its operations. Some inflation will
occur. Capital developments will be curtailed, and urban
living standards will fall. However, we do not believe that
economic factors in themselves will result in the overthrow of the National Front in 1953. . . . Although the
UK believes that lack of oil revenues will result in pro-
gressive economic and political deteriorations in Iran, it
does not appear to regard a Communist takeover in Iran
as imminent.[59]

To deal with the embargo, Mossadeq drew up an "oil-less
budget." He cut state salaries, eliminated chauffeur-driven
cars for senior officials, postponed development projects, restricted luxury imports, issued government bonds, used up
gold and foreign-exchange reserves, printed bank notes, and
gradually devalued the currency—the black-market value of
the dollar rose from 31 rials to 97, and the value of the pound
from 89 rials to 256. He also continued negotiations started
by General Razmara to obtain gold from the Soviet Union as
compensation for the wartime occupation. The British did
not really expect economic pressures to destroy the Iranian
government, but hoped they would compound internal conflicts. As early as 1951 their commercial attaché had warned
that trade sanctions would have little effect on a country that
was still predominantly agrarian.[60]

Economic difficulties, however, gave Baqai, Makki, and
Haerizadeh, as well as Kashani and Qonatabadi, not to mention the royalists and the pro-British deputies, the opportunity to intensify their attacks on Mossadeq. By early 1953,
nine of the twenty who had founded the National Front had
defected. They accused Mossadeq of drowning the country in

worthless bank notes; of undermining the constitution; and of violating property rights by levying income tax, disturbing landlord-peasant relations, establishing state-run bakeries, and threatening to nationalize bus and telephone companies. "Iran," exclaimed Makki, "will soon be like the Soviet Union where the government owns everything and citizens nothing."[61] They further accused him of giving important posts to the Iran Party. "We are now," claimed Haerizadeh, "a dictatorship of the Iran Party." Fatemi later revealed that in drawing up electoral lists Baqai had always insisted his Toilers Party should have as many candidates as the Iran Party.[62] The Iran Party retorted that these critics had "betrayed the cause" and were collaborating with the foreign enemy as well as with the corrupt upper class. It reaffirmed its own commitment to national independence, neutralism, socialism, and constitutionalism.[63]

The opposition furthermore targeted the ministers of education, justice, and health, accusing them of recruiting leftists and collaborating with the Tudeh. Ayatollah Kashani, who earlier had boasted he had been one of the very first to sign the communist-inspired Stockholm Peace Declaration, suddenly discovered that the brother of the education minister had been living in exile in the Soviet Union since 1946. He and his colleagues accused Mossadeq both of enflaming "class warfare" and of collaborating with the "ruling class." They claimed he was reluctant to bring Qavam to account for the July 1952 bloodshed because he was his relative. Kashani took to referring to the premier with his defunct aristocratic title of al-Saltaneh. They even accused Mossadeq of violating *shari'a* by permitting the sale of alcohol, encouraging co-education, protecting foreign schools—especially the famous French lycée named Jeanne D'Arc—transferring funds from religious foundations to state teaching institutions, and contemplating the extension of suffrage to women. Describing women's true place to be at home, Kashani exclaimed "he could not understand what men had done wrong that they deserved to have their women vote." [64] What is more, they discovered that Mossadeq's doctoral thesis, written thirty-five years earlier in Switzerland, had favored secular laws. [65] Mossadeq later reminisced that his opponents had intentionally misconstrued his doctorate to make him out to be a "blasphemer." [66] The State Department cryptically commented that these deputies were "grooming themselves for the premiership." [67]

Makki equated Mossadeq with Hitler. Baqai described him as "worse than Hitler." Not surprisingly, Majles sessions often broke up with fistfights. Baqai's open denunciations eventually split apart the Toilers Party. His close associates— mostly labor organizers from his hometown of Kerman— remained loyal. But the youth and the intellectual sections led by the Khalel Maleki broke away and formed a new party named Niru-ye Sevom (Third Force). Baqai was shocked— shocked—to discover that his former intellectual colleagues had been Marxists. Khalel Maleki was equally shocked to discover Baqai had been "corrupt" in more ways than one. The Toilers Party became one of the most vocal groups against Mossadeq. The Third Force remained, together with the Iran Party, one of Mossadeq's most staunch supporters— even though it vociferously opposed his toleration of the Tudeh. Khalel Maleki assured Mossadeq, "We will follow you all the way even to the gates of hell." Not wanting to put all eggs in one basket, the CIA funneled money to both Baqai and Khalel Maleki. Jalali of the Boscoe Brothers continued to attend meetings of the Third Force. [68] This investment paid off on the actual day of the coup.

These opposition politicians received a wide hearing in part because they had the Majles as a podium; in part because they had access to the country's three major

publications—*Ettela'at, Kayhan,* and *Khandaniha;* and in
part because they themselves had an impressive array of
newspapers—Baqai had *Shahed,* Qonatabadi *Mellat-e Ma,*
and the Fedayan-e Islam *Nabard-e Mellat.* The press in the
West often echoed the charge that Mossadeq was a "dictator." If so, he must have been the first dictator who tolerated
a wide variety of opposition deputies and newspapers.

Although many of these opposition politicians were linked
to the bazaar, much of the bazaar rank-and-file remained
loyal to Mossadeq. Cottam of the CIA writes that one of the
"great lessons" of the Mossadeq period was that when the inevitable break between Mossadeq and Kashani came, the "bazaar unhesitatingly chose Mossadeq," seeing him as the true
"symbol of their nationalism." [69] What is more, a number of
maverick clerics, led by Ayatollahs Ghoruyi and Borquei, as
well as Hojjat al-Islam Abul-Fazl Zanjani and Mahmud Taleqani, continued to support Mossadeq. His charisma as well as
the nationalist cause had trumped other issues.

The differences between Mossadeq and Kashani first
came out into the open only ten days after the July Uprising. When the former requested a year's extension to his
six-month special powers, the latter denounced the request.
When Mossadeq, suspecting palace intrigues, hinted that the
shah should take a vacation abroad, Kashani supporters, led
by Brainless Sha'aban, joined royalists in demonstrating outside the palace. Some three hundred blocked the palace gates
and beseeched the shah not to leave the country. They also
threatened Mossadeq, who happened to be trapped there,
and later in the day used an Army jeep to crash through
his garden gate. Mossadeq was convinced that he had been
invited to the palace so that the pre-arranged crowd could
intimidate him.[70] In a long radio address to the nation, Mossadeq claimed that the idea to travel abroad had been the
shah's, not his; that members of the royal family, especially

the queen mother, were meddling in politics, that he had taken a sacred oath on the Koran to serve the shah as the lawful constitutional monarch, and that the thugs who had assaulted his house were part of a "foreign plot" to kill him. He ended his speech with the familiar slogan the "Shah Should Reign Not Rule." [71] Years later, after the Islamic Revolution, Makki claimed in an interview that during this incident he had warned the shah that a gathering of three hundred did not make a nation.[72]

Tension further increased when the government issued an arrest warrant for General Zahedi, accusing him of plotting a coup. Kashani—as Majles president—gave him sanctuary inside Parliament. Zahedi was accompanied there by Baqai, Qonatabadi, and one of Kashani's sons. Kashani, on a rare visit to the Majles, came to see them. When pro-Mossadeq deputies managed to oust Kashani as Majles president, he denounced the prime minister as no "longer representing the nation." He also denounced him for establishing a "dictatorship worse than the one before 1941." In the weeks before the coup, his supporters were clashing with pro-Mossadeq demonstrators outside his home on an almost daily basis. One demonstrator was killed and two members of his family were arrested. Kashani's heirs later erased this from their history in order to minimize their opposition to Mossadeq. Finally, when Mossadeq called for a referendum and asked supporters to resign from the Majles so that a new Parliament under a reformed electoral law could be formed, Kashani accused him of running roughshod over the constitution and leading the country into a dictatorship. By then at least one-third of the deputies were on the CIA and MI6 payroll.[73] Mossadeq responded by going to the public directly:

The people of Iran—no one else—has the right to judge on this issue. For it was the people of Iran who brought into existence our fundamental laws, our constitution, our Parliament, and our cabinet system. We must remember that the laws were created for the people; not the people for the laws. The nation has the right to express its views, and, if it wishes, to change its laws. In a democratic and constitutional country, the nation is supreme and sovereign.[74]

Mossadeq, the Swiss-trained lawyer who had often cited the constitutional laws against the shah, was now bypassing the same laws and resorting directly to the theory of the general will. The liberal aristocrat who had in the past appealed predominantly to the middle classes was now appealing to the general public. The moderate reformer who had at one time even proposed restricting suffrage to literates was now openly seeking the support of the downtrodden masses. The great admirer of Montesquieu was now echoing Jean-Jacques Rousseau. To ensure victory at the referendum, ballot boxes for "yes" and "no" votes were placed in different locations. As expected, Mossadeq received overwhelming support, obtaining 2,043,300 of the 2,044,600 votes cast throughout the country.[75] The referendum may have exaggerated his support, but there was no doubt he retained his mass following. According to the *New York Times*, the anniversary of the July Uprising was celebrated by a mammoth rally in Tehran—even though Kashani supporters were conspicuously absent.[76] The occasion was also marked by a nationwide general strike.[77]

The Coup Plan

Donald Wilber begins his narrative of the coup in late November 1952.[78] This conveniently leaves out the conclusion reached by both Loy Henderson and George Middleton immediately after the July Uprising that the only way to get rid of Mossadeq was through a military coup. It also leaves out Foreign Minister Eden's earlier request for "more imaginative ways" and the series of joint CIA-MI6 meetings in autumn 1952 to deal with the situation, which were attended by Allen Dulles, the future director of the CIA.[79] Their minutes remain classified.

Wilber starts by listing—in the following order—six major reasons for overthrowing Mossadeq: (1) his "refusal" to accept an oil agreement—the blame was put squarely on his shoulders; (2) his "deficit financing"—by this logic, many governments deserve to be overthrown; (3) his "emotional" politics, drive for "personal power," and his "totally destructive and reckless attitude"; (4) his "extension of tenure" and "disregard for the constitution"—few would have thought the agency had such concern about Iran's 1906 constitution; (5) his undermining of the shah and the armed forces; and (6), his "collaboration with the Tudeh" and his recruitment of its members into the ministries. Wilber does not depict the Tudeh as an immediate threat but leaves the impression that if the existing policies continued, they could possibly sometime in the future pose a serious threat—as had been the case in Czechoslovakia in 1948. But, of course, Iran, with its armed tribes and relatively small urban population, was hardly Czechoslovakia. Wilber stresses that the State Department and the Foreign Office met in November 1952 and asked the CIA and MI6 to prepare a joint plan to overthrow Mossadeq.

The plan was first drafted in early April in Washington; fine-tuned in late April in the British military base in Cyprus; further honed in early June in Beirut; finalized in late June in London; and signed off by the secretary of state and the foreign minister on July 1, and by Eisenhower and Churchill on July 11. The operation was scheduled for mid-August. Loy Henderson was consulted throughout the planning stage; General Zahedi was brought in only later. Communications offices were set up in Tehran, Nicosia, and Washington.

Kermit Roosevelt was named head of field operations. Although he did not speak Persian and had no in-depth knowledge of Iran, Roosevelt had other credentials. He had clandestine experiences from the early years of World War II, when he had worked against the Soviets in Finland. He had some knowledge of the petroleum business, having been recruited in the late 1940s by Foster Dulles into the Overseas Consultants to lobby for oil concessions in Iran.[80] What is more, he could—because of his name—speak to the shah on behalf of the United States. To add to his credentials, Roosevelt visited Churchill on his way to Iran and received the latter's full endorsement. Before leaving Washington, Roosevelt was briefed that Mossadeq was an "ill-tempered, erratic old peasant, continuing on the fringe of responsibility and reality but still judging all problems from his emotional standpoint."[81] The CIA and MI6 named their joint operation "AJAX." A British historian notes that "AJAX" was simply an elaboration of an earlier MI6 plan named "BOOT."[82] These names reveal much about the mentality of the two organizations.

The plan had two component parts: turmoil to destabilize the government; and a conventional military coup to topple the government. Wilber was personally in charge of the "psychological" side of the "war of nerves." He specialized in "white" and "black propaganda," the former being damaging information that was true and attributable; the latter, information that was untrue and deliberately misleading. He boasted that his task was to "weaken the government in any way possible" and to "fan to fever pitch public opinion against Mossadeq."

A crucial component of the plan was to highlight the supposed communist threat, linking the Tudeh to the National Front, exaggerating its strength, inflating its crowds, forging documents to "prove" it had infiltrated the government, claiming it was preparing to pull off a coup, and warning that Mossadeq would wittingly or unwittingly pave the way for the inevitable incorporation of Iran into the Soviet Bloc. News articles in this vein were planted in papers in Britain, America, and Iran. Since they fit well into the public discourse of the time, most newspapers readily ran them. There was not a single mainstream paper in the United States and UK that did not publish at least one major piece on the supposed Red Threat to Iran in the summer of 1953.

Although American and British policymakers readily cited the communist threat in their public statements, they seem to have taken it with a pinch of salt in their private discussions. The very first joint meeting of the State Department and Foreign Office concurred that "the present situation contained no element of Russian incitation and ought not to be seen primarily as part of the immediate short-term 'cold war' problem."[83] When the British Working Party was dragging its feet on accepting the principle of nationalization, it complained the Americans were getting "carried away" with their anti-communist "eloquence."[84] The British ambassador in Washington complained the United States was overemphasizing "the communist angle."[85] The British foreign minister stressed to his American counterpart that "communism was not the only alternative" to Mossadeq.[86] Acheson later wrote, "Eden saw no great crisis or need for haste since for him communist rule was not the only alternative."[87] Acheson himself—according to Roosevelt—did not take the communist threat seriously, even in the summer of 1953.[88]

The Foreign Office, while dismissing the communist

danger, instructed its officials, "We need to stress to the Americans that the danger of communism increases the longer Musaddiq remains in power."[89] During the coup preparations, the British claimed only the military could save the country from communism. MI6 operative Monty Woodhouse—a Cold War warrior if there ever was one—admits in his memoirs that in his transatlantic dealings he intentionally played up the communist threat and downplayed the "need to regain control of the oil industry."[90] Similarly, George Middleton, years later, admitted he had always considered the Tudeh to be more of a "bogeyman" than a real threat, since the whole social structure was not "favourable to a communist take over."[91] Conversely, Acheson, McGhee, and Harriman often cited the communist danger to bring the British in line, but rarely in their later memoirs did they link the coup to this supposed danger.

The communist threat was cited so often that Mossadeq could not resist making fun of the practice. During the last spurt of negotiations on compensation, Loy Henderson complained he would never be able to sell Mossadeq's calculations to the British. Mossadeq quipped, "You can tell them you are saving Iran from communism." Henderson was familiar enough with Mossadeq's humor to get the tease. But historians unfamiliar with the use of irony claim "this use of the cold war sealed his fate.[92] Mossadeq at his trial dismissed talk of the communist danger as a red herring designed to distract attention from the real issues. "I had no concerns about the Tudeh," he argued, "because they had not a single tank or a single machine gun. . . . With future oil revenues we could have alleviated economic problems and thereby diminished their social support."[93] He repeated the same sentiment later in his prison notes.[94] He was unconcerned about the Tudeh for a number of reasons. He knew they lacked the clout to overthrow him. He had confidence

in the ministers whom the opposition denounced as "infiltra-
tors" and "fellow-travelers." He also had daily confirmations
from his trusted nephew and neighbor, Abu Nasr Azod, that
the Tudeh had no plans for a coup and was not even thinking in such terms.[95] Azod, known as the Red Prince, had for a
short while been a member of the Tudeh and kept in touch
with some of his former colleagues.

There are other reasons for not taking the communist
threat at face value. The very same "fellow-travelers" suspected of "penetrating" the National Front were soon permitted to settle in the United States. This would have been a
violation of emigration laws if there had been any substance
in these suspicions. A top-level meeting of the National Security Council held in March 1953 discussed many aspects
of the Iran crisis but hardly touched on the communist danger.[96] Henderson assured Washington on the very eve of the
coup that "so long as security forces remained unaffected
by Tudeh, these forces, together with non-Communist elements, could offer [an] alternative to Mosaddiq other than
the Tudeh."[97] Significantly, the Wilber Report, in its section
on possible "blowbacks"—CIA jargon for costs of failure—
contained next to nothing about a communist takeover but
much on the likelihood of the unearthing of the whole MI6
underground. Instead of dwelling on the possibility of a
communist government, the document laid out contingency
plans for instigating further tribal revolts against the Mossadeq government.[98]

What is more, the CIA had a fairly realistic assessment of
the Tudeh's strengths and weaknesses. It knew from its own
information—supplemented by Iranian G2 reports—that
the party had some 15,000 to 22,000 members; four times
that number of sympathizers; a voting strength of 25,000 in
Tehran; an impressive array of front organizations led by the
Peace Partisans and the Society to Combat the Imperialist

Oil Companies; an even more impressive array of trade unions—60 percent of the rank and file were workers, some women, but most "literate men reasonably well-dressed in western clothes"; and could muster in Tehran on the anniversary of the July Uprising rally some 53,000—which the *New York Times* inflated to more than 100,000.[99] Ghulam-Hussein Sadiqi later complained that Khalel Maleki had insisted on the National Front and the Tudeh having separate rallies, and this had played into the hands of the opposition.[100]

But the CIA also knew that numbers did not necessarily translate into political power. The party was not armed. Its members in the armed forces had been marginalized. It was not talking about revolution. And it was not really preparing either for an uprising or an armed struggle.[101] Its main goal was to bolster Mossadeq and create a united front.[102] The British were intrigued the Tudeh did not "exploit the July disturbances to make a bid for power."[103] One CIA report stated, "The National Front government will remain in power through 1953. The government has the capability to take effective repressive action to check mob violence and Tudeh agitations. . . . The Tudeh will not be able to gain control of the government. Neither the groups opposing the National Front nor the Tudeh Party are likely to develop the strength to overthrow the National Front."[104] Another CIA report stated, "The Tudeh has not made plans for large armed actions of any kind. . . . It has instructed its members to 'protect' the government against possible coup. It does not believe circumstances are favorable for it to seize power."[105] On the eve of the coup, the Foreign Office reported that the Tudeh was limiting its activities to consolidating its labor organizations and it was "difficult to foresee under what circumstances it could attempt a coup."[106] It went on to say that the Iranian military was capable of dealing with any such attempt. The Foreign Office also inadvertently admitted the real problem was that Iranians had a "deep-seated distrust of all foreigners," had difficulty "differentiating between American and Soviet objectives," and, therefore, had serious "illusions about neutralism." [107] In other words, the real problem was not communism but neutralism. These realistic assessments were reconfirmed by the French military attaché, who kept close contact with Saint Cyr–trained Iranians. After a visit from the French attaché, the British ambassador in Kabul reported:

> Colonel Bois [visiting Kabul in June 1953] said that Mussadiq was still fairly firmly in the saddle and had the support of the great majority of the people. He did not seem to think the Tudeh Party had any chance of seizing power in the near future. He said that their strength rose and fell according to whether Mussadiq collaborated with or turned against them. His tactics are apparently to play the Tudeh and the extreme Right off against each other . . . He expects Iran to become a republic like Egypt soon.[108]

The well-known historian William Roger Louis, resorts to "irony" to explain this discrepancy between propaganda and realistic assessments. He writes, "Part of the irony of the story is that the Mussadiq Government was still populist, nationalist, and anti-Communist. Musaddeq remained a figure who touched a basic chord of Iranian nationalism. He had powerful support from the population at large, in part because his social reforms had now begun to take hold." [109]

While beating drums about the communist threat, the CIA and MI6 funneled a regular flow of money—to the tune of $11,000 a week—to some twenty to thirty deputies; to more than twenty newspapers that regularly ran articles written in London and Washington; to the Bakhtiyari chiefs who launched a tribal uprising in February 1953; to an unnamed "terrorist group"—most probably the Fedayan-e Islam—to take "direct action against Mossadeq and his entourage"; to SUMKA, Arya, and the Toilers Party; and—via Ayatollah Behbehani—to preachers and *luti* gangs in southern Tehran. These gangs were considered larger than the small right-wing parties. The money circulating in 1953 became known as Behbehani dollars.

One of the many articles planted in newspapers claimed Hussein Fatemi was a homosexual, a convert to Christianity and Baha'ism, and had been expelled from a missionary school for stealing money.[110] This was an open incitement to murder, since these alleged crimes would have earned him in the eyes of fundamentals the death penalty three times over. In fact, only a year earlier, a member of the Fedayan-e Islam, shouting "Death to the Enemies of Islam," had shot and seriously wounded Fatemi. Mark Gasiorowski, who has interviewed CIA operatives involved in the coup, discovered the propaganda war had included spreading rumors Mossadeq had Jewish ancestry.[111] The CIA and MI6 cannot be faulted for failing to think outside the box.

Wilber forged documents to "prove" Mossadeq was "anti-religious," "corrupted by power," "surrounded by unscrupulous advisers," in favor of "secessionist movements," and "secretly collaborated" with the Tudeh. He also forged documents to show the Tudeh had infiltrated the National Front, was posed to seize power; and planned to kill religious leaders—one ayatollah had his house bombed and many clerics received threatening letters heralding the imminent establishment of a "people's democratic republic." The CIA also forged banknotes, prepared to flood the country with "imitation currency"—it is not clear if this scheme was ever put into effect.

The plan further stipulated that the media—especially Western newspapers—were to stress the "communist danger" and express "concern about Mossadeq's toleration for the Tudeh." Senior U.S. figures were to make an "official statement which would shatter any hope of aid." In early August, the secretary of state made a special point of not stopping in Tehran during his grand tour of the Middle East. The State Department, meanwhile, leaked the president's early private letter to Mossadeq informing him that he could not possibly extend aid to an oil-rich country such as Iran. Reuters quoted Loy Henderson—who, on his way for a "lengthy vacation" in America, had stopped over in Karachi to see Dulles—that the United States had "exhausted all ideas" of how to resolve the Anglo-Iranian dispute. *Time* described this as "shock treatment." [112] The *New York Times,* in an editorial entitled "Mossadegh Plays with Fire," warned, "We know he is a power-hungry, personally ambitious, ruthless demagogue who is trampling over the liberties of his own people. He is encouraging the Tudeh and is following policies which will make the Communists more and more dangerous." [113] The editorial could have been written by Wilber himself.

The most serious act of destabilization came in April, when Baqai supporters—with the active participation of MI6—kidnapped and tortured to death Gen. Mahmoud Afshartous, the police chief and the officer in charge of purging the armed forces. His badly tortured body was dumped outside Tehran to show all and sundry that the government was incapable of protecting even its very top figures. The police issued arrest warrants for Baqai, Zahedi, and fifteen associates, including the editor of *Shahed* and five retired generals. One of the kidnappers later joined SAVAK and was executed after the 1979 revolution for having participated in the murder of Afshartous.[114] The MI6 man involved later told a journalist they had not intended to kill Afshartous but one of the kidnappers had lost his temper and shot him dead.[115] This

would not explain his badly tortured body. The *New York
Times* claimed "Mossadegh attempted to use the Afshartous
affair to discredit all opposition." [116]

The actual military component of the coup relied heavily
on the shah. He was to give the coup a "quasi-legal cover."
He was also deemed the only person with any prestige among
active Army officers. General Zahedi was deemed "venal"
and somewhat of a bluffer. To get the shah's participation,
the CIA and MI6 sent a relay of emissaries: Princess Ashraf,
the shah's "strong willed" twin sister, arrived unannounced
from the Riviera with a secret letter; Gen. Norman Schwarz-
kopf, head of the U.S. gendarmerie mission in 1942–48, used
a regional tour of the Middle East as a cover to make a "social
call"; Assadullah Rashidian brought a coded message to the
shah to prove he spoke on behalf of the UK government; and
Kermit Roosevelt smuggled himself into the palace to assure
the shah that Eisenhower and Churchill were both fully behind the coup. Roosevelt also assured the shah that after the
coup the United States would extend "adequate aid" and the
British would "in spirit of good will and equity" come to a
"generous oil agreement."

The shah, who readily confessed being averse to "risk taking," delayed commitment until Colonel Akhavi, his former
G2 chief, gave him the names of forty active Army officers
willing to actually participate in the coup. He wanted real
names, not vague promises. To further reassure the shah,
General Zahedi agreed to sign an undated letter of resignation as prime minister.[117] The last thing the shah wanted
was to get rid of a civilian premier and then find himself in
the clutches of an Army general. It would be like jumping
from the frying pan into the fire. It was made clear to the
shah that if he did not "come along" the UK and the United
States would go ahead "without him." They warned they
would "cease backing the dynasty," and, consequently, the

"dynasty itself would cease to exist." This sounded more like an ultimatum than a friendly nudge.

The plan laid out the following steps: on an assigned night in mid-August a contingent of Imperial Guards, headed by their commander, Col. Nematullah Naseri, would present Mossadeq with a duly signed *farman* (royal decree) replacing him with Zahedi; another contingent would arrest key ministers; and another headed by General Batmaqalich would take over the telephone-telegraph office, the radio station, and the general staff headquarters. General Batmaqalich—as Zahedi's newly named chief of staff—would issue orders instructing troops and tanks out of their barracks into the capital to crush protests and carry out mass arrests—100 were to be arrested right away and another 4,000 activists in the following days. As a diversion, street gangs would attack offices associated with the Tudeh and the National Front. The plan stipulated that if the "quasi-legal aspect" of the coup failed, its more straightforward military dimension would be implemented. As backup, reinforcements could be rushed in from provincial garrisons—from Kermanshah led by Colonel Bakhtiyar and from Qazvin led by Colonel Qarani. If all else failed, the contingency plan called for tribal uprisings—especially among Bakhtiyaris outside Isfahan and Shahsavens in Azerbaijan. The plan included this note of caution:

The preceding material represents a Western-type plan offered for execution by Orientals. However, it was drafted by authors with an intensive knowledge of the country and its people who endeavored to examine and evaluate all the details from the Iranian point of view. Given the recognized incapacity of Iranians to plan or act in a thoroughly logical manner, we could never expect such a plan to be restudied and executed in the local atmosphere like

a Western staff operation. No precedent for this operation
exists in Iran in recent years. The Reza Shah coup was of
an entirely different nature. Recent coups in other Near
Eastern countries were far easier to carry out since they
were not complicated by a large pro-Communist opposition or hampered by the presence of a head of government
having [a] powerful popular following.[118]

The main obstacle was the command structure of the
Tehran garrison. Soon after the July 1952 uprising, General
Riyahi—Mossadeq's new chief of staff—had completely re-
organized it. Dividing the garrison into five brigades—two
armored and three mountain (light-armored) brigades, he
had housed them in separate barracks; placed them under
the command of colonels he trusted; and set up elaborate
checks to prevent any unauthorized use of tanks, troops,
trucks, ammunition, spare parts, and even fuel. Four of the
five commanders were, like him, French-educated members
of the Iran Party: Col. Ali Parsa, a nephew of Ali Shayegan,
commanded the First Mountain Brigade at Mahabad Airport; Col. Ezatallah Momtaz, the Second Mountain at
Jamshidieh; Col. Ashrafi—the one exception—the Third
Mountain at Eshqabad; Col. Nasser Shahrough, the Second
Armored at Qasr; and Col. Rostom Nowzari, the First Armored at Sultanabad—the largest barracks, with thirty-two
tanks, including sixteen Shermans.[119] Riyahi's trust was well
placed in all but Ashrafi, who happened to be an MI6 operative. Despite this, on the day of the coup Ashrafi refused to
participate and consequently was soon cashiered by the shah.
He lived into old age basking in the reputation of having opposed the coup.[120]

The Imperial Guards—the most royalist section of
the military—had been stripped of heavy armor after the
July Uprising but had been permitted to keep their own

Sa'adabad barracks at Baq-e Shah (Shah's Garden). The only other military contingent in the capital was the Customs Guard. It was commanded by Gen. Muhammad Daftari, Mossadeq's nephew and brother of the Matin-Daftari who served as the premier's main adviser on international law. The Wilber document reports that Mossadeq had chosen his chief of staff well; that Riyahi had chosen his brigade commanders well; and that these commanders had instituted their control over their barracks well. To short-circuit this tight command structure, the coup intended to name a new chief of staff, who would issue instructions directly to deputy barracks commanders and their tank officers—thus undercutting the brigade commanders. The forty names Akhavi passed on to the shah included field officers such as Lt. Cols. Zand-Karimi, Rouhani, and Khosrow-Pana, as well as Cpts. Majed Jahanbani, Akbar Zand, Nasrallah Sepehr, and Akbar Dadstan. The plan emphasized the "military aspect of the coup" would succeed only if Tudeh crowds were kept off the streets. It also emphasized that too much reliance should not be placed on the royalist street "gangs," since they could muster at most a mere 3,000 men.[121]

Counterfeit Revolt

The operation was launched in the late hours of August 15. Three contingents of Imperial Guards left their barracks in Baq-e Shah as planned. Colonel Naseri headed straight for Mossadeq's residence with a convoy formed of one armored vehicle, two jeeps, and two trucks full of armed guards. The second contingent, formed of two trucks full of guards, drove to northern Tehran to the summer house shared by Riyahi and some members of the cabinet—Fatemi, Haqshenas, and Zirakzadeh. The third, led by General Batqamalich and Col. Hussein Azmoudeh, made its way to the telegraph office and the general-staff headquarters in central Tehran. Only the second had any success. After a short exchange of fire, it managed to seize Fatemi, Haqshenas, and Zirakzadeh. Riyahi had been tipped off and had rushed to his staff headquarters.

Naseri, on reaching Mossadeq's residence, found himself confronted by a much larger force. Waiting for him was Colonel Momtaz, commander of the Second Mountain Brigade, with four tanks. Instead of Naseri arresting Mossadeq, Mossadeq had Naseri arrested. Mossadeq dismissed the *farman* as a forgery, arguing that the shah did not have the constitutional authority to appoint or dismiss prime ministers; that authority, according to Mossadeq, resided in the Majles. Similarly, when Batmaqalich arrived at the staff headquarters, he found himself confronted by a much superior force—including a tank. He fled, but his assistant Azmoudeh was arrested. Wilber was mystified by what had gone awry.

In fact, a young member of the Imperial Guard, Capt. Mehdi Homayuni, who also happened to be a member of the clandestine military branch of the Tudeh, had warned his party superiors of the impending coup. His organization had relayed the information to Nuraldin Kianuri, the main liaison between the party's central committee and its clandestine military network. Kianuri had been able to quickly communicate the information to Mossadeq because their wives were close family relatives and knew each other's personal phone numbers. Kianuri had warned Mossadeq over the phone of the impending coup, providing him with specifics on Naseri's movements.[122] Mossadeq, in turn, had instructed Riyahi to take necessary precautions. Reinforcements—including tanks—had been rushed both to the premier's home and the staff headquarters. Mossadeq confirmed the general thrust of this account at his trial. He narrated how a certain *shakhsi* (person) had phoned his wife at seven p.m. at home and warned of the planned coup that same evening. The same unnamed person, he elaborated, had read him the names of the specific officers involved.[123]

By five a.m. the next day, normalcy had returned to the capital. Lifting martial law, the government announced that thirty arrest warrants had been issued. Naseri and fourteen Imperial Guards—including Capt. Mehdi Homayuni—were already under arrest. Others, led by Zahedi, Batqamalich, Farzandegan, and Perron, went into hiding—Zahedi into the home of an American diplomat. When a cabinet minister suggested that Naseri should be executed, Mossadeq dismissed the idea as not only illegal but absurd.[124] Meanwhile, the shah, together with his wife and personal pilot, flew a small plane to Baghdad—as planned in case of failure.

A G2 lawyer appointed by Mossadeq to investigate the attempted coup got much of the story right.[125] His report—which he wrote down immediately—was not published until after the 1979 revolution. He identified most of the leading participants and mentioned the involvement of both a United Press correspondent and an "unknown American" who had smuggled himself into the palace. He recommended the arrest of both Colonel Akhavi and General Daftari. However, the former, an old friend of Riyahi, threatened to blow out his own brains in front of his friend. He was permitted to check into a hospital, "sick." The latter, Mossadeq's nephew, was retained as commander of the Customs Guards after he tearfully denied involvement and swore personal allegiance to his uncle. This was still an age when a "gentleman's word" counted. The CIA spread rumors that the arrested were about to be executed. In fact, they were placed in a low-level security jail, together with previous detainees such as Baqai and Brainless Sha'aban. All had easy access to the outside world.

The day after the failed coup, large spontaneous crowds—formed of the National Front as well as the Tudeh—celebrated in Ferdowsi Square and in Lalezar, Naderi, and

Istanbul Avenues. They changed the street names, tore down
the shah's pictures, and toppled royal statues—notably that
of Reza Shah in Cannon Square. Ahmad Zirakzadeh later
wrote that his Iran Party had eagerly participated in these
actions. Fatemi informed colleagues such activities had
been condoned by Mossadeq.[126] It was later revealed that
Mossadeq told Riyahi not to interfere because the "people
needed an outlet to vent their justifiable anger." [127] Similar
crowds toppled statues in most provincial towns—with the
notable exception of Shahi (Qiyamshahr) where the Pahlavis had invested substantial sums in the local economies as
well as in their large estates.[128]

That same evening, a much larger but orderly rally convened in Parliament Square to hear government spokesmen.
The main speakers were Fatemi, Shayegan, Haqshenas,
Razavi, and Zirakzadeh. The rally was sponsored by the National Front—especially the Iran Party, the Third Force,
and the Union of Bazaar Guilds and Tradesmen. It was also
supported by the Tudeh and its affiliated trade unions. The
speakers, with the notable exception of Fatemi, spoke in favor
of forming a council to resolve the constitutional issue. They
stressed once more that the shah should reign not rule. Fatemi, however, spoke of the need to establish a republic and
put "traitors" on trial who had tried to pull off the coup. He
drew parallels between Farouk, the recently deposed king of
Egypt, and the "young man" who had just fled to Baghdad.
That morning Fatemi had quietly taken Ali Dehkhoda—the
icon of the intelligentsia and veteran of the constitutional
revolution—to Mossadeq's home to explore the possibility of
naming him president of a prospective republic.[129] The rally
ended with a resolution calling for the formation of a council
to resolve the constitutional crisis. Mossadeq had insisted on
such a council, having told his ministers he had taken a vow
on the Koran to be faithful to the constitutional monarchy.

Fatemi later wrote the only time Mossadeq had ever raised his voice with him was over this issue.[130]

Sporadic attacks on statues and royal symbols continued well into the night. That same evening, Fatemi published in his *Bakhtar-e Emruz* an article pronouncing the monarchy dead and buried. It described the court as a "center of corruption," the shah as "capricious and bloodthirsty," a "servant of the British," and a "thief of Baghdad," and the shah's father as a dictator who had signed the notorious 1933 oil concession.[131] The article, as well as this speech, later sealed Fatemi's fate.[132] Earlier, he had told his assistant in *Bakhtar-e Emruz* he felt confident since he knew that the defection of Ayatollah Kashani and other "opportunists" had little influence, that the economy could manage without oil, and that the West was intentionally exaggerating the Tudeh threat. "Dr. Fatemi," his assistant later wrote, "did not perceive the communist threat as either clear or present.... His view substantially reflected those of Dr. Mossadegh."[133]

Immediately after the Naseri fiasco, some at CIA and MI6 headquarters concluded that the whole coup had failed. Washington instructed Roosevelt to leave. Robert McClure thought the remaining hope was that General Riyahi would eventually carry out his own coup. The undersecretary of state, with little knowledge of the situation on the ground wrote, "We now have to take a whole new look at the Iranian situation and probably have to snuggle up to Mossadeq if we're going to save anything there."[134] Others, however, notably Roosevelt, concluded that only the "quasi-legal" aspect of the coup had failed. They argued that their core network—especially the military component—remained very much intact, and that with some improvisations the original plan could still be carried out. Roosevelt claims he threatened to shoot anyone indulging in "defeatist talk." Henderson, who had taken a "prolonged vacation" so as to be absent during the coup, was in Beirut when he heard of the fiasco. He immediately rushed back to Tehran on a military plane and was greeted at the airport by Mossadeq's son. On his way from the airport he saw jubilant crowds toppling statues. Straightaway he met Roosevelt in the American embassy. He then requested an urgent meeting with Mossadeq. He was granted such a meeting for the very next day—on August 18.

The vital importance of this meeting has often been overlooked. Mossadeq admirers prefer to gloss over it. Wilber ignores it entirely; instead he resorts to vague language on how a "situation" was created in which the "military plan could be implemented." [135] Henderson himself sent Washington a sanitized summary, leaving out his own instrumental role in the actual coup.[136] After all, august ambassadors are not supposed to be in the cloak-and-dagger business—that territory belongs to the CIA. He would offer a less sanitized version twenty years later to the oral history project at Columbia University.[137] He also leaked—of course anonymously—to *Time* a similar version immediately after the coup.[138] His own private papers—opened after his death—confirm the *Time* account. They reveal that he issued Mossadeq an ultimatum and that immediately before the meeting he had hammered out a strategy together with Roosevelt.[139] This is further confirmed by historian Stephen Ambrose who, in writing *Ike's Spies: Eisenhower and the Espionage Establishment*, had free access to other Henderson papers.

According to Henderson, the meeting lasted a full hour and began on a polite note. Mossadeq, wearing a suit instead of his "usual pajamas," was his "courteous self" but expressed a "certain amount of smoldering resentment." He blamed the British for the coup attempt, although he must have known from his G2 report that Americans, especially McClure, were implicated as well. Henderson expressed "sorrow" for the chain of events that had taken place during his absence. Mossadeq gave a "sarcastic smile."

The tone, however, drastically shifted when Henderson turned to the "extreme serious" matter at hand: the abysmal failure of law enforcement to protect American lives. His Isfahan consul had just phoned him with the news that dangerous "mobs" had converged on his building with such slogans as "Down with the U.S.," and "Yankee, Go Home." His own military attaché's car had been attacked and the driver had been stabbed. Henderson then issued Mossadeq the not-so-subtle ultimatum that if the authorities did not act forcefully to establish law and order in the streets, he would have no choice but to request that all Americans leave Iran forthwith. He stressed the United States could not continue to recognize Mossadeq as the head of government since the government could no longer control the streets. He also mentioned in passing that he had heard the shah had dismissed him. This raised the question whether he was even still the lawful prime minister. In reporting back to his ministers, Mossadeq highlighted that Henderson questioned his authority.[140] Mossadeq reported that he had firmly pointed out that the monarch did not have the constitutional authority to dismiss prime ministers. While threatening Mossadeq, Henderson held out the promise of future financial assistance and continued recognition if strong action was taken immediately to reestablish law and order in the streets. Sadiqi, the interior minister, later recounted that Mossadeq had requested that people stay off the streets to oblige Henderson, who had vehemently complained about the anti-American demonstrations.[141] A later U.S. embassy report on the coup obliquely mentioned that in the course of the conversation Henderson had raised the sensitive issue of who was the legal premier.[142]

Ambrose, relying on Henderson's private papers, writes that the ambassador on his return to Tehran had "demanded an immediate audience" with Mossadeq, had vigorously "protested the mob attacks" on Westerners, and had threatened to evacuate all Americans if the streets were not cleared. Mossadeq—according to Henderson—had "lost his nerve," picked up the phone, and ordered his chief of police to "restore order in the streets." This, he concludes, was the "old man's fatal mistake." [143]

Mossadeq fell for the bait. He issued a formal ban on all demonstrations.[144] General Riyahi also announced that his troops had instructions to shoot if necessary. *Time*, in its postmortem of the coup, reported that "things began to happen" immediately after the Henderson interview. "When Henderson left the room Mossadegh was firmly convinced that the US was undecided as to whether to continue to recognize him as Iran's Premier. . . . Shaken, the old man went to the phone and ordered the army and police to drive the rioting Reds off the streets. That call, turning the army loose on the most powerful street support he had, was Mossadegh's fatal mistake." A similar account of the meeting appeared in *Newsweek*.[145] Henderson himself, in his interview twenty years later, stated that Mossadeq "in my presence picked up the phone, called the chief of police, and gave orders that the police be instructed immediately to restore order to the streets, to break up the roving gangs who were moving around indulging in violence." In his official account, however, Henderson admitted the importance of Mossadeq's order but avoided mentioning his own role. He simply wrote Mossadeq had "ordered the streets cleared and cessation of demonstrations." [146] Things just happened.

A Foreign Office expert given access to some of the correspondence between the U.S. embassy in Tehran and the State Department in Washington reported that the "first significant break in the situation" came when Mossadeq ordered the "clearing of the streets." [147] A much longer postmortem

written for the Foreign Office—probably by Kermit Roosevelt himself—and published recently by the State Department with gaping redactions states, "Mr. Henderson called
on the Prime Minister during the afternoon. . . . Their meeting ended abruptly. According to well placed sources, it was
soon after this that the plans for the events of the 19th of
August were put into operation." [148]

The *New York Times* correspondent wrote that the government on August 18 banned all street demonstrations because
unruly Tudeh and National Front mobs were fighting each
other.[149] The same correspondent also gave the misleading
information that Zahedi had been sighted in faraway Azerbaijan. In fact, he was hiding out in Tehran—most probably with Americans. Late that same day, Colonel Ashrafi,
now military governor of Tehran as well as commander of
the Third Mountain Brigade, called in Tudeh and National
Front representatives to read to them Mossadeq's explicit instructions to stay off the streets.[150]

The following morning, the Tudeh as well as the National
Front observed Mossadeq's instructions.[151] The Third Force
declared the danger from the right to be dead and buried,
but that from the Tudeh to be still well and alive.[152] The
Boscoe Brothers had done a good job with the Third Force.
Meanwhile, six opposition papers—still free to publish—
prominently displayed the royal decree naming General
Zahedi prime minister. The six included Kashani's *Setareh-e
Islam* (Star of Islam). Hojjat al-Islam Taleqani later revealed that forgers had been busy all night in Ayatollah
Behbehani's home, rolling out leaflets under the name of
the Tudeh heralding the dawn of a "democratic people's republic." They also threatened to hang from lampposts clerical leaders, including Grand Ayatollah Boroujerdi.[153] At six
thirty a.m., cabinet members convened in Mossadeq's home
to discuss plans for a referendum to determine the fate of the

monarchy. Sadiqi, the interior minister, was entrusted with
the task of preparing the ballot boxes. At eight a.m. he sent
out instructions to provincial governors to prepare for the expected referendum.[154]

At about the same hour, a gang of some three hundred
men armed with knives, rocks, and heavy clubs made their
way from southern Tehran through the bazaar toward the
city's northern areas.[155] It was led by Tayeb—the colleague
of Brainless Sha'aban. The reporter for the *New York Times*
wrote that these "street fighters from the slums" provided
a useful pretext for military intervention.[156] Cottam—who
had firsthand knowledge of the coup—gives this description
of the street gang:

> The athletic clubs of the mob leaders are centers for ath-
> letic young toughs, known as chaqu keshan (knife wield-
> ers), who can be hired for any kind of corrupt or terroristic
> activity. Generally, also, the mob leader will control a
> number of brothels and gambling houses. He and his men
> are for hire by politicians, and when a sizeable political
> demonstration is desired the mob leaders purchase the
> participation of large numbers of unskilled laborers. . . .
> The chaqu keshan mobs are most frequently purchased
> by rightist and royalist politicians. The mob that appeared
> from the slums of South Tehran on August 19, 1953, and
> presented the rightist Army generals with victory over
> Mossadeq were mullah and chaqu keshan–led.
>
>   There is no doubt that the mob that appeared on Au-
> gust 19, 1953, and toppled Mossadeq from power was a
> conglomeration of south Tehran illiterates collected by
> Behbehani's organization with the assistance of Kashani,
> other lesser mullahs, and a wide assortment of chaqu ke-
> shan leaders. The mob screamed pro-Shah slogans, and
> no doubt some individuals did so with conviction; but

sustained royalist support could not be expected from this quarter.[157]

Christopher de Bellaigue, a contemporary British writer who has spent much time talking to *zurkhaneh* athletes and Tayeb fans, gives a similar description:

> On 18 August 1953, Tayeb sent word to his closest asso-
> ciates to gather in the fruit and vegetable market. The
> following morning, some three hundred came; they car-
> ried knives and other weapons. Tayeb doled out money
> that he had received from a trio of banking brothers
> who were active as a conduit for CIA money. Swollen by
> more local lads, the crowd set off from the market, rais-
> ing anti-Mossadegh slogans, beating up people wearing
> white shirts (a fashion associated with Communists), and
> forcing passing cars to hoot in support of the Shah. Along
> the route, Tayeb's band joined forces with a second group,
> led by Icy Ramazan. As they marched north, the accre-
> tions continued. The most picturesque group came from
> the New Town (Red Light District) and was composed of
> celebrated prostitutes of the day. . . . The actions of Tayeb
> and the others allowed the coup makers to portray the
> events of 19 August as an expression of popular will —
> rather than a CIA-sponsored plot.[158]

The gang dismantled newspaper stands carrying pro-government publications; beat up pedestrians and drivers refusing to shout "Long Live the Shah"; threatened to loot shops unless they closed; ransacked the Sa'adi Theatre—a social center for leftist intellectuals; and burned down the offices of the Iran Party, the Third Force, *Bakhtar-e Emruz*, and *Besu-ye Ayandeh*—the main Tudeh newspaper. As they moved into the city center they were joined by what Kermit

Roosevelt described as "unemployed persons transported free by hired lorries"; by some Fedayan-e Islam supporters as well as members of the Toilers, SUMKA, and Arya Parties; by peasants trucked in from the royal estates at Veramin; and, most important of all, by prisoners released from the central jail.[159] Captain Homayuni—the Imperial Guard who had sabotaged the early coup—writes in his memoirs that around nine a.m. the street gangs freed him and others in the central jail.[160] By two p.m. Imperial Guards—many wearing civilian clothes—were driving trucks from their barracks into the city.[161] The total in this royalist "crowd" was no more than three to four thousand.

Whereas an American reporter sympathetic to the CIA later described them as a "grotesque procession," royalists were quick to hail them as a spontaneous "crowd" that brought about a "Popular Revolt (*Qiyam*)"—even a "Shah-People's Revolution (*Enqelab*)."[162] Four thousand did not make a crowd—especially in a country where rallies easily numbered more than fifty thousand. Neither was this force instrumental in the coup. It merely provided an acoustical side effect to the real show—a conventional military coup. An eyewitness to the assault on the offices of the Third Force wrote that the gangs were too small to take over the building. They had to wait for truckloads of soldiers to arrive. They then pillaged the building under the supervision of Army officers.[163]

While gangs were ransacking, Army commanders drove their tanks into the city. One eyewitness claims Colonel Nowzari, the trustworthy commander of the First Armored Brigade, himself rushed to Sultanabad Barracks in the early morning and ordered Captain Jahanbani—a secret royalist—to rush tanks into the city to implement Mossadeq's order to clear the streets.[164] It is still not clear whether other brigade commanders did the same on their own or whether

their deputies were instructed to do so by General Daftari—
the hastily appointed military governor and police chief.[165]
Daftari, commander of the Customs Guards, had been given
these important posts over the objections of G2 and the chief
of staff. Mossadeq felt the situation would be handled best
by his close relative. In his memoirs, Sadiqi writes that at
eleven a.m. the prime minister phoned him with instructions
to hand over the posts of police chief and military governor
to General Daftari.[166] In other words, one of the coup con-
spirators now held three key positions—that of military governor, police chief, and Customs Guard commander. Captain
Homayuni writes the new military governor promptly dispatched royalist officers to arrest brigade commanders still
holding out for Mossadeq—especially Colonel Parsa of the
First Mountain Brigade in Mahabad Barracks.[167]

Fatemi's assistant in *Bakhtar-e Emruz* years later claimed
that Mossadeq himself had instructed the barracks to permit
tanks to leave so as to establish law and order in the city.[168]
Thus the main obstacle set up to prevent a coup had been overcome. Once some thirty-two tanks and trucks full of troops
were permitted out of their barracks, they headed not for the
ransacking gangs but straight for the strategic posts assigned
in the original plans. Colonel Momtaz later admitted the
tanks dispatched to defend the government ended up attacking that same government.[169] In the course of the day, tanks
captured the staff headquarters; the telephone-telegraph
building, breaking communications between the government and the barracks under pro-Mossadeq commanders;
the interior ministry—Sadiqi escaped to Mossadeq's house;
and the radio station—among the first to address the country
were Zahedi, the shah's brother, Kashani's son, and editors of
the main royalist newspapers.

By five p.m., tanks driven by royalist officers and street
gangs led by Brainless Sha'aban converged on Mossadeq's

home. During the day, Mossadeq had periodic meetings with most of his advisers—Shayegan, Fatemi, Nariman, Hassebi, Razavi, Zirakzadeh, Sadiqi, and the Moazemi brothers. Although the final firefight dragged out for two full hours, the result was predictable. Colonel Momtaz, protecting the house, had only three tanks. Colonels Rouhani and Afkhami, attacking the house, had twenty-four, including two lethal Shermans. Momtaz later narrated that on that fatal day, his side had a grand total of five tanks—three guarding Mossadeq's home, one protecting the Officers Academy, and one outside Baq-e Shah.[170] He informed Mossadeq that his light tanks were no match for the heavy Shermans bombarding the house.[171]

At around seven p.m., with bullets flying into the house, Mossadeq ordered Momtaz to cease firing. As the badly damaged house was being ransacked, Mossadeq and fifteen colleagues—including Shayegan, Sadiqi, Zirakzadeh, Nariman, Razavi, Sheifullah Moazemi, and Hassebi—climbed over the wall into the neighboring house. In the process, Zirakzadeh broke his ankle and Mossadeq cut his head. From there they dispersed to other houses farther down the road. Mossadeq, Shayegan, Sadiqi, Razavi, and Sheifullah Moazemi made their way to the latter's home nearby, and from there they got in touch with Jafar Sharef-Emami, a staunch royalist and a future premier. Sharef-Emami happened to be Moazemi's brother-in-law. They were first detained at the Officers Club, where they were received by General Batqamalich, the new chief of staff, who was related by marriage to Sadiqi. They were then transported to Sultanabad Barracks. A few of the other ministers, notably Fatemi, avoided arrest for the time being.

During the chaotic day, National Front militants had pleaded with Mossadeq to form a National Force, call supporters into the streets, and, if necessary, distribute arms.[172]

Similarly, the Tudeh—after an emergency executive committee meeting—had sent a delegation to his house be-
seeching him to do the same.[173] Kianuri again phoned with
information that Imperial Guards were being trucked
into the city. He was told not to *panek* (panic), because
the situation was under control.[174] Shayegan, in his memoirs, writes that three Tudeh emissaries—one of whom he
knew personally—came to the house requesting active re-
sistance.[175] Although these requests were supported by Fatemi, Sanjabi, and a Qashqayi khan present at the meetings,
Mossadeq rejected them on the grounds that he did not want
to "pour oil over a burning fire." Shayegan admits that for
much of the day they were confident that trusted officers
such as Generals Riyahi and Daftari had the "situation under control." "The one lesson I learnt," he wrote years later,
"is that in a country like Iran you can never trust the army."
Zirakzadeh, Azar, Shayegan, and other National Front leaders later told interviewers that Mossadeq had been reluctant
to act because he belonged to an "old style of politics" and
abhorred the thought of a bloody civil war. He also feared
that such strife could bring foreign intervention and partition off the country—as in 1907.[176] A member of the Tudeh
central committee writes that Mossadeq in his final phone
conversation with Kianuri had exclaimed that the country's
fate now lay in the hands of Keram al-Kateben (The Angels
of Judgment Day).[177] The British embassy later confirmed
that on that fatal day Mossadeq had adamantly refused all
requests to distribute arms.[178]

In estimating casualties, the city's medical office gave the
figure of forty-one killed and seventy-five injured.[179] The
U.S. embassy claimed seventy-three dead and one hundred
wounded. Western newspapers, however, in preparation
for Mossadeq's trial, asserted as many as three hundred had
been shot dead besieging his house.[180] One journalist claimed

Mossadeq had surrendered in the nick of time, since Zahedi was preparing to call for airstrikes.

The shah returned on August 22—just six days after his flight. He was welcomed at the airport by Zahedi, Naseri, Batqamalich, Daftari, and Brainless Sha'aban. When he saw Naseri wearing a general's insignia, he inquired who had promoted him. On being told it was Zahedi, the shah abruptly retorted only he had the authority to make such promotions. His drive into the city was marked by strewn flowers and hastily made triumphant arches. That evening Zahedi made a well-publicized visit to Kashani. The shah himself made a quiet visit the next day. The Iraqi ambassador confidentially told Reuters that the shah had made the "unprecedented step of calling on Kashani at his house in order to thank him for his cooperation in the restoration of the monarchy." [181] In the following week, the main newspapers displayed large pictures of Zahedi posing with Kashani, Baqai, Makki, Haerizadeh, and Qonatabadi.[182] Years later, Sayyed Mahmud Kashani, the ayatollah's son and the Islamic Republic's representative at the Hague, claimed the coup had succeeded because Mossadeq had rejected his father's advice—especially his advice to arrest Zahedi. According to him, Mossadeq had betrayed the real patriotic movement led by his brave father.[183]

In a brief postmortem, Loy Henderson informed the State Department that the shah on his return had wasted no time in reestablishing the previous chain of command—issuing orders to the chief of staff and military heads, bypassing the prime minister. He had repeated his long-standing insistence he was "Commander-in-Chief of the Armed Forces in effect as well as in name." Henderson commented the shah feared that without this power he would "sink into insignificance and eventually be forced to abdicate." He concluded, "The Shah is living in a dream world. He seems to think his restoration was due entirely to his popularity with his people." [184] In an aside, the U.S. embassy admitted, "The majority of people probably still favor Dr. Musaddiq—leaving aside the Tudeh." [185]

Coverage

Soon after Mossadeq's overthrow, G.K. Reddy, a socialist deputy in the Indian parliament, wrote a series of articles on the coup for the *Times of India.*[186] Talking to diplomats and politically aware Iranians, he drew a fairly accurate picture—in fact, so accurate that the Foreign Office recommended the articles for in-house reading even though its printed circulars kept the official line that "a surprising outburst of popular opinion had swept away Dr. Musaddiq himself." [187] "These articles," wrote a Foreign Office hand, "are of outstanding interest and worth reading." [188] Reddy gave a blow-by-blow account of the pertinent events—the "mysterious visits" of Princess Ashraf and General Schwartzkopf; the public rebuffs given by Eisenhower and Dulles; the United States siding with the UK over the issue of "fair compensation"; the close contacts between Army officers and American military advisers; the long-standing ties between the British and the tribes (he claimed most of the "troublesome tribal chiefs were on the British payroll"); the growing liaison between the palace and the Americans; the reputed asylum taken by Zahedi in the American embassy; the Tudeh's forestalling of the coup; the rushed return of Henderson and his questioning of Mossadeq's legitimacy; and, finally, the tanks brought to clear the streets but used to carry out the coup. He concluded:

A good many people in Iran, especially the middle class intelligentsia seem to believe that the real royalist coup d'état was largely inspired if not actually engineered by

foreign elements, notably the United States. . . . Dr. Mossadeq's supporters have put forward a book full of circumstantial evidence to prove their accusation that the United
States actively backed the recent coup. . . . A good many
people feel sorry that a national hero and symbol of Iranian patriotism should have fallen. The people have deep
faith in Dr. Mossadeq. In some ways the picture is darker
now than before the coup. Half the army has to keep an
eye on the tribes; the other half on the cities.[189]

If an Indian visitor could get the story right, Western
journalists and academics could be expected to do the same.
They, however, took their cue from President Eisenhower,
who, immediately after the coup, gave a well-publicized
speech entitled "Peace with Justice." Apparently without
any sense of irony, he claimed that Iranians had spontane-
ously risen up against a seemingly "irresistible dictator" because of their fear of communism. *Time* headlined its coup
story as "Iran Mob, Riot for their Shah." [190] It claimed three
hundred had died so that the "people could take over." The
London *Observer* explained events in the context of the "Crisis in Islam"—especially the intrusion of Western ideas and
technologies into traditional societies.[191] It argued the West
still needed to woo secular nationalists to be able to win
the war against communism. *The Reporter*, in an article on
"Oil, Blood, and Politics," explained the crisis in terms of
Mossadeq being like Goebbels and the shah having "half-
mystical powers" over his people.[192] The *Christian Science
Monitor* claimed a "communist coup" had been averted just
in time because of public revulsion against Mossadeq's acts of
"treason"—especially his arrest of the royal messenger.[193] It
described the shah as "liberal," "benevolent," and "constitutional." "What saved the throne," it claimed, "was the shah
was truly the champion of reform. . . . The main question

remaining is that of moral principles. Only moral principles
can sustain a people these days." Clearly there was no surfeit
of moral principles in August 1953.

The *New York Times* outdid others. It billed Zahedi as a
"farmer," "lifelong royalist," "strong anti-British nationalist," and "unknown" in Washington; the royalist gangs as
"huge mobs" awed by the Shadow of God on Earth; the coup
as a "sudden reversal" and "popular uprising"; and Mossadeq as "old," "wealthy, "aristocratic," and the "richest
man in Iran." It further described him as "a dictator who
had eliminated all means of orderly change," claimed he'd
"done practically nothing but watch the country go down the
drain," and because of his "intense nationalism and hatred of
the British failed to reach an oil agreement"—even rejecting
the "reasonable compromise" proposed by the International
Bank.[194] It quoted the shah, claiming 99 percent of the population supported him and the change of premiers had been
legal since the monarch had the authority to appoint prime
ministers. It described his return as "triumphant," "widely
acclaimed," and "prestige at peak." It even claimed there
had been such a marked shift in public opinion toward the
United States and against the USSR that Zahedi had to place
a tank outside the Soviet embassy to protect it from angry
crowds led by Brainless Sha'aban. Kennett Love, the *New
York Times* correspondent who wrote many of these pieces,
years later in an unpublished analysis of the coup expressed
regret for having been unwittingly used by the CIA.[195] He
noted that although the United States had played a major
role in the coup and the Iranian public knew it, the American public did not. In fact, even State Department experts
on Iran remained ignorant. One such expert, who had been
taught Persian, trained to work in Iran, and sent there in the
mid-1950s, remained oblivious until 1960—when he heard
it for the first time from an Iranian.[196]

No better was the coverage given by academics—especially academics with connections to the two secret services. Peter Avery of Cambridge University claimed the "tide completely turned" on August 19 because of Mossadeq's own shortcomings—his tantrums, dictatorial methods, flirtations with the Tudeh, and, of course, inability to compromise on the oil issue. "Mossadeq," he speculated, "was in bed during these last hours when his house was about to be stormed. When he heard the rifle fire and the rumble of tanks approaching, he pulled a sheet over his head and snuggled down giggling and saying, 'Look what I have done.' " [197]

Professor George Lenczowski of Berkeley, who at one point had spent many hours interviewing Ayatollah Kashani, wrote that nationalization had ruined the country and brought it to the abyss of communism but the situation had been saved at the last moment. "It was only," he proclaimed, "through the major exertions of a group of Iranians dedicated to preserving the existing political system and the country's independence that this dangerous alternative was avoided." [198] Professor J.C. Hurewitz of Columbia was more circumspect. He wrote, "When Muhammad Reza Shah and Queen Suraya fled Iran on 16 August 1953, many experts predicted that the secret and hasty departure marked the end of the Pahlavi dynasty and perhaps of the monarchy. In less than a week the shah returned to Tehran in triumph, his political opponents vanquished." [199] Roger Savory of Toronto University was starry-eyed on how the monarchy was saved because of the "principle of homeostasis"—2,500 years of monarchy, organic stability, and opposition to rapid change: "The warmth and spontaneity of the Shah's welcome by the people when he returned to Iran on 22 August 1953 seems to have astonished many foreign observers and commentators, but should not have occasioned any surprise to the student of Persian history." [200] Elizabeth Monroe, the Foreign Office adviser and author of *Britain's Moment in the Middle East*, outdid her colleagues. In a piece published in the *New York Times* entitled "Key Force in the Middle East—The Mob," she claimed that the "thousands" who poured out to "battle" Mossadeq in his "Hitler-like bunker" were the same people who a day earlier had been out shouting their enthusiastic support for him. "Provide Tehran," she insinuated, "with a political stir and out pours the mob from its slums and shanty towns no matter what the pretext for a demonstration." [201] Gustav Le Bon, the nineteenth-century arch-conservative, would have applauded.

These weighty analyses managed to avoid unseemly topics such as the CIA or MI6. They even avoided the term "coup." Instead they portrayed the overthrow in much the same way as did the Pahlavi dynasty—as the "nation's revolt" and "people's revolution." Some historians have argued that Edward Said's well-known and highly controversial book *Orientalism* unfairly exaggerates the links between academia and the foreign-policy establishment. Fortunately for them, Edward Said was unaware of the nitty-gritty of these links in the 1953 coup. They were far greater than even he could have possibly imagined. More cautious academics wisely kept silent and pretended to be pure scholars uninterested in such unseemly subjects as politics. The whole sorry story tended to widen the gap on how Iranians and Westerners saw not only the coup but also the history of Iran's relations with the West.

4

Legacy

The evil that men do lives after them.

—Shakespeare, *Julius Caesar*, Act III, Scene 2

The 1953 coup in Iran had far-reaching consequences in other parts of the world. It induced American policy makers to conclude that troublesome governments elsewhere could easily be overthrown. In the years to come, the CIA carried out strikingly similar coups in Guatemala, Indonesia, and Chile. Some resulted in mass killings on a genocidal scale. The killing fields of Guatemala and Indonesia could well match the best known horrors of the twentieth century. Conversely, it led many to suspect that the United States was planning coups here, there, and everywhere. Whenever governments—whether in the Congo, Brazil, Argentina, South Vietnam, Cambodia, Iraq, or Pakistan—were overthrown by their military, suspicion automatically fell on the CIA. The United States, which in previous decades had liked to portray itself as champion of liberal democracy, was increasingly identified with right-wing authoritarian military dictatorship. It was reduced to arguing that at least such regimes were better than totalitarian dictatorships.

What is more, the coup set back by at least two decades the whole process of oil nationalization throughout the world—especially in the Middle East and North Africa. The Seven Sisters lost no opportunity immediately after

1953 in pointing out to oil-producing countries the costs of "abrogating sacred contracts." History, however, caught up with them in the 1970s. In that decade, one country after another—radical states such as Libya, Iraq, and Algeria, as well as conservative monarchies such as Kuwait and Saudi Arabia—took over their oil resources, and, having learned from the past, took precautions to make sure the oil companies would not return victorious. For those eager for instant gratification, 1953 was a resounding success. For those thinking about long-term repercussions, 1953 harbored innumerable dangers—some that continue to haunt us in the twenty-first century.

The coup, however, cast its darkest shadow over Iran—but not necessarily in the most obvious ways. Some argue that if Mossadeq had not been overthrown, political pluralism would have taken root and eventually blossomed into full democracy. Others argue he would have inevitably been faced with foreign-instigated tribal revolts. Then he would have been overthrown or else would have had to resort to high-handed methods—in which case he would have further sacrificed old-fashioned liberalism for strident forms of militant nationalism more in line with that of Nasser and other Third World leaders. Still others argue that internal uprisings would have paved the way for civil war, which would have tempted foreign intervention, which, in turn, would have brought about another repartitioning of Iran.

These "ifs" and counterfactual histories, while intriguing, are nevertheless purely speculative. We can fantasize endlessly without reaching any firm conclusions. We do, however, know that the coup did produce the following four substantial legacies: (1) the denationalization of the oil industry; (2) the destruction of the secular opposition; (3) the fatal delegitimization of the monarchy; and (4) the further intensification of the already intense paranoid style prevalent throughout Iranian politics. In other words, the coup left a deep imprint on the country—not only on its polity and economy but also on its popular culture and what some would call mentality.

The shah settled the oil dispute after a decent interval—mid-1954. He signed a complex 50/50 profit-sharing agreement with a Consortium. In the Consortium, 40 percent of the shares were held by the AIOC—renamed British Petroleum; 14 percent by Royal Dutch Shell; 6 percent by Compagnie Français (it was brought in reluctantly); 35 percent by the five American "majors" (7 percent each by Gulf, Texaco, Mobil, Standard Oil of New Jersey, and Standard Oil of California); and the remaining 5 percent by smaller American companies known as the independents.

Before signing, the Consortium made it clear to both the State Department and the Foreign Office that it "needed to be granted certain rights and powers in respect of producing and refining operations, including the exclusive right to explore for, drill for, produce and refine, as well as the right to transport and export oil and gas together with the right of effective control and management of these operations."[1] It wanted these to last a full twenty-five years. William Knox D'Arcy could not have asked for more. The newly arrived British ambassador summed up the immediate dilemma:

The articulate part of the Persian public has I believe realized that oil settlement is desirable. Nevertheless, they accept the facts reluctantly. The blow to their foolish hopes has left their nationalism still extremely sensitive. It is liable to break loose from any shackles of logic. We have to deal with a government which is unusually well-disposed and to whose survival quick agreement is essential. It understands the oil problem in broad terms, and is quite realistic about it, but can not afford an agreement

which does not look presentable. If either in the course
of the negotiations or at the time of the conclusion of an
agreement, it appears to be selling the pass on any of the
subjects liable to arouse mass emotions (the degree of Persian control and compensation are the obvious examples)
it may be swept out of office. . . . It is like a meeting of
co-executives of the estate of an elderly crank as troublesome in death as in life. He has left an eccentric will to
which the settlement must outwardly conform, but the
executors are really engaged together in a conspiracy to
interpret the will liberally enough to enable the monies
to be invested in such a way as to bring maximum profit
to all the beneficiaries.[2]

The Consortium got all it wanted. In the words of Sir Den-
nis Wright, the new British charge d'affaires and future ambassador, "a formula" was found to make it appear that Iran
kept "sovereignty" while the Consortium retained the "control it considered essential for the running of operations."[3]
Herbert Hoover, who had been taking a keen interest in Iran
ever since 1943, signed on behalf of the Consortium. The
chairman of Shell was appointed managing director of the
Consortium. In effect, the oil industry was denationalized.
The agreement was ratified in October 1954 by a closed session of the seventeenth Majles. This Majles—closed down by
Mossadeq—had been reopened once the shah felt confident
he could safely orchestrate new elections.

The British triumph was greater than it would appear, for
Shell, despite its full name, was in many ways British. In the
early 1940s, when the major companies had made secret bids
for new concessions in Iran, the State Department as well as
the Foreign Office treated Shell as British.[4] In 1948, the AIOC
and Shell signed a joint twenty-year agreement to coordinate
all their activities—especially over prices, production, and

working within the sterling area.[5] In 1952—when the International Bank offered its new "compromise"—the State Department noted that Churchill's cabinet, particularly his Treasury, "handled Royal Dutch Shell as a British enterprise."[6] The Ministry of Fuel had so trusted Shell that it had proposed a similar consortium in early 1951:

> It is essential that the majority of the oil should accrue to a British controlled purchasing organisation such as the Anglo-Iranian or Shell and be sold for sterling, since in that way we can reap the foreign currency earnings from the sale of oil for sterling and get the benefit of oil sales in bilateral negotiations with foreign countries. So long as the Shell/Treasury agreement remains in force, it would make no difference if the oil should accrue to a Dutch member of the Shell group since under that agreement all sales of oil are made for sterling through London whether the oil is owned by British or Dutch members of the group. . . . We could contemplate a consortium.[7]

With BP holding 40 percent and Shell 14 percent, the British in effect had controlling shares in the Consortium. In short, they had won the oil struggle hands down. This is invariably overlooked, since it does not fit the narrative of the British Empire in steady decline after World War II. History, however, does not always move in a straight line. As soon as the agreement was finalized, AIOC shares tripled and the company distributed £80 million as dividends to its shareholders.[8]

To save face—something the regime desperately needed—the pretense was preserved that the industry remained fully nationalized. As the Iranian ambassador in Washington stressed, "his government wanted a decent window dressing."[9] The final agreement declared that the NIOC would keep overall "ownership rights" over resources, but would "lease out operations." The NIOC would manage the Kermanshah refinery as well as the company's health, education, and transport facilities. It paid the AIOC only $25 million as compensation—much of this came from the $45 million rushed to Iran by the United States. To soothe national sensibilities, the Consortium was incorporated not in Britain but in the Netherlands. The British government was more than happy giving it a Dutch identity. Some clauses in the final agreement remained opaque—reminiscent of the 1933 Agreement. Consortium members could make special arrangements among themselves about prices and production levels without consulting or even informing the NIOC.[10] The shah was soon complaining—of course privately—that the Consortium had a habit of making crucial decisions without taking into account Iran's needs.[11]

In the 1970s, the NIOC gained a few advantages. It nibbled at the territory conceded to the Consortium. It signed concessions with others—especially with the Italian ENI—and barter deals with foreign states. What is more, the shah increasingly resorted to bluster. He touted the spectacular rise in oil revenues, which increased in part because of higher production but in most part because of the 1973 Arab-Israeli War and the subsequent Arab embargo against the United States. Iran's oil revenues rose from $34 million in 1955 to $5.6 billion in 1973; and, after the quadrupling of prices in 1973–74, to nearly $20 billion in 1976.[12] On one hand, the shah denounced Western consumers for wasting scarce resources and exhorted OPEC to drastically jack up prices—which would have required restricting and even cutting production. On the other hand, he pressured the Consortium to drastically increase production in Iran—which would have glutted the world market and thus limited the price rise.

Bluster, thus, hid the reality that the Consortium continued to control the oil industry in Iran after 1953. As the 1979
revolution unfolded, the *Financial Times* reported that foreign companies, fearful of assassinations, were hastily evac-
uating their technicians, and that the NIOC was preparing
to "take over" the actual running of the industry.[13] It added
that whatever the outcome of the revolution, it was obvious
that the Consortium would lose its "control over production"
and would be reduced from an operating entity into a mere
purchasing one.[14] It further added that the Consortium had
controlled 90 percent of production and shared a common
interest with the shah—that of increased production. It was
now losing control and facing a government that favored
lower production. The Iran of 1979 caught up with the Iran
of 1951–53. In other words, Iran, the very first country in the
region to nationalize its oil, became one of the last to complete the process.

The destruction of the opposition was swift and decisive.
The dismantling of the National Front was relatively easy,
since its central pillar, the Iran Party, had refrained from
establishing grassroots organizations. Its main function had
been to provide Mossadeq with ministers, advisers, technocrats, and civil servants. Twenty-three leading figures from
the fallen administration were immediately rounded up and
hauled before military tribunals. Initially accused of high
treason and charged with the death penalty, most ended up
receiving relatively light sentences—often three years. Mossadeq himself was tried in the Sultanabad Barracks before a
select audience of 150. He denounced his military judges as
"foreign stooges," ridiculed the main charge of "undermining the constitutional monarchy," and retorted that he was
on trial for having "resisted imperialism" by nationalizing
the oil industry. "On account of age," he was sentenced to
only three year's imprisonment. The U.S. embassy deemed

the trial a "serious blunder," since it gave the defendant the opportunity to turn the tables against the prosecution. The embassy would have preferred a swift closed trial.[15] The embassy also admitted that Mossadeq was still deemed a "demigod" retaining "hold over the public" and "symbolizing the nationalist ideal." [16]

The British ambassador later remarked that Mossadeq retained public support because his "movement had been a revolutionary drive of the three lower classes against the upper class and the British who were identified with that class." [17] During the trial, the Tudeh offered to arrange Mossadeq's escape, but he declined with the remark that he had no desire to spend the rest of his life hiding.[18] After serving three years, Mossadeq was banished to his village of Ahmadabad. He died there nine years later. He left a will requesting to be buried in the main Tehran cemetery next to the "martyrs" of the July Uprising. His request was denied by the shah. Instead he was buried in his own sitting room near a mantelpiece displaying a picture of Gandhi.

Only two prominent figures from the National Front were killed. Hussein Fatemi, who had dismissed the shah as "that young traitor," was captured after hiding seven months in the Tudeh underground. He was sentenced to death, taken from the hospital where he was still recovering from earlier wounds, and executed. Royalists later made the unlikely claim that the shah had pardoned Fatemi but gungho officers had executed him before the royal pardon had reached them.[19] His parting cry was "Long Live Mossadeq." Bakhtiyari khans, his longtime family friends, had failed to persuade the shah to commute the death sentence. Fatemi is the only National Front figure to be honored by the Islamic Republic with a street name. The other victim, Karem-Pour Shirazi, editor of a gadfly paper that had lampooned members of the royal family, was doused with paraffin and torched to death in prison.

The crackdown on the Tudeh and its affiliated organizations, especially the trade unions, was much harder than on the National Front. The regime readily accepted the ominous "principle" articulated by the U.S. embassy that since communism was not produced by socioeconomic grievances, massive repression was the only sure way to stamp it out. "The notion," the embassy argued, "that communism feeds on suppression may be accepted to be communist inspired. . . . What they fear is firm police action."[20] The regime rounded up 1,200 party members immediately after the coup. The figure grew to nearly 2,500 in the following months; and further to more than 3,000 in August 1954, when the secret service, with the help of the CIA, uncovered the military organization of the Tudeh Party with more than 500 members—30 of whom managed to escape abroad.[21]

Officers and party leaders—especially those without social connections—were dealt with harshly; most of the others were gradually released. Seven remained incarcerated until the 1979 revolution. They became, together with Nelson Mandela, the longest-serving political prisoners in the world. Thirty-one were executed; eleven were tortured to death; fifty-two had their death sentences commuted to life; another ninety-two were sentenced to life; and hundreds were given terms varying from one to fifteen years. According to British and American confidential reports, the earlier executions were given much "gory publicity," but the later ones were kept secret because of "public revulsion"; because of the victims' "bravado" and "uncompromising defiance"—they faced death denouncing the regime and praising their party; because of the reluctance of firing squads to shoot straight; and, most important of all, because of the "widespread suspicion" the United States had pressured the shah into such "un-Persian" behavior.[22] The United States suspected the shah was spreading such rumors. To contain the bad publicity, the chief prosecutor spread the added false rumors that prison wardens had given tranquilizers to the condemned to soothe their nerves.

Capt. Khosrow Rouzbeh—a leading figure in the military organization—was one of the last to be captured and executed. The British embassy described him as the "Red Pimpernel, who, in a series of disguises walked in and out of innumerable police traps with the swashbuckling courage which made him a figure of legendary proportions, both to the party, the security authorities, and the general public."[23] Rouzbeh's final testament was circulated widely by the Communist International. To eradicate the opposition, especially the Tudeh, the regime in 1957 created—with the help of the CIA, MI6, and Mossad—a new national security organization. Known by its Persian acronym SAVAK, it became an important pillar of state for the next two decades—until the Islamic Revolution of 1979.

The seemingly impressive size of the Tudeh military organization led many to wonder why the communists had not carried out their own coup—as some in the West had feared; or at least successfully forestalled the CIA one. Tudeh leaders, especially Nuraldin Kianuri, have provided three explanations.[24] First, more than 120 of the 500 joined after the coup. Second, the overall figure was not that substantial when placed within an institution that was remarkably top-heavy. The armed forces in 1953 had as many as 15,000 commissioned and 51,000 noncommissioned officers. The 500 constituted less than 1 percent of the officer corps. Third, few held positions that could have been instrumental in a prospective coup. Almost all were either cadets; members of the medical, engineering, and teaching corps; or police and gendarmerie officers—many in distant provinces. Only twenty-six were in the cavalry; two commanding tanks in Tehran—one defended Mossadeq's house, the other at the radio station. Over the years, G2—with the helping hand of MI6—had carefully purged leftists both from the armored divisions and from the Tehran garrison. Riyahi had contin- ued this policy. Kianuri admits that the Tudeh had almost no access to arms and ammunition. The party, however, did have a few people in highly sensitive positions—four members of the royal family, three of them in the Imperial Guards; and two G2 officers, who, at various times, were en- trusted with the personal safety of General Zahedi, the shah, and Vice President Nixon during his 1953 visit. Although the Tudeh was never in a position to seize power, it did have the ability to terminate with extreme prejudice any of these top figures—if such had been its policy.

The dismantling of the Tudeh and the National Front left a gaping political vacuum—one filled eventually by the Is- lamic movement. In 1963–64, when the shah granted Amer- ican military advisers immunity from Iranian law, Ayatollah Khomeini—relatively unknown at that time—made his grand entry into national politics by forcefully denounc- ing the concession as a humiliating submission reminiscent of the notorious nineteenth-century Capitulations extracted by the European imperial powers. Even members of the handpicked Majles objected, with one deputy openly argu- ing that if an American sergeant ran over his child he would not be able to turn to the judicial system and would have to resort to personal revenge.[25] The subsequent riots that erupted in major cities used not the language of national- ism and socialism but of Islam. Those in Tehran were led by Tayeb Haj Rezayi, the same *luti* who had been instrumental in the 1953 coup. This time he was promptly executed. The movement that eventually triumphed in the 1979 revolution traces its very birth to these riots. In short, the shah had inadvertently replaced the secular opposition with a religious one that proved in the long run to be far more lethal.

British and American diplomats liked to depict the shah as a Hamlet-esque figure incapable of making up his mind whether to resist or appease Mossadeq. His form of tragedy, however, was less like Hamlet and more like a protagonist in Greek drama. He knew that specific actions would inevitably lead to his own doom but nevertheless was carried away toward that same destination against his better judgment by forces far beyond his control—by Fate, Providence, History, and, in this case, the United States and UK. They had eventually presented him with the ultimatum that they would carry out the coup with or without him. They had coupled this with the not-so-subtle threat that if he did not cooperate, they could not guarantee the survival of the monarchy and his dynasty.

From the very inception of the crisis in 1949, the shah— unlike many foreign observers—was savvy enough to understand that the oil issue was the country's cause célèbre; that it was comparable to independence movements sweeping other parts of the former colonial world; that Mossadeq articulated and epitomized these nationalist aspirations; and that those foolhardy enough to oppose oil nationalization would inevitably lose credibility and end up on the wrong side of history. By being swept along into the coup, the shah ended up in the deep hole he had tried to avoid. Even though after the coup Mossadeq was airbrushed out of history and his name could not be mentioned in the royal presence, his ghost continued to haunt the shah. The MI6 man in Tehran during the Islamic Revolution noted that the shah continued for the rest of his life to suffer from an acute "inferiority complex" vis-à-vis Mossadeq.[26] Asadollah Alam, the shah's personal confidant, writes in his private diaries:

Audience. Offered my congratulations on the thirty-third anniversary of HIM's succession. "Just think what calamities we've been through since then," he said. I agreed, remarking how hard things had been during the last war, but he brushed this aside. "The war years weren't really that difficult," he said, "since we had no alternative but passive resignation. No, the worst years of my reign, indeed of my entire life, came when Mosaddiq was Prime Minister. The bastard was out for blood and every morning I woke with the sensation that today might be my last on the throne. Every night I went to bed having been subjected to unspeakable insults in the press."[27]

To minimize the damage, the shah did his best to pretend he had preserved the nationalized oil industry. His bluster, however, could not hide the harsh reality that Iran after 1953 found itself chained to the chariot wheels of the West. On a long list of issues, the shah openly sided with the First World against not only the Second but also against the Non-Aligned Third World. He took Iran into the Baghdad Pact, later named CENTO; had his ever-expanding armed forces trained almost entirely by the United States and UK; signed the controversial Capitulation Treaty granting American military advisers exemption from Iranian law; spent billions on Western arms; permitted the United States to place monitoring networks in the country; opposed Nasser's Pan-Arab cause—even during the 1967 Arab-Israeli War; gave de facto recognition to Israel and appeared to side with it against the Palestinians; sold oil to South Africa at a time when much of the Third World was calling for a boycott of the Apartheid regime; and, to top it all, in the mid-1970s, when the drain of the Vietnam War led America to the Nixon doctrine, he eagerly volunteered to be America's policeman in the Persian Gulf and even beyond, in the Indian Ocean. For the shah, this was the perfect opportunity to project power into the region. For Iranian nationalists, this reconfirmed their deep-seated conviction that he was a Western stooge.

On the eve of the Islamic Revolution, Abul-Hussein Bani-Sadr—soon to be elected the first president of the Islamic Republic—in his émigré paper accused the regime of "fifty acts of treason in fifty years of tyranny." [28] The list began with the 1953 coup and the undoing of oil nationalization. It then cited the gross violation of the 1906 constitution, the opening up of the market to Western businesses, the dissemination of "cultural imperialism," and the alliance with the United States against the Third World—especially over the Arab-Israeli conflict. Bani-Sadr would have fully concurred with Henry Kissinger's assessment that the shah "was for the US the rarest of leaders, an unconditional ally." [29] No doubt, there were occasional strains between Tehran and Washington that royalists later used to claim the shah was truly independent. But then, there had been occasional differences between Vidkun Quisling and his patron without anyone being able to claim the former had been truly independent. Marvin Zonis, in his biography of the shah entitled *Majestic Failure,* writes:

> US policy was Shah-centric because over the years he had been such a faithful ally. He consistently followed policies consonant with American interests. He remained staunchly anti-Soviet. His diplomatic agreements and weapon deals with the USSR never threatened US policy-makers. In addition, the Shah was especially strident in his opposition to pro-Soviet Marxist "liberation" movements. The Shah sent Iranian troops to Oman to aid the sultan in quelling the Dhofar rebellion supported by the Soviets and aided by the Marxist-dominated People's Democratic Republic of Yemen. No nonaligned movements decrying

"imperialism" and colonialism for the Shah. In short, the Shah willingly served as a regional superpower and, under the Nixon doctrine, striving to ensure regional stability and the perpetuation of pro-Western regimes.[30]

The eventual collapse not only destroyed the monarchy but also inflicted collateral damage on the armed forces. Since the Pahlavi dynasty had created the modern armed forces, expanded and pampered them, made them its central pillar, and owed its 1953 survival partly to them, the general public, as well as the opposition, saw the two as inseparable. No shah, no army. After all, the Pahlavi dynasty had always been a military monarchy. In the final days of the revolution, Khomeini, cognizant of Mossadeq's fatal mistake, exhorted followers not to stay at home and instead to pour into the streets to physically prevent troops from moving into the city. Tens of thousands did so—staying out even through the night. The eventual debacle came when these demonstrators broke into armories, prompting the shah's last premier to order the chief of staff to use heavy artillery. The chief of staff refused, suspecting the prime minister had "lost touch with reality."[31] Immediately after the revolution, Khomeini did not hesitate in decapitating the high command, purging the officer corps, and then creating the Revolutionary Guards to overshadow the regular armed forces. The 1953 coup had delegitimized not only the monarchy but also the regular military. The United States, which had invested so much both in the monarchy and the army ever since 1941, ended up as a major loser. No regular army; no U.S. influence.

The coup's most enduring influence is on collective memory. It not only further intensified the paranoid attitudes already prevalent in the political culture but also brought the United States into the picture. Politically conscious citizens—irrespective of ideology—were now more than ever before convinced that real power lay in "hidden hands" and that the figures visible on the national stage were mere "marionettes" controlled by "foreign strings." Soon after the coup, the British ambassador reported back to the Foreign Office that "Iranians are still hypnotized by the neurosis that foreign, and particularly British, influence is present in every village and valley in Iran." [32] The political lexicon became replete—and remains to this day—with terms such as *tuteh* (plot-conspiracy), *jasouz* (spy), *khiyanat* (treason), *dast-e panha* (hidden hand), *poshteh-e pardeh* (behind the curtain), *poshteh-e sahneh* (behind the scenes), *avamel kharejeh* (foreign agents), *'ummal-e kharejeh* (foreign hands), *nafouz-e beganeh* (alien influence), *nokar-e kharejeh* (foreign servant), *naqsheh* (design-scheme), *'arousak* (puppet), *vabasteh* (dependent), *setun-e panjum* (fifth column), and *khatar-e kharjeh* (foreign danger). The old word *este'mar* (colonialism-imperialism) now competed with such new terms as Western *estekbar* (arrogance) and Western *tahajum-e farhange-ye gharb* (cultural aggression). [33]

Although the paranoid style cut across political lines, whom viewers identified as nefarious depended very much on where they themselves stood in the political spectrum. For the traditional left, namely the Tudeh, the threat came from imperialism—Britain in the past, and now America in alliance with Britain. The coup confirmed the accepted notion that America had replaced Britain as the main imperial power in the world. For many in the political center—both secular and religious—the threat came from all the major powers, including the Soviet Union. [34] Immediately after the revolution, remnants of the Third Force produced a remarkable book replete with elaborate charts "proving" that the Tudeh and some of the senior clergy were "linked" to the Soviet Union; the Freemasons, the Fedayan-e Islam, and much of the Shi'i hierarchy to Britain; and the Army, the "Islamic liberals," and most of the old regime to America. It insisted that the Islamic Revolution had been a joint Anglo-American-Russian *prozheh* (project)—just like the 1953 coup.[35]

The paranoid style was by no means confined to radicals. Royalists had their own version. The shah, always suspicious of British and American intentions, distrusted even those who had worked closely with the CIA and MI6 to restore him to the throne. By the late 1950s, many of the key coup figures had been removed from the national scene. General Zahedi had been sent off to his luxury mansion in Switzerland; the Rashidians to their Knightsbridge residence; and Colonel Farzandegan to ITT in America. General Bakhtiyar, who had founded SAVAK, had been exiled and then assassinated by his own organization. Others, such as Colonels Akhavi, Gilanshah, and Qarani, had become nonpersons. The 1953 coup left no recognizable heroes; instead it was glorified as the "Shah-People Revolt."

The shah's final testament, his *Answer to History*, reads like the ramblings of a paranoid.[36] He claims the British invaded the country in 1941 with the primary aim of getting rid of his father, who had roused their wrath by canceling the oil concession.[37] The British had "a hand" in the creation and growth of the Tudeh Party. They had plotted with the Tudeh and the Fedayan-e Islam to assassinate him in 1949, but had been forestalled then as well as at other times by divine intervention. They had also secretly helped Mossadeq to "clip his [royal] wings" and impede his ambitious modernization programs. "We always suspected," he writes, "that [Mossadeq] was a British agent, a suspicion his future posturing as an anti-British nationalist did not diminish." The British, together with the oil companies and "reactionary clerics," had engineered the Islamic Revolution in retaliation for his championing of OPEC and the Palestinian cause. The Palestinians, as well as the Israelis, would have been surprised to hear that. Of course, the Russians since Catherine the Great had been working incessantly to take over Iran in order to acquire warm seaports on the Persian Gulf and Indian Ocean. On his deathbed, the shah claimed that the CIA, together with MI6, had engineered the 1979 revolution on the grounds that the whole enterprise would have been too complex for the KGB. "Who," he asked rhetorically, "paid for the demonstrations dotted with black and blond manes, rarely found in Iran?" In other places, his *Answer to History* sounded more restrained:

> Throughout the seventies opposition mounted and in the end created a strange confluence of interests—the international oil consortium, the British and American governments, the international media, reactionary religious circles in my own country, and the relentless drive of the Communists who had managed to infiltrate some of Iran's institutions. I do not believe that this convergence of forces represented an organized plot against me in which each part meshed with the others. But clearly all the forces involved had their own reasons for pushing me offstage. . . . I believe they somehow had foreknowledge of the events that were to take place later that year. I also believe that members of the Carter Administration—especially the McGovernites in the second echelon of the State department—were anxious to see me leave in favor of this new so-called "Islamic Republic."

William Sullivan, the American ambassador during the revolution, was "astounded" by the shah's explanation for the protests:

> Suddenly it all tumbled out. For nearly ten minutes, the shah related incident after incident that had taken place

throughout the country, each one constituting an assault
on the government's authority and on the forces of law
and order. He traced them not only to students but also
to industrial workers, to members of the various factions,
and to the Shi'a ulama itself, and to the merchants of the
bazaar. He said the pattern was widespread and that it was
like an outbreak of [a] sudden rash in the country. He said
it gave evidence of sophisticated planning and was not the
work of spontaneous oppositionists. He then turned to me
and in an almost supplicant tone said he had thought this
over at great length and had concluded that the actions
he had just outlined represented the work of foreign intrigue. What bothered him, he said, was that the intrigue
went beyond the capabilities of the Soviet KGB and must
therefore also involve the British and the American CIA.
He said he could understand the British intrigue to some
extent because there were those in the United Kingdom
who had never forgiven him for nationalizing the oil
industry. . . . What bothered him most, he continued, was
the role of the CIA. Why was the CIA suddenly turning
against him? What had he done to deserve this sort of action from the United States? . . . Had we and the Soviets
reached some grand design in which we had decided to
divide up Iran between ourselves as part of an overall division of power throughout the entire world?[38]

The Islamic Republic can compete with the shah in developing elaborate conspiracy theories. For Khomeini, foreign conspiracies lurked here, there, and everywhere. He
blamed them for age-old problems: the decline of Islamic
civilization; the conservative "distortions" of Islam; and the
conflicts between Sunnis and Shi'is as well as between rival
states within the Muslim world. He claimed colonial powers had for years dispatched Orientalists into the Muslim

world to misinterpret Islam and the Koran. They had also conspired to undermine Islam with religious quietism, with new sects such as the Baha'is and Freemasons, and with secular ideologies—especially communism, socialism, liberalism, monarchism, and nationalism. "Those who drafted the 1906 constitution," he declared, "were receiving instructions directly from their British masters." [39] Of course, he blamed them for a host of contemporary problems:

> The Big Powers, and among them especially the United States, have since long ago been busy scheming. And preceding them was Britain. For a long time now they have been putting together the sporadic bits of information and intelligence which they have gathered about the various countries of the world and especially those upon which they have preyed. What we have in terms of natural resources, they know better than we do. Even before the advent of motorcars they would dispatch their experts here on horseback or camel to make a survey of our resources, including our oil as well as our valuable stones. I recall I mentioned in an earlier speech my meeting with a member of the Qom Theological School during my trip to Hamadan many years ago. He was the son of a well-reputed personality in the city and he brought me the map which was strewn with small dots. I asked him what the dots represented and he told me the map had been drawn by agents of a foreign power and the dots represented the presence of mineral resources. It was a fully detailed map showing even the smallest villages. Therefore, as you can see, even at a time when automobiles were not in vogue, they had surveyed our country, including our deserts, and had at the same time studied the ethnic life the people, as well as their social life, their habits, their

religion, their tastes, their inclinations, and their relations
with the clergy.[40]

Such suspicions came in handy. In November 1979, when
the newborn regime was striving to consolidate itself, Khomeini's entourage exhorted college students to break into the
American embassy compound on the pretext that the CIA
was plotting a repeat performance of 1953 from the very
same grounds. Much of the public was convinced that the
CIA was capable and willing to do so. Thus began the famous 444-day American hostage crisis. Americans who knew
little of the events of 1953 were mystified; Iranians were not.
The specter of coup had come to haunt U.S.-Iranian relations. Similarly, on March 5, 1981, when more than 100,000
gathered at Tehran University to commemorate Mossadeq's
death and call for the establishment of a democratic rather
than an Islamic republic, Hojjat al-Islam Ali Khamenie—
Khomeini's future successor—declared ominously: "We are
not liberals, like Allende, willing to be snuffed out by the
CIA."[41] When, a few months later, the Mujahedin—an organization formed of anticlerical radical Muslims—tried to
overthrow the government, the regime proceeded to execute
more than one thousand protestors, including teenage girls.
They were charged with "warring against God" on behalf of
"satanic foreign powers."

The 1953 crisis also came in handy during the long-drawn-
out standoff between the United States and Iran over the
nuclear program—with the former suspecting the program
harbored military intentions and the latter insisting it was designed purely for peaceful civilian purposes. Throughout the
standoff, the regime implicitly and explicitly referred back
to 1951–53. It drew parallels between a country's sovereign
right to enrich uranium and to nationalize its own natural

resources. It also drew parallels between earlier Western claims that Iranians lacked the technical knowledge to run the oil industry and now the moral credibility to be entrusted with nuclear know-how. It equated the U.S.-led sanctions with the economic embargo organized by the British. It also equated the two sets of drawn-out negotiations, arguing that in both cases the Western powers in public pretended to be willing to accept a "fair compromise" but in reality and in private persistently insisted on tough demands unacceptable to Iran. In 1951–53, the real intention had been the over-throw of Mossadeq. The intention now, claimed the regime, was the overthrow of the Islamic Republic.

The paranoid style reached a new peak in 2009. When more than two million took to the streets to protest the rig-ging of the presidential elections, the regime's automatic re-action was to hold show trials and accuse opposition leaders of plotting a "velvet revolution" in the style of the "colored" ones that had recently swept through Eastern Europe. They were accused of working in cahoots not only with the CIA and MI6 but also with an elaborate international web, in-cluding the BBC, the Voice of America, Columbia Univer-sity, Harvard University, the Hoover Institution, the Ford Foundation, PEN, Freedom House, Chatham House, the Council on Foreign Relations, and, of course, the omnipres-ent and ominous Soros Foundation. They were also accused of being led astray from Islam by the pernicious ideas of Max Weber, Talcott Parsons, Richard Rorty, and, most danger-ous of all, Jürgen Habermas. Regimes that tremble before Weber and Habermas have much to fear. This would have appealed to Mossadeq's sense of humor. He would have been further amused by the knowledge that the United States now had to deal with the likes of Khomenie and Khamenei.

NOTES

Introduction

1. William Roger Louis, "Britain and the Overthrow of the Mosaddeq Government," in *Mohammad Mosaddeq and the 1953 Coup in Iran*, ed. Mark Gasiorowski and Malcolm Byrne (Syracuse, NY: Syracuse University Press, 2004), 135, 148.

2. Mark Gasiorowski, "The Truth About the 1953 Coup," *Le Monde Diplomatique*, October 2000. See also Mark Gasiorowski, "The 1953 Coup d'État Against Mosaddeq," in *Mohammad Mosaddeq and the 1953 Coup in Iran*, 229; "The 1953 Coup d'État in Iran," *International Journal of Middle East Studies* 19, no. 3 (1987), 261–86; and "The CIA Looks Back at the 1953 Coup in Iran," *Middle East Report* 216 (Fall 2000), 4–5.

3. U.S. Government, *Foreign Relations of the United States, 1952–54*, vol. 10 (Iran) (Washington, DC: U.S. Government Printing House, 1989); *Foreign Relations of the United States, 1951*, vol. 5 (Iran) (Washington, DC: U.S. Government Printing House, 1982). See also Warren Kimball, "Classified!" *Perspectives* (February 1997), 9–10, 22–24; Stephen Weissman, "Why Is US Withholding Old Documents on Covert Ops in Congo, Iran?" *Christian Science Monitor*, March 27, 2011.

4. Stephen Weissman, "Censoring American Diplomatic History," *Perspectives* (September 2011), 48–49.

5. Ibid. See also Tim Weiner, "CIA Is Slow to Tell Early Cold War Secrets," *New York Times*, April 8, 1996; "CIA Destroyed Files on 1953 Iran Coup," *New York Times*, May 29, 1997; and "CIA Breaking Promises, Puts Off Release of Cold War Files," *New York Times*, July 15, 1998.

6. Malcolm Byrne, "The Secret CIA History of the Iran Coup," http://www.gwu.edu/-nsarchiv/NSAEBB/NSAEBB28/index.html. See also "CIA Sued over Broken Promises on Declassification," http://www.gwu.edu/nsarchiv/news/19990513/19990513.html.

7. Edward Wong, "Web Site Lists Iran Coup Names," *New York Times*, June 24, 2000, http://www.nytimes.com/library/world/mideast/062400iran-report.html; Donald Wilber, "Overthrow of Premier Mossadeq of Iran,

November 1952–August 1953" (Washington, DC: CIA Historical Division, 1954), http://cryptome.org/cia-iran-all.htm. The document—with some names redacted—was later published as a book: Donald Wilber, *Regime Change in Iran: Overthrow of Premier Mossadeq of Iran, November 1952–August 1953* (London: Russell Press, 2006).

8. James Risen, "How a Plot Convulsed Iran in '53 (and in '79)," *New York Times*, April 16, 2000.

9. *The Guardian*, April 17, 2000.

10. Byrne, "Secret CIA History of the Iran Coup, 1953."

11. Habib Ladjevardi, *Reference Guide to the Iranian Oral History Collection* (Cambridge: Harvard University Press, 1993). See also http://ted.lib.harvard.edu/ted/deliver/home?_collections=iohp.

12. Hamid Ahmadi, *An Introduction to the Iranian Left Oral History Project* (Amsterdam: International Institute of Social History, 1996). See also http://www.iisg.nl/images-sound/video/iran.php.

1. Oil Nationalization

1. Adam Hochschild, *King Leopold's Ghost: A Story of Greed, Terror, and Heroism in Colonial Africa* (New York: Houghton Mifflin, 1999), 71.

2. L.P. Elwell-Sutton, *Persian Oil: A Study in Power Politics* (London: Lawrence & Wishart, 1955), 24.

3. David Mitchell, "History of AIOC (1935)," *FO 371*/Persia 1951/34-91525.

4. A. Rothnie, "Degree of Interference of HMG in Administration of AIOC," *FO 371*/Persia 1951/34-91621.

5. Persian Oil Working Party, "Approach to a New Persian Government (September 1951)," *FO 248*/Persia 1951/34-1529.

6. Elwell-Sutton, *Persian Oil*, 24.

7. Mitchell, "History of AIOC (1935)."

8. Cited by Mostafa Fateh, *Panjah Sal-e Naft* (Fifty Years of Oil) (Tehran: 1979), 315.

9. Ministry of Fuel, "Effect on the Sterling Area," *BP*/066896.

10. Foreign Office, "Memorandum on AIOC Holdings," *FO 248*/Persia 1951/1526.

11. A. Badakhshan & F. Najmabadi, "Oil Industry," *Encyclopedia Iranica*.

12. Foreign Office, July 30, 1951, *FO 248*/Persia 1951/1258.

13. Foreign Office, "Note on the Effect of UK Tax Policy on Persian Oil Royalties (April 19, 1949)," *FO 371*/Persia 1951/34-1531.

14. Daniel Yergin, *The Prize: The Epic Quest for Oil, Money, and Power* (New York: Simon & Schuster, 1991), 277.

15. Ibid., 448.

16. Fateh, *Fifty Years of Oil*, 414.

17. AIOC, "Note on Payments (July 17, 1951)," *BP*/00003565.

18. AIOC, "Brief Review of Events Leading up to the Present (May 1951)," *BP*/00003565.

19. Foreign Office, Memorandum (August 24, 1949), *FO 371*/Persia 1949/34-75491.

20. Foreign Office, "Sale of Oil to the Admiralty," *FO 371*/Persia 1951/34-91620.

21. Abul-Fazel Lusani, *Tala-ye Siyah ya Bala-ye Iran* (Black Gold or Iran's Calamity) (Tehran: 1950).

22. British Embassy, "Letter from AIOC Employees," *FO 371*/Persia 1949/34-75498.

23. "Tape Transcript of Interview with Derbyshire on the 1953 Coup." Interview for the television program *End of Empire* (Granada Channel 4 [UK], 1985).

24. Elwell-Sutton, *Persian Oil*, 101–03.

25. A.B., *Naft* (Oil) (Tehran: 1947), 1–70.

26. British Consul in Bushire, "Bolshevik Activity in the South," *FO 371*/Persia 1929/34-13783.

27. British Minister in Tehran, "The Strike in Abadan," *FO 371*/Persia 1929/34-13783.

28. British Consul in Khorramshahr, "Report on Tudeh Activities in the Oil Industry," *FO 371*/Persia 1946/34-52714.

29. British Military Attaché, July 23, 1946/*Persia 1946*/34-52711; British Labour Attaché, "Memorandum on Tudeh Activities Against AIOC," *FO 371*/Persia 1946/34-52713; Khorramshahr Consul, July 14, 1946, *FO 371*/Persia 1946/34-52713; Khorramshahr Consul, "June Report," *FO 371*/Persia 1946/34-52742.

30. Ahwaz Consul, July 16, 1946, *FO 248*/Persia 1946.

31. Cabinet Notes, June 26, 1946, *FO 371*/Persia 1946/34-52717.

32. J.H. Jones, "My Visit to the Persian Oilfields," *Journal of the Royal Central Asian Society* 34, Part 1 (January 1947), 65.

33. Khorramshahr Consul, September 25, 1946, *FO 371*/Persia 1946/34-52724.

34. Philip Noel-Baker, July 31, 1946/*FO 371*/Persia 1946/34-52719.

35. "Letter to the Foreign Office," July 18, 1946/Persia 1946/34-52720.

36. Mr. Glennie, "Anglo-Iranian Oil Company Position in Iran," *BP*/127728.

37. Labour Attaché, "Labour Conditions in AIOC," *FO 371*/Persia 1946/34-61984.

38. U.S. Congress, Committee on Foreign Relations, *The Strategy and Tactics of World Communism* (Washington, DC: 1949), 8.

39. Ahwaz Consul, "British Employees Grievances," *FO 371*/Persia 1944/34-40158.

40. Ministry of Fuel and Power, "Notes on 17 March 1944," *FO 371*/Persia 1944/34-40158.

230 NOTES TO PAGES 23–31

41. AIOC, *AIOC and Iran: A Description of the Company's Contribution to Iran's Revenue and National Economy; and of Its Welfare Activities for Employees in Iran* (London: AIOC Publication, 1951), 1–20.

42. Elwell-Sutton, *Persian Oil*, 86–96.

43. Foreign Office, "Notes About AIOC Activities in South Persia (February 21, 1951)," *FO 371*/Persia 1951/34-91449.

44. George Curzon, *Persia and the Persian Question* (London: Longmans, 1892), vol. 2, 631.

45. Reader Bullard, *Letters from Tehran* (London: I.B. Tauris, 1991), 154, 270.

46. British Minister, "Annual Report for Persia (1922)," *FO 371*/Persia 1923/34-10848.

47. Harold Nicolson, *Curzon: The Last Phase* (London: Constable, 1934), 3, 129.

48. Antony Wynn, *Persia in the Great Game* (London: Murray, 2003), 316.

49. James Balfour, *Recent Happenings in Persia* (London: Blackwood, 1922), 133.

50. Gen. William R. Dickson, *Documents on British Foreign Policy* (London: Government Printing House, 1948), vol. 13, 485.

51. British Minister, "Annual Report for Persia (1922)," *FO 371*/Persia 1923/34-10848.

52. Mohammad Majd, *The Great Famine and Genocide in Persia, 1917–1919* (Lanham, MD: University Press of America, 1984).

53. British Minister, "Annual Report for Persia (1922)," *FO 371*/Persia 1923/34-10848.

54. Fateh, *Fifty Years of Oil*, 304–24.

55. James Bamberg, *The History of British Petroleum* (Cambridge: Cambridge University Press, 1994), vol. 2, 37.

56. British Embassy, "Taqizadeh's Speech," *FO 371*/Persia 1949/34-75495.

57. Foreign Office, "Correspondence Relating to Arthur Moore," *FO 371*/Persia 1951/34-91606.

58. Khan-Malek Sassani, *Dast-e Panhan-e Siyasat-e Ingles dar Iran* (The Hidden English Hand in Iran) (Tehran: 1952); and Mahmud Mahmud, *Tarekh-e Ravabet-e Siyasat-e Ingles dar Qaran-e Nouzdahum-e Meladi* (History of Anglo-Iranian Political Relations in the Nineteenth Century) (Tehran: 1949–54), vols. 1–8.

59. Ahmad Ashraf, *Toure-ye Tuteh dar Iran* (Conspiracy Theory in Iran) (Tehran: 1993), 69–120.

60. British Embassy, "Annual Political Report for 1941," *India Office*/L/P&S/12-3472A.

61. British Ambassador, March 19, 1946, *FO 371*/Persia 1946/34-52670.

62. General Patrick Hurley, "Memorandum to the President, State Department," *Foreign Relations of the United States: 1943* (Washington, DC: U.S. Government Printing Office, 1964), vol. 4, 364–66.

63. Homa Katouzian, ed., *Musaddiq's Memoirs* (London: Jebhe Publications, 1988), 114.

64. Habib Ladjevardi, "Interview with Ghulam-Hussein Mossadeq," *The Iranian Oral History Project* (Cambridge: Harvard University Press, 1993).

65. Katouzian, *Musaddiq's Memoirs*, 163.

66. British Legation, "Leading Personalities in Persia (1927)," *FO 371/ Persia* 1927/23-12300.

67. Katouzian, *Musaddiq's Memoirs*, 254.

68. British Legation, "Leading Personalities in Persia (1927)," *FO 371/ Persia* 1927/34-12300.

69. British Ambassador, January 20–22, 1944, *FO 371/Persia* 1944/34-4086.

70. Veronica Horwath, "Dissimulating Friendship: Italian-Iranian Relations in the 1930s" (unpublished paper, City University of New York Graduate Center, Spring 2009), 30–31.

71. Muhammad Mossadeq, May 23, 1950, *Muzakerat-e Majles Showra-ye Melli* (Parliamentary Debates) (Tehran: Government Printing House, 1950), sixteenth Majles.

72. Vernon Walters, *Silent Missions* (New York: Doubleday, 1978), 253.

73. Muhammad Mossadeq, "New Proposals for Electoral Reform," *Ayandeh* 3, no. 2 (1944), 61–63.

74. Hussein Key-Ostovan, *Siyasat-e Muvazeneh-e Manfi dar Majles-e Chahardahum* (The Policy of Negative Equilibrium in the Fourteenth Majles), 2 vols. (Tehran: 1949).

75. Muhammad Mossadeq, October 19, 1944, *Parliamentary Debates.*

76. Daniel Yergin, *Shattered Peace: The Origins of the Cold War and the National Security State* (Boston: Houghton Mifflin, 1977), 180.

77. Foreign Office, "Comment in London (October 3, 1944)," *FO 371/ Persia* 1944/34-40241; U.S. Embassy, May 16, 1944, *Foreign Relations of the United States: 1944*, vol. 4, 449.

78. Ibid.

79. Foreign Office, "Comment in London (January 8, 1945)," *FO 371/ Persia* 1945/34-45443.

80. U.S. Embassy to the State Department, December 23, 1943, *Foreign Relations of the United States: 1943*, vol. 4, 627.

81. U.S. Embassy to the State Department, April 3, 1944, *Foreign Relations of the United States: 1944*, vol. 4, 446–47.

82. U.S. Embassy to the State Department, July 12, 1944, *Foreign Relations of the United States: 1944*, vol. 4, 341.

83. Clarmont Skrine, *World War in Iran* (London: Constable, 1962), 227.

84. Foreign Office, April 20, 1949, *FO 371/Persia* 1949/34-75475.

85. U.S. Embassy, October 1944, *Foreign Relations of the United States: 1944*, vol. 5, 45.

86. George Kennan to the Secretary of State, November 7, 1944, *Foreign Relations of the United States: 1944*, vol. 4, 470.

87. British Embassy in Moscow, March 9, 1946, *FO 371*/Persia 1946/34-52663.

88. British Embassy, "Reasons for Opposing Russian Concession," *FO 371*/Persia 1945/34-45443; Foreign Office, April 9, 1946, *FO 371*/Persia 1946/34-52670.

89. U.S. Embassy, September 25, 1945, *Foreign Relations of the United States: 1945*, 417.

90. British Ambassador, "Memorandum on Withdrawal of British Troops (25 May 1945)," in *State Department Unpublished Declassified Files*, July 30, 1946, NND 760050.

91. British Ambassador, September 30, 1947, *FO 371*/Persia 1947/34-91972.

92. Foreign Office, "Memorandum on Persian Oil (September 1946)," *FO 371*/Persia 1946/34-52729.

93. British Ambassador, December 27, 1944/*FO 371*/Persia 1944/34-40243.

94. U.S. Embassy, March 22, 1946, *Foreign Relations of the United States: 1946*, vol. 7, 369–73.

95. U.S. Ambassador, January 11, 1947, *Foreign Relations of the United States: 1947*, vol. 5, 891–93.

96. U.S. Ambassador, July 26, 1947, *Foreign Relations of the United States: 1947*, vol. 5, 923.

97. British Ambassador, "Annual Report for Persia (1947)," *India Office*/L/P&S/12-3472B.

98. Foreign Office, "Annual for Persia (December 31, 1952)," *FO 416*/Persia 1954/106.

99. Foreign Office, "Notes on the Soviet-Persian Oil Agreement of 1946," *FO 371*/Persia 194734-91530.

100. British Ambassador, October 25, 1945, *FO 371*/Persia 1944/34-40241.

101. Foreign Office, "The Anglo-Iranian Oil Company," *FO 371*/Persia 1950/34-1531.

102. Max Thornburg, "General Summary of My Activities Concerning Persia Oil," *FO 248*/Persia 1951/1530.

103. Secretary of State, "Notes (March 24, 1949)," *FO 371*/Persia 1949/34-75495.

104. "The Crisis in Iran," *The Economist*, March 10, 1951.

105. Sam Falle, *My Lucky Life* (London: The Book Guild, 1996), 72.

106. Ladjevardi, "Interview with Sir George Middleton," *Iranian Oral History Project*.

107. Ibid.

108. British Embassy, "Leading Personalities in Persia (1952)," *FO 416*/Persia 1952/105.

109. British Embassy, October 29, 1951, *FO 371*/Persia 1951/34-61608.

110. British Embassy, November 23, 1945, *FO 371*/Persia 1945/File 31.

111. British Embassy, "Handwritten Notes on Iran Party (1950)," *FO 371*/Persia 1950/34-82310.

112. Falle, *My Lucky Life*, 75.

113. Razavian Archive, "18 Unpublished Photos," www.cloob.com/club/article/show/clubname/mosadegh.

114. Iraj Afshar, ed., *Taqrerat-e Mossadeq dar Zendan* (Mossadeq's Comments in Prison) (Tehran: 1980), 116–17.

115. Ahmad Shayegan, ed., *Sayyed Ali Shayegan* (Tehran: 2004), vol. 2, 350–52.

116. They were: Arsalan Khalatbari, a lawyer, member of the Iran Party, and grandson of the important magnate who had supported the constitutional revolution; Yusef Moshar (Moshar Azam), a patrician politician who had been forcefully retired by Reza Shah; Sayyed Muhammad-Reza Jalali-Naini, a lawyer and editor of yet another gadfly paper *Keshvar* (Country); Dr. Shams al-Din Jazayeri, a lawyer and the editor of *Montaq* (Logic); Ayatollah Sayyed Jafar Ghoruyi, a Tehran cleric who tended to keep himself in the background; and Dr. Muhammad Kaviyani, a lawyer and family friend of Shayegan (when the latter had served as Qavam's minister of education, Kaviyani had acted as his deputy minister).

117. Ahmad Maleki, "How the National Front Was Created," *Khandaniha* February 3–March 5, 1955.

118. National Front, "Platform and Statutes," *Shahed*, October 12–24, 1949; and July 1, 1950.

119. For a study of the *lutis*, see Philippe Rochard, "The Identities of the Iranian *Zurkhanah*," *Iranian Studies* 35, no. 4 (Fall 2002), 313–40.

120. British Embassy, "Leading Personalities in Persia (1952)," *FO 371/* Persia 1952/105.

121. "Biography of Ayatollah Kashani," *Khandaniha* 8, no. 78 (June 1, 1948).

122. Muhammad Dahnavi, *Mujma'ahyi az Maktabahat, Sokhanraniha va Paymanha-ye Ayatollah Kashani* (Ayatollah Kashani's Collected Writings, Speeches, and Messages) (Tehran: 1982), vols. 1–3.

123. British Embassy, "Leading Personalities in Persia (1952)," *FO 416/* Persia 1952/105.

124. British Embassy, "An Islamic Call," *FO 371/*Persia 1952/34-D8719.

125. British Embassy, "Leading Personalities in Persia (1952)," *FO 371/* Persia 1952/105.

126. Fedayan-e Islam, *'Elamiyeh* (Proclamation) (Tehran, 1950), 1–25.

127. British Embassy, September 20, 1949, *FO 371/*Persia 1949/33-75500.

128. Foreign Office, March 17, 1950, *FO 371/*Persia 1950/34-82311.

129. Abbas Masoudi, "The Oil Question," *Ettela'at*, May 28, 1949.

130. British Labour Attaché, "Six Monthly Review," *FO 371/*Persia 1952/34-98732; British Embassy, December 14, 1951, *FO 371/*Persia 1951/34-98595.

131. British Ambassador, February 25, 1952, *FO 248/*Persia 1952/34-1531.

132. British Ambassador, "The Mansur Government," *FO 371/*Persia 1950/34-82312.

133. Foreign Office, "Notes," *FO 371*/Persia 1950/34-82377; and Foreign Secretary, "Letter to British Ambassador in Tehran," December 15, 1950, *FO 248*/Persia 1950/34-1512.

134. British Ambassador, "Conversations with the Prime Minister," *FO 248*/Persia 1950/34-1512.

135. Walters, *Silent Missions*, 254.

136. British Military Attaché, July 1–8, 1946, *India Office*/L/P&S/12-3505.

137. Foreign Office, January 19, 1951, *FO 371*/Persia 1951/34-91522.

138. Foreign Office, February 6, 1951, *FO 371*/Persia 1951/34-91522.

139. Foreign Office, "Minutes of Meeting (February 28, 1950)," *FO 248*/Persia 1950/34-1512.

140. Katouzian, "Editor's Note," *Musaddiq's Memoirs*, 30–31.

141. British Embassy, April 15, 1951, *FO 371*/Persia 1951/34-91454.

142. Thornburg, "General Summary of My Activities Concerning Persian Oil."

143. British Embassy, March 27, 1951, *FO 371*/Persia 1951/34-91524.

144. Foreign Office, "Minutes of the Meeting (March 16, 1951)," *FO 371*/Persia 1951/34-01522.

145. Foreign Office, "Notes on Ala," *FO 248*/1541.

146. British Ambassador, April 23, 1951, *FO 248*/Persia 1951/34-15126.

147. Khorramshahr Consul, July 19, 1946, *India Office*/L&S/12-3490A.

148. Foreign Office, "Notes by H. G. Gee," *FO 371*/Persia 1949/34-75500.

149. Khorramshahr Consul, "Report for October–December 1948," *FO 371*/Persia 1948/34-75501.

150. Khorramshahr Consul, May 5, 1948, *FO 371*/Persia 1948/34-68734.

151. Labour Attaché, "Six Monthly Report (November 18, 1949)," *FO 371*/Persia 1949/34-75470.

152. Labour Attaché, "Report on AIOC," *FO 371*/Persia 1950/34-82378.

153. Labour Attaché, December 31, 1948, *FO 371*/Persia 1949/34-75469.

154. Labour Attaché, "Report for April–June 1951," *FO 371*/Persia 1951/34-91628.

155. British Embassy, March 11, 1950, *FO 248*/Persia 1950/1512.

156. British Embassy, March 1950, *FO 371*/Persia 1950/34-82378.

157. Labour Attaché, "Report on AIOC," *FO 371*/Persia 1950/34-82378.

158. Foreign Office, "AIOC Housing," *FO 371*/Persia 1950/34-82379.

159. British Embassy, "Tudeh Activities in the Last Year," *FO 248*/Persia 1950/1493.

160. Minister of Fuel and Power, November 15, 1950, *FO 371*/Persia 1950/34-91628.

161. AIOC to Chairman, "Memo (January 16, 1950)," *BP*/101108.

162. A.E.C. Drake, "Letter 20 May 1951," *BP*/066896.

163. Foreign Office, March 28, 1951, *FO 371*/Persia 1951/34-91524.

164. Foreign Office, April 13, 1951, *FO 371*/Persia 1951/34-91456.

165. "Abadan on Fire and in Blood," *Ettela'at-e Haftegi* (Weekly News), April 19, 1951.

166. Khuzestan Consul General, "Report on Khuzestan," *FO 248*/Persia 1951/1524.

167. A.E.C. Drake, April 17, 1951, *BP*/068908.

168. *Ettela'at-e Haftegi*, April 12, 1951.

169. AIOC, "Tudeh Proclamation," *BP*/068908.

170. Khuzestan Consul General, "Washington Telegram," *FO 248*/Persia 1951/1524.

171. Gad Selia, "AIOC's Primitive Labour," *Jerusalem Post*, July 6, 1951. Discussed in Foreign Office, *FO 371*/Persia 1951/34-91628.

172. Khuzestan Consul General, "Reports for February–June 1951," *FO 248*/Persia 1951/1524.

173. British Embassy, May 7, 1951, *FO 371*/Persia 1951/34-91524.

174. Ministry of Fuel and Power, "Effect on Sterling (March 20, 1951)," *BP*/066896.

175. Hussein Ala, April 12, 1951, *Parliamentary Debates,* sixteenth Majles.

176. The Shah, "Message to the Nation," *Tehran Mosavar*, May 10, 1951.

177. British Ambassador (in Washington), May 9, 1951, *FO 371*/Persia 1951/34-91493.

178. Reza Shafaq, April 13, 1951, *Parliamentary Debates*, First Senate.

179. Katouzian, *Musaddiq's Memoirs*; and Farhad Diba, *Mohammad Mossadegh: A Political Biography* (London: Croom Helm, 1986).

180. Sepehr Zabih, *The Mossadegh Era* (Chicago: Lake View Press, 1982), 26.

181. Fakhreddin Azimi, *Iran: The Crisis of Democracy 1941–53* (New York: St. Martin's Press, 1989), 249–50.

182. Hedayat Matin-Daftari, ed., *Vezeh-e Mossadeq* (Special Issue on Mossadeq), *Azadi* 2, nos. 26–27 (Summer–Autumn 2001), 81–93.

183. Fateh, *Fifty Years of Oil*, 409.

184. Mustafa Fateh, "Letters to Mr. Gass," *BP*/00009249.

185. Jamal Emami, April 27, 1951, *Parliamentary Debates*, sixteenth Majles.

186. Falle, *My Lucky Life*, 75.

187. British Embassy, "Letter on Two Party System in Iran (August 17, 1957)," *FO 371*/Persia 1957/34-127074.

188. British Embassy, "Minutes of Meetings with Sayyed Ziya," *FO 248*/Persia 1951/34-1514.

189. Don North, "Interview with Dr. Claude Forkner (1986)," *Oral History Research Office* (Columbia University, 1986).

190. Foreign Office, "Conversations with Mr. Loombe of the Bank of England (May 1, 1951)," *FO 371*/Persia 1951/34-91530.

191. Ibid.

192. George McGhee, *Envoy to the Middle World* (New York: Harper & Row, 1983), 327.

193. U.S. Embassy, "Popularity and Prestige of Prime Minister Mossadeq (July 1, 1953)," in *FO 371*/Persia 1953/34-104568.

194. Muhammad Mossadeq, "May Day Address," *Ettela'at*, May 2, 1951.

195. They included Amir-Timour Kalali (Sardar Nasrat), a wealthy tribal chief, as minister of labor; Javad Busheri (Amir Homayun), a prominent businessman, as minister of roads; Hassan Ali Farmand (Zia al-Mulk), an aristocratic landlord, as minister of agriculture; Dr. Hassan Adham (Hakim al-Dawleh), brother of the court physician, as minister of health; Muhammad Ali Varasteh, a career civil servant who had served in a number of cabinets, as minister of finance; Ali Hayat, a judge with close ties to the palace, as minister of justice; and Gen. Ali Asghar Naqdi as minister of war.

196. British Embassy, May 2, 1951, *FO 371*/Persia 1951/34-91457.

197. British Ambassador, "Interview with the Prime Minister (May 7, 1951)," *FO 248*/Persia 1951/34-1526.

198. The others were: Morteza Qoli Bayat (Saham al-Sultan), another former premier, who was also related to Mossadeq both through marriage and through blood ties; Nasser Qoli Ardalan, a frequent provincial governor, who came from a Kurdish tribe that had caused much trouble for the British in both world wars; Abdul-Qassem Najm (al-Mamalek), a former finance minister, who during the war had served as ambassador to Japan; Muhammad Sorouri, another former minister, who had in the past worked closely with Bayat; and Reza Shafaq, a former ambassador to the UN and law professor reputed to be anti-British.

2. Anglo-Iranian Negotiations

1. Ministry of Fuel and Power, "Letter to the Foreign Office," *FO 371*/Persia 1945/34-45443.

2. Foreign Office, January 4, 1951, *FO 371*/Persia 1951/34-91521.

3. Foreign Office, "Record of Special Meeting (March 20, 1951)," *FO 371*/Persia 1951/34-91525.

4. Foreign Office, "Memorandum (April 11, 1951)," *FO 371*/Persia 1951/34-91470.

5. Secretary of State, "Telegram to the State Department (November 5, 1951)," *FO 371*/Persia 1951/34-91608.

6. Foreign Office, "First Meeting Held in the State Department (April 9, 1951)," *FO 371*/Persia 1951/34-91471.

7. Ibid.

8. Foreign Office, "Second Meeting Held in the State Department (April 10, 1951)," *FO 371*/Persia 1951/34-91471.

9. Foreign Office, May 9, 1952, *FO 371*/Persia 1952/34-98654.

10. Foreign Office, "Third Meeting Held in the State Department (April 17, 1951)," *FO 371*/Persia 1951/34-91471.

11. Foreign Office, "Notes (November 13, 1951)," *FO 371*/Persia 1951/34-91613.

12. British Ambassador, "Conduct of the Anglo-Persian Oil Question (January 4, 1951)," *FO 371*/Persia 1951/34-91521.

32737

13. Petroleum Division, "Memo of Conversations (June 5, 1951)," *BP/*Persia 1951/00043859.

14. Ministry of Fuel and Power, June 15, 1951, *FO 371*/Persia 1951/34-91544; Foreign Office, "Telegram (November 6, 1951)," *FO 248*/Persia 1951/34-1530.

15. British Ambassador, October 23, 1951, *FO 371*/Persia 1951/34-91606.

16. British Ambassador, "Letter to the Foreign Office (August 13, 1951)," *FO 371*/Persia 1951/34-91576.

17. Treasury Department, "Memo (October 19, 1951)," *FO 371*/Persia 1951/34-91606.

18. Foreign Office, "Notes (May 5, 1952)," *FO 371*/Persia 1952/34-9859.

19. Foreign Office, "Telegram of May 14, 1951," *FO 371*/Persia 1951/34-91533.

20. Working Party, June 23, 1951, *FO 371*/Persia 1951/34-91497.

21. Working Party, "Policy Paper (June 9, 1951)," *FO 371*/Persia 1951/34-91543.

22. Foreign Office, "Notes Made by Mr. Pyman (May 5, 1952), *FO 371*/Persia 1952/34-9859.

23. Working Party, July 6, 1951, *FO 371*/Persia 1951/34-91544.

24. Prime Minister, "Telegram to British Ambassador in Washington," *FO 371*/Persia 1951/34-91533.

25. Clement Attlee, "Letter to the British Ambassador in Washington," *FO 371*/Persia 1951/34-91541; and *FO 248*/Persia 1951/34-1527.

26. Treasury Department, March 31, 1951, *FO 371*/Persia 1951/34-9162; Foreign Office, "Telegram (October 12, 1951)," *FO 371*/Persia 1951/34-91602.

27. Foreign Office, "Memo of Conversations (February 14, 1951)," *FO 371*/Persia 1951/34-98608; and Foreign Office, "Record of Conversations with the State Department," *FO 371*/Persia 1951/34-91471.

28. Working Party Meeting, "Minutes of Meeting," *FO 371*/Persia 1951/34-91497.

29. British Ambassador, "Telegram (January 13, 1952)," *FO 371*/Persia 1952/34-98647.

30. British Embassy, May 1, 1951, *FO 248*/Persia 1951/34-1526.

31. British Ambassador, "Letter to the Foreign Office (May 19, 1951)," *FO 371*/Persia 1951/34-91535.

32. Foreign Office, "Second Meeting Held in the State Department," *FO 371*/Persia 1951/34-91471.

33. British Ambassador, "Letter to the Foreign Office (May 30, 1951)," *FO 371*/Persia 1951/34-91541.

34. Foreign Office, "Persian Oil Dispute: Views of Miss Lambton," *FO 371*/Persia 1951/34-91609; Foreign Office, January 2, 1952, *FO 371*/Persia 1952/34-98608.

35. British Ambassador, September 18, 1951, *FO 248*/Persia 1951/34-1514.

36. British Ambassador, "Report of Events in Persia (September 1951)," *FO 371*/Persia 1951/34-91451.

37. Ministry of Fuel and Power, September 5, 1951, *FO 371*/Persia 1951/34-91587.

38. Foreign Office, October 22, 1951, *FO 371*/Persia 1951/34-91606.

39. Deputy Assistant Secretary of State, "Memo to Secretary of State (March 15, 1951)," *Foreign Relations of the US, 1951–54*, vol. 10, 9.

40. British Ambassador, "Letter to Foreign Office (March 19, 1951)," *FO 371*/Persia 1951/34-91524.

41. George McGhee, *Envoy to the Middle World* (New York: Harper & Row, 1983), 327.

42. Sam Falle, *My Lucky Life* (London: The Book Guild, 1986), 83.

43. British Ambassador (in Washington), "Anglo-US Talks in Washington," *BP*/Persia 1951/00043859; State Department, "Memo of Conversations (April 18, 1951)," *Foreign Relations of the US, 1951–54*, vol. 10, 41.

44. British Ambassador (in Washington), April 11, 1951, *FO 371*/Persia 1951/34-91470; April 2, 1951, *FO 371*/Persia 1951/34-91470.

45. McGhee, *Envoy to the Middle World*, 327, 335.

46. State Department, "Memo of Conversations in Washington (April 17, 1951), *Foreign Relations of the US, 1951–54*, vol. 10, 34.

47. State Department, "Meeting on AIOC Problem with US Oil Companies Operating in the Middle East," *Foreign Relations of the US, 1951–54*, vol. 5, 309.

48. James Goode, *The United States and Iran: In the Shadow of Mussadiq* (New York: St. Martin's Press, 1997), 29–30.

49. Secretary of State, "Letter to the U.S. Embassy in Tehran (May 11, 1951)," *Foreign Relations of the US, 1951–54*, vol. 10, 53.

50. AIOC, "Persian Oil—An American View (June 14, 1951)," *BP*/ 00003565.

51. Foreign Office, "Notes on the Situation," *FO 371*/Persia 1951/34-91498.

52. Goode, *United States and Iran*, 128.

53. *New York Times*, May 17, 1951.

54. Defence Ministry, "Meeting with Sir William Fraser (May 23, 1951)," *FO 371*/Persia 1951/34-91537.

55. Foreign Office, "Minutes of Persian Working Party," *FO 371*/Persia 1951/34-91497.

56. Foreign Office, "Fraser's Visit to the Foreign Office," *FO 371*/Persia 1951/34-91533.

57. Foreign Office, "Minutes (May 7, 1951)," *FO 371*/Persia 1951/34-91533.

58. British Residency in Bahrain, "Thornburg Memo (March 31, 1951)," *FO 371*/Persia 1951/34-91619.

59. British Embassy (in Washington), June 7, 1951, *FO 248*/Persia 1951/34-31986

60. British Embassy, July 19, 1951, *FO 248*/Persia 1951/34-1528.

61. British Embassy (in Washington), "Telegram (May 4, 1951)," *FO 371*/Persia 1951/34-91530.

62. British Embassy, August 20, 1951, *FO 371*/Persia 1951/34-91580; Ministry of Fuel and Power, "Conversations with Mr. Walter Levy (May 23, 1951)," *FO 371*/Persia 1951/34-91537.

63. Max Thornburg, "General Summary of My Activities Concerning Persian Oil," *FO 248*/Persia 1951/34-1930.

64. AIOC, "Grady's Article," *BP*/Persia 1951/106249.

65. Reader Bullard, "Oil Crisis in Iran," *BP*/Persia 1951/106249.

66. Reader Bullard, *Letters from Tehran* (London: I.B. Tauris, 1991), 154, 164, 174, 265.

67. Don North, "Interview with Loy Henderson," *Oral History Research Office* (Columbia University, 1972).

68. Charles Issawi, "A Set of Accidents?" in *Paths to the Middle East*, ed. Thomas Naff (Albany: SUNY Press, 1993), 160.

69. Charles Issawi, *Oil, the Middle East, and the World* (New York: Library Press, 1972), 16.

70. "Iran and the World," *New York Times*, August 21, 1953.

71. "Dervish in Pin-Striped Suit," *Time*, June 4, 1951.

72. British Ambassador, May 21, 1951, *FO 371*/Persia 1951/34-91459.

73. George Middleton, "Annual Report on Persia for 1951," *FO 371*/Persia 1951/34-98593.

74. Habib Ladjevardi, "Interview with Sir George Middleton," *The Iranian Oral History Project* (Cambridge: Harvard University Press, 1993).

75. British Ambassador, "Report on Events in Persia in 1951," *FO 371*/Persia 1951/34-98593.

76. British Embassy, September 4, 1951, *FO 248*/Persia 1951/34-1514.

77. British Embassy, August 2, 1952, *FO 248*/1952/34-1531.

78. Drew Pearson, "USSR Wants Long Peace Parley," *Washington Post*, July 11, 1951. Cuttings of this article were sent by the British embassy in Washington to Tehran to show that the press attaché was doing his job. *FO 248*/Persia 1951/34-1528.

79. British Embassy (in Washington), "Letter to the Foreign Office," *FO 371*/Persia 1951/34-98608.

80. Foreign Office, May 5, 1951, *FO 371*/Persia 1951/34-91533.

81. "Challenge of the East," *Time*, January 7, 1951. See also "Dervish in Pin-Striped Suit." The British embassy in Washington sent copies of these articles to both London and Tehran. *FO 248*/Persia 1951/34-1541.

82. British Embassy (in Washington), "Letter to the British Embassy in Tehran," *FO 248*/Persia 1951/34-1527.

83. British Embassy (in Washington), May 5, 1951, *FO 371*/Persia 1951/34-91533.

84. British Ambassador (in Washington), November 26, 1951, *FO 371*/Persia 1951/34-91615.

85. Foreign Office, "Telegram from Tehran to Washington," *FO 371/* Persia 1951/34-91530.

86. Foreign Minister, "Letter to Webb (October 10, 1951)," *FO 371/*Persia 1951/34-9160.

87. "Profile of Mohammad Moussadek," *Observer*, May 20, 1951.

88. Special Correspondent, "Persia's Present Leaders," *The Times*, August 22, 1951.

89. Special Correspondent, "The Crisis in Persia: Internal Issues Behind the Oil Demands," *The Times*, March 22, 1951; "Persia's Oil Claim: Motives Behind the Demand for Nationalization," *The Times*, May 23, 1951.

90. British Ambassador, August 5, 1951, *FO 371/*Persia 1951/34-91548

91. Foreign Office, "Notes on Professor Elwell-Sutton," *FO 371/*Persia 1957/34-127074.

92. L.P. Elwell-Sutton, *Persian Oil: A Study in Power Politics* (London: Lawrence and Wishart, 1955).

93. Foreign Office, "Propaganda Line," *FO 248/*Persia 1951/34-1527.

94. Foreign Office, "Notes on the *Daily Telegraph* and the *Observer*," *FO 371/*Persia 1953/34-104177.

95. British Ambassador, "A Comparison Between Persian and Asian Nationalism in General," *FO 371/*Persia 1951/34-91464.

96. British Ambassador, "Comments to the Foreign Office," *FO 371/*Persia 1951/34-91459.

97. British Embassy, "The Persian Social and Political Scene," *FO 371/* Persia 1951/34-91460.

98. Persian Oil Working Party, "The Persian Character," *FO 371/*Persia 1951/34-91539.

99. Daniel Yergin, *The Prize: The Epic Quest for Oil, Money, and Power* (New York: Simon & Schuster, 1991), 450–78, 583.

100. Barry Rubin, *Paved with Good Intentions: The American Experience in Iran* (New York: Oxford University Press, 1980), 57–67.

101. Peter Avery, *Modern Iran* (London: Ernest Benn, 1965), 416–39.

102. Cyrus Arjani (pseudonym), "Review of *Musaddiq, Iranian Nationalism and Oil*, ed. James Bill and Roger Louis," *Bulletin of the British Journal of Middle Eastern Studies* 16, no. 2 (1989), 207–12.

103. Sireen Hunter, *The Future of Islam and the West: Clash of Civilizations or Peaceful Coexistence* (London: Praeger, 1996), 137.

104. Ronald Ferrier, "Review of Homa Katouzian's *Mussadiq and the Struggle for Power in Iran*," *Bulletin of the School of Oriental and African Studies* 55, Part 2 (1992), 340–42.

105. Falle, *My Lucky Life*, 75.

106. McGhee, *Envoy to the Middle World*, 400.

107. Elaine Sciolino, "Mossadegh: Eccentric Nationalist Begets Strange History," *New York Times*, April 16, 2000.

108. Mark Gasiorowski, "The Truth About the 1953 Coup," *Le Monde Di-*

plomatique, October 17, 2000; "The 1953 Coup Revisited" (paper presented to the Center for Iranian Research and Analysis).

109. Stephen Kinzer, *All the King's Men: The Hidden Story of the CIA's Coup in Iran* (New York: Wiley, 2003), 106.

110. Farah Pahlavi, *An Enduring Love: My Life with the Shah* (New York: Hyperion, 1987), 46–47.

111. Abbas Milani, *The Shah* (New York: Palgrave Macmillan, 2011), 145.

112. Gholam Reza Afkhami, *The Life and Times of the Shah* (Berkeley: University of California Press, 2009), 145.

113. UK Government, "Anglo-Iranian Oil Company Case," *FO 371*/Persia 1951/34-91604.

114. Foreign Office, "An Account of American Ambassador's Visit (January 1, 1951)," *FO 371*/Persia 1952/34-98647.

115. Foreign Office, "HMG's Ambassador's Notes (April 1951)," *FO 371*/Persia 1951/34-91615.

116. Foreign Office, "General Measures Voluntarily Taken by AIOC (1951)," *FO 371*/Persia 1951/34-91538.

117. AIOC, "Plan for Shut-down of Fields, Production, and Abadan Refinery (July 2, 1951)," *BP*/00043857.

118. Foreign Office, "Meeting with Herr A. Stahmer (November 29, 1951)," *FO 371*/Persia 1951/34-91617.

119. Ministry of Fuel and Power, October 8, 1951, *FO 371*/Persia 1951/34-91599.

120. Foreign Office, "Attempts to Dispose of Persian Oil," *FO 371*/Persia 1951/34-98657.

121. Foreign Office, Memo (June 28, 1951), *FO 371*/Persia 1951/34-91495.

122. British Cabinet, "Persian Ability to Produce and Sell Oil," *FO 371*/Persia 1951/34-91617.

123. U.S. Ambassador, August 27, 1951, *Foreign Relations of the United States, 1951–54*, vol. 10, 149.

124. Cabinet Defence Committee, "Military Possibility of Seizing Abadan Island (June 1951)," *FO 371*/Persia 1951/34-91461.

125. Ministry of Defence, "Notes (May 21, 1951)," *FO 371*/Persia 1951/34-91459.

126. Ministry of Defence, "Notes (May 24, 1951)," *FO 371*/Persia 1951/34-91459.

127. Lord Mountbatten, "Memo to the Admiralty (April 5, 1951)," *FO 371*/Persia 1951/34-91620.

128. Cited by James Cable, *Intervention at Abadan: Plan Buccaneer* (New York: St. Martin's Press, 1991), 117.

129. Foreign Office, July 13, 1951, *FO 248*/Persia 1951/34-1527.

130. British Ambassador, "Oil Problem in Iran (October 13, 1951)," *FO 248*/1951/34-1529.

131. British Ambassador (at UN), "Telegram (October 13, 1951)," *FO 371/* Persia 1951/34-9160.

132. British Embassy (in Washington), August 20, 1951, *FO 371*/Persia 1951/34-91580.

133. Kermit Roosevelt, *Countercoup: The Struggle for the Control of Iran* (New York: McGraw Hill, 1979), 98.

134. *Dad*, July 16, 1953; *Bakhtar-e Emruz*, July 16, 1953.

135. AIOC Office in Tehran, "Letter to London (July 16, 1951)," *BP*/126359; British Embassy, "Telegram (August 2, 1951)," *FO 416*/Persia 1951/104.

136. Hedayat Matin-Daftari, *Doktor Hussein Fatemi: Neveshtehha-ye Makhfegah va Zendan* (Dr. Hussein Fatemi: Writings from Underground and Prison) (London: 2005), 55.

137. British Ambassador, "Activities and Development of Tudeh Party," *FO 416*/Persia 1951/104.

138. British Ambassador, June 7, 1951, *FO 248*/Persia 1951/34-1527.

139. Don North, "Interview with Loy Henderson (December 1970)," *Oral History Research Office* (Columbia University, 1972).

140. Averell Harriman, "Memo to the State Department (July 24, 1951)," *Foreign Relations of the United States 1951–54*, vol. 10, 109–10.

141. Vernon Walters, *Silent Missions* (New York: Doubleday, 1978) 259.

142. Norman Seddon, "Letter to London (July 29, 1951)," *BP*/126359.

143. Treasury Chambers, "Persia: Policy to be Adopted by the Mission to Tehran," *FO 248*/Persia 1951/34-1527.

144. Tek, "Letter to Fraser (August 10, 1951)," *BP*/00043854.

145. Foreign Office, "Minutes of the Second Meeting Between the Stokes Mission and the Persian Government Delegation (August 8, 1951)," *FO 371/* Persia 1951/34-91577.

146. Foreign Office, "Record of the Lord Privy Seal's Conversations with the Shah (August 13, 1953)," *FO 371*/Persia 1951/34-91583.

147. Foreign Office, "Reply of the Persian Delegation," *FO 371*/Persia 1951/34-91583.

148. U.S. Ambassador, "Telegram (September 30, 1951)," *Foreign Relations of the US, 1951–54*, vol. 10, 186–87.

149. These forgeries were amateurish; they used the wrong numbering and transliteration. See *FO 371*/Persia 1951/34-91593.

150. British Ambassador, "Oil Problem in Persia (October 18, 1951)," *FO 248*/Persia 1951/34-1529.

151. British Ambassador, "Telegram (August 25, 1951)," *FO 371*/Persia 1951/34-91582; and "Telegram (August 26, 1951)," *FO 371*/Persia 951/344-91584.

152. Ministry of Fuel and Power, September 5–6, 1951, *FO 371*/Persia 1951/34-91589.

153. United Nations, Five Hundred and Sixteenth Meeting (October 15, 1951).

154. Foreign Office, October 23, 1951, *FO 371*/Persia 1951/34-91603.

155. British Ambassador (at the UN), October 15, 1951, *FO 371*/Persia 1951/34-91602.

156. James Goode, *The United States and Iran: In the Shadow of Musaddiq* (New York: St. Martin's Press, 1997), 57.

157. State Department, "Memorandum for the President Concerning Meeting with Prime Minister Mossadeq (October 22, 1951)," *Declassified Documents*/White House/1979/Doc. 78.

158. Foreign Office, "Telegram (November 6, 1951)," *FO 248*/Persia 1951/34-1530.

159. Ibid.

160. Ministerial Committee, October 25, 1951, *FO 371*/Persia 1951/34-91605.

161. Ministry of Fuel and Power, "Meeting with Representatives of Oil Companies (November 17, 1951)," *FO 371*/Persia 1951/34-91611; Foreign Office, November 6, 1951, *FO 371*/Persia 1951/34-91610.

162. Goode, *United States and Iran*, 60.

163. Foreign Office, "Political Issues Involved in the Present Situation in Persia (November 13, 1951)," *FO 371*/Persia 1951/34-91611.

164. Foreign Office, Handwritten Note on November 8, 1951, *FO 371*/Persia 1951/34-91610.

165. Foreign Office, December 8, 1951, *FO 371*/Persia 1951/34-91616.

166. British Ambassador, "Telegram (October 23, 1951)," *FO 371*/Persia 1951/34-91606.

167. McGhee, *Envoy to the Middle World*, 403.

168. Walters, *Silent Missions*, 262.

169. Dean Acheson, *Present at the Creation: My Years in the State Department* (New York: Norton, 1969), 504.

170. Secretary of State, "Memo to the State Department (November 10, 1951)," *Foreign Relations of the US, 1952–54*, vol. 10, 278–79.

171. Muhammad Mossadeq, Speech, *Parliamentary Debates*, November 24, 1951.

172. Muhammad Mossadeq, Speech, *Parliamentary Debates*, December 11, 1951.

173. British Embassy, December 17, 1951, *FO 371*/Persia 1951/34-91466.

174. British Embassy (in Washington), December 22, 1951, *FO 381*/Persia 1951/34-91618.

175. British Embassy, "Telegram to the Foreign Secretary on the Persian Situation," *FO 248*/Persia 1951/34-1514.

176. British Charge d'Affaires, "Brief for the Ministerial Committee (March 7, 1952)," *FO 371*/Persia 1952/34-98649.

177. Foreign Office, February 14, 1952, *FO 371*/Persia 1952/34-98608.

178. British Embassy, March 10, 1952, *FO 248*/Persia 1952/34-1531.

179. Robin Zaehner, "Conversation with Sayyed Ziya," *FO 248*/Persia 1952/34-1531.

180. British Embassy, "The Shah and Kashani (January 8, 1952)," *FO 248*/Persia 1952/34-1541; January 28, 1952, *FO 248*/Persia 1952/34-1541.

181. British Embassy, May 26, 1952, *FO 248*/Persia 1952/34-1531.

182. British Embassy, July 13, 1952, *FO 248*/Persia 1952/34-1539.

183. Foreign Office, May 28, 1952, *FO 248*/Persia 1952/34-1531.

184. British Embassy, June 28, 1952, *FO 248*/Persia 1952/34-1531.

185. British Embassy, July 13, 1952, *FO 248*/Persia 1952/34-1539.

186. British Embassy, April 16, 1952, *FO 248*/Persia 1952/34-1531.

187. U.S. Ambassador, January 4, 1952, *Foreign Relations of the US, 1952–54*, vol. 10, 302.

188. U.S. Ambassador, May 24, 1952, *Foreign Relations of the US, 1952–54*, vol. 10, 382.

189. British Embassy, June 11, 1952, *FO 248*/Persia 1952/34-1531.

190. Foreign Office, "Letter to the British Ambassador (July 18, 1951)," *FO 416*/Persia 1951/34-105.

191. U.S. Government, *Foreign Relations of the US, 1952–54*, vol. 10, 410–46.

192. British Embassy, August 21, 1952, *FO 248*/Persia 1952/34-1531; January 28, 1952, *FO 248*/Persia 1052/1531.

193. British Embassy, "Confidential Conversation with an Informant (August 21, 1952)," *FO 248*/Persia 1952/1521.

194. Masoud Hejazi, *Davare-ye Khaterat* (Judgments of Memory) (Tehran: 1996), 46–48.

195. U.S. Ambassador, June 27, 1952, *Foreign Relations of the US, 1952–54*, vol. 10, 405; British Embassy, "Letter to the Foreign Office (July 28, 1952)," *FO 248*/Persia 1952/1531.

196. British Embassy, June 21, 1952, *FO 248*/Persia 1952/34-1531.

197. Foreign Office, May 28, 1952, *FO 248*/Persia 1952/34-1531.

198. British Embassy, July 16, 1952, *FO 248*/Persia 1952/34-1539.

199. British Embassy, "Conversation with Perron," *FO 248*/Persia 1952/34-1531.

200. British Embassy, July 8, 1952, *FO 248*/Persia 1952/34-1541.

201. British Embassy, July 28, 1952, *FO 248*/Persia 1952/34-1541.

202. Muhammad Mossadeq, "Resignation Speech," *Ettela'at*, July 17, 1952.

203. British Embassy, July 19, 1952, *FO 248*/Persia 1952/34-1539; Britannica House, "Chronology on Persia," *BP*/1052-113549.

204. Hassan Arsanjani, *Yaddashtha-ye Siyasi: Siyeh-e Tir* (Political Memoirs: 30th Tir) (Tehran: 1956), 1–80.

205. Ayatollah Kashani, "Proclamation," *Shahed* (Witness), July 19, 1952.

206. British Embassy, "The Tudeh Party Policy," *FO 416*/Persia 1952/105.

207. *New York Times*, July 23, 1952.

208. Mostafa Fateh, *Panjah Sal-e Naft* (Fifty Years of Oil) (Tehran: 1979), 606–7; Arsanjani, *Political Memoirs*, 48–50.

209. Nuraldin Kianuri, *Khaterat* (Memoirs) (Tehran: 1992), 217–90.

210. British Embassy, "Review of the Present Crisis (July 28, 1952)," *FO 371*/Persia 1952/34-98602.

211. British Embassy, "Developments in the Persian Internal Situation (July 30, 1952)," *FO 416*/Persia 1952/34-105.

212. British Embassy, July 28, 1952, *FO 248*/Persia 1952/34-1541.

213. British Embassy, "Telegram (July 21, 1952)," *FO 248*/Persia 1952/34-1539.

214. British Embassy, "Summary of Events-Persia-1952," *FO 416*/Persia 1952/106.

215. Ladjevardi, "Interview with Sir George Middleton," *Iranian Oral History Project.*

216. British Embassy, "Correspondence Respecting Persia in 1953," *FO 416*/Persia 1953/106.

217. British Embassy, July 28, 1952, *FO 248*/Persia 1952/34-1541.

218. Falle, *My Lucky Life*, 81.

219. Loy Henderson, "Letter to the State Department (July 28, 1952)," *Foreign Relations of the US, 1952–54*, vol. 10, 416–17.

220. *Tehran Mosavar* (Tehran Illustrated), July 15, 1953.

221. Ibrahim Safai, *Rahbaran-e Mashrutiyat* (Leaders of the Constitution) (Tehran: 1965), 702.

222. Arsanjani, *Political Memoirs*, 66–68.

223. *Ettela'at*, July 21, 1952.

224. *Washington Star*, July 25, 1952.

225. Sam Falle, "Confidential Report on the *Washington Star*," *FO 248*/Persia 1952/1531.

226. American Embassy, "Report on High-Level Army Appointments," *FO 371*/Persia 1953/34-104601.

227. British Embassy, "Telegraph (July 28, 1952)," *FO 371*/Persia 1952/34-98602.

228. Secretary of State, "Letter to the U.S. Ambassador in London (July 26, 1952)," *Foreign Relations of the US, 1952–54*, vol. 10, 415–16.

229. British Embassy, "Letter to Anthony Eden (August 25, 1952)," *FO 248*/Persia 1952/1531.

230. British Embassy, "Review of the Present Crisis (July 28, 1952)," *FO 371*/Persia 1952/34-98602.

231. British Embassy, "Memorandum from Tehran (July 22, 1952)," *FO 248*/Persia 1952/34-153.

232. British Embassy, "Telegram (July 28, 1952)," *FO 371*/Persia 1952/34-98602.

233. American Ambassador to the Secretary of State, "Telegrams (July 30–31, 1952)," *Foreign Relations of the US, 1952–54*, vol. 10, 424–25.

234. Foreign Office, "Telegram (July 29, 1952)," *FO 371*/Persia 1952/34-98602.

235. War Office, "Telegram (July 29, 1952)," *FO 371*/Persia 1952/34-98602.

236. British Embassy, "Telegram to the War Office (August 4, 1952)," *FO 371*/Persia 1952/34-98602.

3. The Coup

1. Tim Heald, ed., *My Dear Hugh: Letters from Richard Cobb to Hugh Trevor-Roper* (London: Frances Lincoln, 2011), 159.

2. Hussein Fardoust, "The August 19th Coup," *Kayhan-e Hava'i*, October 2, 1991; Fardoust's *Khaterat* (Memoirs) (Tehran: 1988), serialized in *Kayhan-e Hava'i*, November 30, 1988–June 1, 1994. They were later published as *Zohur va Soqut-e Saltanat-e Pahlavi* (Emergence and Fall of the Pahlavi Dynasty) (Tehran: 1991).

3. Military Attaché, "Annual Report on the Persian Army for 1951," *FO 371*/Persia 1952/34-98638.

4. British Military Attaché, "Weekly Reports (February 17, 1946)," *India Office*, L/P &S/12-3505.

5. These MI6 files, of course, are unavailable, but parts occasionally do appear in the Foreign Office. See "Personalities in Persia—Military Supplement (1947)," *FO 371*/Persia 1947/34-62035.

6. Donald Wilber, *Overthrow of Premier Mossadeq of Iran, 1951–53*, http://cyrptome.org/cia-iran-all.htm. Appendix E.

7. Sam Falle, *My Lucky Life* (London: The Book Guild, 1996), 81.

8. Foreign Office, "Comment, (February 28, 1957)," *FO 371*/Persia 1957/34-127074; British Embassy, "Report on Political Parties," *FO 371*/ Peresia 1957/34-127075; Foreign Office, "Comment, March 26, 1958)," *FO 371*/Persia 1958/34-120713.

9. British Embassy, "Confidential Report to the Foreign Office (May 1952)," *FO 371*/Persia 1952/34-38572.

10. Robin Zaehner, "The Fida'iyan-e Islam (March 1, 1952)," *FO 248*/ Persia 1952/34-1540.

11. Roy Melbourne, "Development of Fedayan Islam (1952)," *Declassified U.S. Documents*/1975/308/Doc. C.

12. John Glubb, "Letter to the Foreign Office," *FO 248*/Persia 1951/34-1529.

13. Homa Sarshar, *Sha'aban Jafari* (Sha'aban Jafari) (Beverly Hills: Naab Publishers, 2002), 30.

14. Lane Pyman, "Conversations with Sayyed Ziya," *FO 248*/Persia 1951/34-1528.

15. Sam Falle, "Conversations with Sayyed Muhammad Reza Behbehani, (May 18, 1952)" *FO 248*/Persia 1952/34-1571.

16. British Embassy, "Leading Personalities in Persia (1957)," *FO 371*/ Persia 1957/34-127072.

17. Robin Zaehner, "Meeting with Sayyed Tabatabai (May 15, 1952)," *FO 248*/Persia 1952/34-38572.

18. Falle, *My Lucky Life*, 89.

19. British Embassy, "Letter to the War Office (August 4, 1952)," *FO 371*/Persia 1952/34-98602.

20. British Embassy, "Zahedi's Shadow Cabinet," *FO 248*/Persia 1952/34-1531.

21. Ibid.

22. Robin Zaehner, "Conversation with Perron," *FO 248*/Persia 1952/34-1531.

23. Robin Zaehner, "Conversations with an Informant," *FO 248*/Persia 1952/34-1531.

24. Robin Zaehner, "Conversations with Khalatbari," *FO 248*/Persia 1952/34-1531.

25. Sam Falle, "Confidential Conversation with General Zahedi (August 7, 1952)," *FO 248*/Persia 1952/1531.

26. British Embassy, October 13, 1952, *FO 248*/Persia 1952/34-1531.

27. British Embassy, "Telegram (July 28, 1952)," *FO 248*/Persia 1952/34-1531.

28. Foreign Office, "Note on Diplomatic Status," *FO 371*/Persia 1952/34-98606.

29. British Embassy, "Point Four Program in Persia," *FO 416*/Persia 1952/34-105.

30. G.K. Reddy, "Iranian Round-Up," *Times of India*, June 1–3, 1953.

31. British Embassy (Kabul), "Views of the French Military Attaché in Tehran," *FO 371*/Persia 1953/34-104572.

32. U.S. Embassy, "Letter to the State Department," *FO 371*/Persia 1952/34-9859.

33. Interview with General Riyahi in Ghulam-Reza Nejati, *Jonbesh-e Mellishudan-e Naft va Kudeta-ye Best-u-Hasht-e Mordad* (The Movement to Nationalize Oil and the Coup of August 19) (Tehran: 1986), 371.

34. Reddy, "Iranian Round-Up."

35. Donald Wilber, *Adventures in the Middle East* (Princeton: Darwin Press, 1986), 187–90.

36. Safa al-Din Tabaraian, "Sumka and the Reproduction of Nazism," *Motale'at-e Iran* (Iranian Studies) 1 no. 1 (Autumn 2003), 17–106.

37. British Embassy, October 13, 1952, *FO 248*/Persia 1952/34-1531; British Embassy, "Report on the Arya Party," *FO 371*/Persia 1953/34-104569; Foreign Office, "Persian Oil Dispute: Views of Miss Lambton," *FO 371*/Persia 1951/34-91609.

38. British Embassy, "Note on R. Cottam," *FO 248*/Persia 1951/1517.

39. Esfandiar Bozorgmehr, *Karavan-e Omr* (Life's Caravan) (London: 1993), 188, 190, 209.

40. Kermit Roosevelt, *Countercoup: The Struggle for the Control of Iran* (New York: McGraw Hill, 1979), 16.

41. British Embassy, August 11, 1952, *FO 248*/Persia 1952/34-1531.

42. Loy Henderson, September 20, 1952, *Foreign Relations of the US, 1952–54*, vol. 10, 475.

43. CIA, "Memo for the President," *Foreign Relations of the US, 1952–54*, vol. 10, 689.

44. Foreign Office, Handwritten Notes, *FO 371*/Persia 1953/34-104606.

45. Loy Henderson, March 9, 1953, *Foreign Relations of the US, 1952–54*, vol. 10, 705.

46. AIOC, "Notes on Compensation (January 9, 1953)," *BP*/05926.

47. Foreign Office, "Minutes of the Persian Official Meeting," *FO 371*/Persia 1952/34-98647.

48. British Embassy, "Henderson's Conversation with Musaddiq (January 8, 1953)," *FO 371*/Persia 1953/34-104574.

49. State Department, "Memo of Meeting with UK Foreign Office (January 9, 1952)," *Foreign Relations of the US, 1952–54*, vol. 10, 303.

50. Habib Ladjevardi, "Interview with Sir George Middleton," *The Iranian Oral History Project* (Cambridge: Harvard University Press, 1993).

51. Harlan Cleveland, "Oil, Blood, and Politics," *The Reporter*, November 10, 1953.

52. State Department, "Memorandum of Discussion at the Meeting of the National Security Council," *Foreign Relations of the US, 1952–54*, vol. 10, 711–13.

53. "Taped Transcript of Interview with Derbyshire on the 1953 Coup," Interview for the television program *End of Empire* (Granada Channel 4 [UK], 1985).

54. Foreign Office, "Summary of Political Developments in 1953," *FO 371*/1953/34-104571.

55. Homa Katouzian, ed., *Musaddiq's Memoirs* (London: Jebhe Publications, 1988), 44–45.

56. Vernon Walters, *Silent Missions* (New York: Doubleday, 1978), 252.

57. AIOC, "Letter to the Ministry of Fuel (April 23, 1953)," *BP*/066260.

58. G.K. Reddy, "The Economic Crisis," *Times of India*, June 3, 1953.

59. CIA, "Probable Developments in Iran Through 1953," Declassified Documents, 1–8.

60. Commercial Counsellor, June 1, 1951, *FO 371*/Persia 1951/34-91497.

61. For Majles attacks, see Iranian Government, *Muzakerat-e Majles* (Parliamentary Debates), seventeenth Majles, February 28–August 20, 1953.

62. Hedayat Matin-Daftari, *Doktor Hussein Fatemi: Neveshtehha-ye Makhfegah va Zendan* (Dr. Hussein Fatemi) (London: 2005), 62.

63. Editorial, "The People Rule, the Shah Reigns," *Jebe'eh-e Azadi*, March 10, 1953.

64. Muhammad Dahnavi, *Mujma'ahyi az Maktabahat, Sokhanraniha va Paymanha-ye Ayatollah Kashani* (Ayatollah Kashani's Collected Writings, Speeches, and Messages) (Tehran: 1982), vol. 3, 192.

65. Atesh (pseudonym), *Qiyam dar Rah-e Saltanat* (Uprising for the Monarchist Road) (Tehran: 1954), 50–56.

66. Katouzian, *Musaddiq's Memoirs*, 192.

67. U.S. Embassy, "Iran's Political Trends Since the Departure of the British Embassy (April 24, 1953)," *FO 371*/Persia 1953/34-104567.

68. Masoud Hejazi, *Davare-ye Khaterat* (Judgments of Memory) (Tehran: 1996), 54. Hejazi did not appear to realize that Ali Jalali was a CIA agent.

69. Richard Cottam, *Nationalism in Iran* (Pittsburgh: University of Pittsburgh Press, 1964), 154–55.

70. Mehdi Azar, "Did Foreigners Carry Out the 1953 Coup?" *Mehregan* 5, no. 2 (Summer 1996), 47–52.

71. U.S. Embassy, April 8, 1953, *FO 371*/Persia 1953/34-104567.

72. Morteza Rasuli, "Interview with Hussein Makki," *Tarekh-e Mo'aser-e Iran* (Contemporary History of Iran), no. 1 (Fall 1997), 176–216.

73. William Roger Louis, "How Musaddeq Was Ousted," *Times Literary Supplement*, June 29, 2001.

74. Muhammad Mossadeq, "Speech to the Nation," *Bakhtar-e Emruz*, July 17, 1953.

75. *New York Times*, August 4–14, 1953.

76. *New York Times*, July 23, 1953.

77. *New York Times*, July 22, 1953.

78. Wilber, *Overthrow of Premier Mossadeq*, iv.

79. Robert Scheer, "CIA's Role in the 1953 Iran Coup," *Los Angeles Times*, March 29, 1979.

80. Stephen Dorril, *MI6: Inside the Covert World of Her Majesty's Secret Intelligence Service* (New York: Free Press, 2000), 566.

81. Roosevelt, *Countercoup*, 77.

82. Dorril, *MI6*, 578.

83. Foreign Office, "First Joint-Meeting of the State Department and the Foreign Office (April 9, 1951)," *FO 371*/Persia 1951/34-91471.

84. Working Party, "Memorandum (October 15, 1951)," *FO 371*/Persia 1951/34-91607.

85. State Department, "Memo of Conversations with the British Ambassador, *Foreign Relations of the US, 1951*, vol. 5, 189–90.

86. Foreign Office, "Telegram to the Washington Embassy (November 11, 1951)," *FO 248*/Persia 1951/1530.

87. Dean Acheson, *Present at the Creation: My Years in the State Department* (New York: Norton, 1969), 680.

88. Roosevelt, *Countercoup*, 88.

89. Foreign Office, November 26, 1951, *FO 371*/Persia 1951/34-91615.

90. Christopher Woodhouse, *Something Ventured* (London: Granada, 1982), 117.

91. Ladjevardi, "Interview with Sir George Middleton," *Iranian Oral History Project.*

92. Steve Marsh, "The United States, Iran and Operation "Ajax,' " *Middle Eastern Studies* 39, no. 3 (July 2003), 24.

93. Jalil Bozorgmehr, *Muhammad Mossadeq dar Dadgah-e Nezami* (Muhammad Mossadeq in Military Court) (Tehran: 1984), vol. 1, 573–74.

94. Iraj Afshar, ed., *Taqrerat-e Mossadeq dar Zendan* (Mossadeq's Comments in Prison) (Tehran: 1980), 134.

95. Abu Nasr Azod Qajar, *Baznegar-e dar Tarekh* (A Review of History) (Bethesda, MD: 1996).

96. State Department, "Memorandum on the Meeting of the National Security Council (March 4, 1953), *Foreign Relations of the US, 1952–54,* vol. 10, 692–701.

97. American Embassy, August 12, 1953, *Foreign Relations of the US, 1952–54,* vol. 10, 743–74.

98. Wilber, *Overthrow of Premier Mossadeq*, Appendix E.

99. U.S. Embassy, "Estimate of Tudeh Numerical Strength," *FO 371/* Persia 1953/34-104573.

100. "Interview with Dr. Ghulam-Hussein Sadiqi, *Ruznameh-e Donya,* September 11, 1979.

101. CIA, August 18, 1953, telegram declassified on August 12, 1982. I would like to thank Mark Gasiorowski for making these documents available.

102. CIA, April 4, 1953, telegram declassified on August 12, 1982.

103. Foreign Office, "The Tudeh Party," *FO 975/*Persia 1953/69.

104. CIA, "Probable Developments in Iran Through 1953," declassified report, 1–7.

105. CIA, "Report on Iran (August 18, 1953), *Declassified Documents* (Microfiche)/1981/276 D.

106. Foreign Office, "The Tudeh Party," *FO 975/*Persia 1953/69.

107. Foreign Office, "Press Reports on Ambassador Sadchikov (June 25, 1953)," *FO 371/*Persia 1953/34-104576.

108. British Ambassador (Afghanistan), "Views of the French Military Attaché (June 10, 1953)," *FO 371/*Persia 1953/34-104576.

109. Louis, "How Mussadeq Was Ousted."

110. *FO 371/*Persia 1953/34-10456. The article was planted in the newspaper *Joshan* in Isfahan.

111. Mark Gasiorowski, "The 1953 Coup d'État in Iran," *International Journal of Middle East Studies* 19, no. 3 (August 1987), 284.

112. *Time,* July 20, 1953.

113. Editorial, "Mossadeq Plays with Fire," *New York Times,* August 15, 1953.

114. Hamid Seifzadeh, *Hafez-e Tarekh-e Afshartous Keybud?* (Who Kept the Secret of Afshartous?) (Tehran: 1984).

115. "Interview Tape with Derbyshire on the 1953 Coup," *End of Empire.* This part of the interview was not televised.

116. Kennett Love, "Army Seizes Helm," *New York Times,* August 20, 1953.

117. Foreign Office, "Report on U.S. Memo Sent from Tehran to Washington," *FO 371/*Persia 1953/34-104564.

118. Wilber, *Overthrow of Premier Mossadeq*, Appendix B.

119. Muhammad-Jafar Mohammadi, "Account of Military Activities in the August 19 Coup," *Nimrouz*, October 8–December 26, 1999.

120. "Interview with Two Officers Who Defended Dr. Mossadeq," *Ettela'at*, August 19, 1979.

121. Wilber, *Overthrow of Premier Mossadeq*, Appendix B.

122. Muhammad-Jafar Muhammadi, *Raz-e Pirouzi-ye Kudeta-ye Best-u-Hasht-e Mordad* (Secret of the Success of the August 19 Coup) (Tehran: 2006). Captain Homayuni was arrested after the failed coup, together with other Imperial Guards; promoted to rank of major a few days later when the shah returned triumphant; rearrested and sentenced to life imprisonment two years later when he was unmasked as a member of the Tudeh Party. He recounted his experiences to Muhammadi, a fellow Tudeh member. For extracts from his memoirs, see Muhammad-Hussein Khosrowpanah, *Sazman-e Afsaran-e Hezb-e Tudeh-e Iran* (The Military Organization of the Tudeh Party of Iran) (Tehran: 1998), 241–74.

For variations on this account with another Imperial Guard, Major Abdul-Samad Khair-Khah—giving the warning, see F.M. Javansher, *Tajrabeh-e Best-u-Hasht-e Mordad* (The Experience of August 19) (Tehran: 1980), 288–89; and Nuraldin Kianuri, *Khaterat* (Memoirs) (Tehran: 1992), 264–66.

Hussein Fardoust, in his memoirs, writes that the Tudeh had two members among the elite Imperial Guard: Majors Khair-Khah and Nazer. Both were highly trusted by the shah and G2; the former because he was highly efficient; the latter because he was related to the shah via the queen mother. Nazer escaped to the Soviet Union in 1954 and did not return until the Islamic Revolution. See Fardoust, *Memoirs*.

Some sources claim that it was Colonel Muhammad-Ali Mobasheri, head of the Tudeh military organization, who personally phoned and warned Mossadeq of the impending coup. See "The Tudeh Party Informed Mossadeq of the Coup," *Sharvand-e Emruz*, August 13, 2001. Mobasheri, however, was unlikely to have had direct lines of communications with the prime minister. Former Tudeh members who opposed Kianuri's later leadership had their own reasons for trying to minimize his role.

123. Bozorgmehr, *Muhammad Mossadeq in Military Court*, vol. 1, 440–41.

124. Mehdi Azar, "Did Foreigners Carry Out the 1953 Coup?"

125. Ismail Elmieh, "Notes on the Investigation," in Ghulam-Reza Nejati, *Jonbesh-e Mellishudan-e Naft va Kudeta-ye Best-u-Hasht-e Mordad* (The Movement to Nationalize Oil and the Coup of August 19) (Tehran: 1986), 469–85.

126. Ladjevardi, "Interview with Ahmad Zirakzadeh," *Iranian Oral History Project*.

127. Bozorgmehr, *Muhammad Mossadeq in Military Court*, vol. 1, 121.

128. U.S. Embassy, "Summary of Political Events in Iran," *FO 371*/Persia 1953/34-104569.

129. Muhammad-Ali Safari, *Qalam va Siyasat* (Pen and Politics) (Tehran: 1992), 853.

130. Matin-Daftari, *Doktor Hussein Fatemi*, 36.

131. Nasrallah Shefteh, *Zendeginameh va Mobarezat-e Siyasi-ye Doktor Sayyed Hussein Fatemi* (The Life and Political Struggles of Dr. Sayyed Hussein Fatemi) (Tehran: 1985), 366–70.

132. Safari, *Pen and Politics*, 830–35.

133. Sepehr Zabih, *The Mossadegh Era* (Chicago: Lake View Press, 1982), 133–34.

134. Undersecretary of State, "Memorandum (August 18, 1953)," *Foreign Relations of the US, 1952–54*, vol. 10, 748.

135. Wilber, *Overthrow of Premier Mossadeq*, Summary.

136. U.S. Embassy, "The Ambassador's Interview with Mossadeq," *FO 371*/Persia 1953/34-104570; Loy Henderson, "Memorandum on Meeting with Mossadeq (August 18, 1953)," *Foreign Relations of the US, 1952–54*, vol. 10, 748–52.

137. Don North, "Interview with Henderson," *Oral History Research Office* (Columbia University, 1972).

138. "Iran Mob, Riot for the Shah," *Time*, August 31, 1953. The detailed information in this article must have been leaked by Henderson since there were only three people at the meeting: Mossadeq, Henderson, and his interpreter.

139. Loy Henderson's Private Papers, Manuscript Division of the Library of Congress. For a summary of this meeting, see Moyara De Morales Ruehsen, "Operation 'Ajax' Revisited: Iran, 1953," *Middle Eastern Studies* 29, no. 3 (July 1993), 479–80, 485–86.

140. Hussein Azabi, ed., *Yadnameh-e Mohandes Hassebi* (Memoirs of Engineer Hassebi) (Tehran: 1991), 124.

141. "Interview with Dr. Ghulam-Hussein Sadiqi," *Ruznameh-e Donya*, September 11, 1979.

142. Roy Melbourne (of U.S. embassy), "Political Situation from April to Overthrow of Mossadeq on August 19," in *FO 371*/Persia 1953/34-104572.

143. Stephen Ambrose, *Ike's Spies: Eisenhower and the Espionage Establishment* (Jackson: University of Mississippi Press, 1981), 208–9.

144. Military Governor, "Proclamation," *Ettela'at*, August 18, 1953.

145. Arnaud de Burchgrace, "Shah Returns in Triumph," *Newsweek*, August 31, 1953.

146. U.S. Ambassador, "Dispatch to the State Department (August 20, 1953)," *Foreign Relations of the US, 1952–54*, 10, 762.

147. Foreign Office, "Notes on a U.S. Telegram (August 20, 1953)," *FO 371*/Persia 1953/34-104570.

148. British Memorandum, "Political Review of the Recent Crisis (September 2, 1953)," *Foreign Relations of the US, 1952–54*, 10, 780–88.

149. Kennett Love, "Extremist Riot in Teheran," *New York Times*, August 19, 1953.

150. Parvez Babayi, "The August 19 Coup," *Andisheh-e Jam'eh* (Social Thought), no. 12 (August 2000), 8–10.

151. Baqer Momeni, "From July to August," *Aresh*, no. 75 (August 1994), 32–35. The whole issue is devoted to reminiscences from leftist students in August 1953.

152. Hejazi, *Judgments of Memory*, 114–21, 681.

153. Ali Rahnema, *Niruha-ye Mazhabi* (Religious Forces) (Tehran: 2005), 952.

154. Parvez Varjaved, ed., *Yadnameh-e Doktor Ghulam-Hussein Sadiqi* (Memoirs of Dr. Ghulam-Hussein Sadiqi) (Tehran: 1992), 120–22.

155. Richard and Gladys Harkness, "The Mysterious Doings of the CIA," *Saturday Evening Post*, October 30–November 13, 1954. See also Stella Marigold, "The Streets of Tehran," *The Reporter*, November 10, 1953.

156. Kennett Love, "The American Role in the Pahlavi Restoration" (Princeton University, unpublished paper, 1960), 2.

157. Cottam, *Nationalism in Iran*, 37–38, 155.

158. Christopher de Bellaigue, *In the Rose Garden of the Martyrs: A Memoir of Iran* (New York: HarperCollins, 2004), 173.

159. British Memorandum, "The Political Review of the Recent Crisis (September 2, 1953)," *Foreign Relations of the US, 1952–54*, vol. 10, 780–88; *Ettela'at-e Haftegi*, August 1953; Shams al-Din Amir-Alai, *Khaterat-e Man* (My Memoirs) (Tehran: 1984), 393–97.

160. Homayuni, "Memoirs," in Khosrowpanah, *Military Organization of the Tudeh Party of Iran*, 251–53.

161. Babak Amir-Khosrovi, *Nazar az daroun beh Naqsh-e Hezb-e Tudeh-e Iran* (Internal Look at the Role of the Tudeh Party of Iran) (Tehran: 1996), 666.

162. Harkness, "Mysterious Doings of the CIA."

163. Hejazi, *Judgments of Memory*, 109–12.

164. Cited by Muhammadi, "Account of Military Activities in the August 19 Coup," *Nimrouz*, November 5, 1999.

165. Bozorgmehr, *Muhammad Mossadeq in Military Court*, 481.

166. Varjaved, *Memoirs of Dr. Ghulam-Hussein Sadiqi*, 123–24.

167. Homayuni, "Memoirs," 254–55.

168. Shefteh, *Life and Political Struggles of Dr. Sayyed Hussein Fatemi*, 314.

169. Bozorgmehr, *Muhammad Mossadeq in Military Court*, vol. 2, 56–59.

170. "Interview with Colonel Momtaz," *Majaleh-e Iran*, August 18, 1999.

171. Varjaved, *Memoirs of Dr. Ghulam-Hussein Sadiqi*, 127.

172. Masallah Varaqa, *Chand-u-Chun Variyzi-ye Dowlat-e Mossadeq* (Sketches on the Downfall of Mossadeq's Government) (Tehran: 2007), 338.

173. Zabih, *Mossadegh Era*, 135.

174. Kianuri, *Memoirs*, 276–78.

175. Ahmad Shayegan, ed., *Sayyed Ali Shayegan* (Tehran: 2004), vol. 2, 9–11.

176. Ladjevardi, "Interview with Ahmad Zirakzadeh" and "Interview with Mehdi Azar," *Iranian Oral History Project*; Shefteh, *Life and Political Struggles of Dr. Sayyed Hussein Fatemi*, 315; Karem Sanjabi, *Omidha va Na Omidiha* (Hopes and Despairs) (London: Jebhe Publications, 1989), 148.

177. Sadeq Ansari, *Az Zendegi-ye Man* (From My Life) (Los Angeles: Nashr-e Ketab, 1996), 336.

178. British Embassy, "Notes on Political Parties (August 16, 1957), *FO 371*/Persia 1953/34-127075.

179. Rahnema, *Religious Forces*, 955.

180. Joseph Mazandi, "Shah's Men Overthrow Mussadiq," *Times of India*, August 20, 1953.

181. Foreign Office, "Notes on Conversation Between Iraqi Ambassador and Reuters Correspondent," *FO 371*/Persia 1953/34-104571.

182. Amir-Alai, *My Memoirs*, 405.

183. Mahmud Kashani, "Was It Really a Military Coup?" paper presented at a conference on Muhammad Mossadeq and the 1953 Coup, at St. Antony's College, Oxford, UK, on June 8–10, 2002.

184. U.S. Embassy, "Conversation Between Mr. Henderson and the Shah (September 14, 1954)," *FO 371*/Persia 1954/34-104571.

185. U.S. Embassy, "Report on the Political Situation (February 12, 1954)," *FO 371*/Persia 1954/34-109986.

186. G.K. Reddy, "Iran's Royalist Coup," *Times of India*, September 16–18, 1953.

187. Foreign Office "Persia: Quarterly Political Report—July to September 1953," *FO 416*/Persia 1953/106.

188. Foreign Office, Handwritten Notes, *FO 371*/Persia 1953/34-104568.

189. G.K. Reddy, "An Unexpected Victory," *Times of India*, September 17, 1953.

190. "Iran Mob, Riot for Their Shah," *Time*, August 31, 1953.

191. Robert Stephen, "Crisis in Islam," *The Observer*, August 23, 1953.

192. Harlan Cleveland, "Oil, Blood, and Politics," *The Reporter*, November 10, 1953.

193. Elgin Groseclose, "Iran," *Christian Science Monitor*, September 21–22, 1953. Cuttings in *FO 371*/Persia 1953/34-104571.

194. Kennett Love, "Army Seized Helm," *New York Times*, August 20, 1953; "New Iran Premier Lifelong Royalist," *New York Times*, August 20, 1953; "Mossadegh Quits," *New York Times*, August 21, 1953; "Iran's Army Now Hold the Balance of Power, *New York Times*, August 23, 1953; "Shah, Back in Iran, Wildly Acclaimed; Prestige at Peak," *New York Times*, August 23, 1953; "Reversal in Iran," *New York Times*, August 23, 1953.

195. Kennett Love, "The American Role in the Pahlavi Restoration" (unpublished paper, 1960), 1–41.

196. Personal communication with Edward Thomas, retired State Department officer.

197. Peter Avery, *Modern Iran* (London: Ernest Benn, 1965), 416–39.

198. George Lenczowski, ed., *Iran Under the Pahlavis* (Stanford: Hoover Institution, 1978), 443.

199. J.C. Hurewitz, *Middle East Politics: The Military Dimension* (New York: Praeger, 1969), 266.

200. Roger Savory, "The Principle of Homeostasis Considered in Relation to Political Events in Iran," *International Journal of Middle East Studies* 3, no. 3 (July 1972), 286.

201. Elizabeth Monroe, "Key Force in the Middle East—The Mob," *New York Times*, August 30, 1953.

4. Legacy

1. Roger Stevens, "Telegram (April 14, 1954)," *FO 371*/Persia 1954/34-110060.

2. Roger Stevens, "Letter to the Foreign Office (March 13, 1954)," *FO 371*/Persia 1954/34-110060.

3. British Chargé d'Affaires, "Annual for Persia (1954)," *FO 371*/Persia 1954/34-114805.

4. Foreign Office, "Comments in London (October 3, 1944)," *FO 371*/Persia 1944/34-40241; U.S. Embassy, May 16, 1944, *Foreign Relations of the US, 1944*, vol. 4, 449.

5. AIOC, "AIOC-Shell Agreement (December 30, 1948)," *BP*/00009249.

6. State Department, September 20, 1952, *Foreign Relations of the US, 1952–54*, vol. 10, 475.

7. Ministry of Fuel and Power, "Persia (October 29, 1951)," *FO 371*/Persia 1951/34-91607.

8. Anthony Sampson, *The Seven Sisters: The Great Oil Companies and the World They Make* (New York: Viking, 1975), 134.

9. British Ambassador (Washington), "Letter to the Foreign Office (March 27, 1954)," *FO 371*/Persia 1954/34-110060.

10. Sampson, *Seven Sisters*, 131.

11. Asadollah Alam, *The Shah and I* (New York: St. Martin's Press, 1991), 248.

12. Andrew Whitley and Anthony McDermott, "Iran Without Oil," *Financial Times*, January 17, 1979.

13. Patrick Cockburn, "Iran May Run Own Oilfields," *Financial Times*, January 25, 1979.

14. Andrew Whitley, "Reduced Role for Oil Consortium," *Financial Times*, February 10, 1979.

15. Foreign Office, "U.S. Report on the Zahedi Cabinet," *FO 371*/Persia 1953/Persia 1953/34-104572.

16. U.S. Embassy, Political Environment of the Zahedi Government," *FO 371*/Persia 1953/34-104572.

17. British Ambassador, "The New Iranian Cabinet (April 9, 1957)," *FO 371*/Persia 1957/34-127074.

18. Mehdi Homayuni, "Memoirs," in Muhammad-Hussein Khosrowpa-nah, *Sazman-e Afsaran-e Hezb-e Tudeh-e Iran* (The Military Organization of the Tudeh Party of Iran) (Tehran: 1998), 262–68.

19. Gholam Reza Afkhami, *The Life and Times of the Shah* (Berkeley: University of California Press, 2009), 193.

20. U.S. Embassy, "Recent Tudeh Activities and Government Counter Measures" (October 9, 1953), *FO 381*/Persia 1953/34-104573.

21. Military Governor of Tehran, *Ketab-e Siyah darbareh-e Sazman-e Afsaran-e Tudeh* (Black Book on the Tudeh Officers' Organization) (Tehran: 1956); Ali Zibayi, *Kommunism dar Iran* (Communism in Iran) (unpublished SAVAK document), vol. 1–2; Khosrowpanah, *Military Organization of the Tudeh Party of Iran*.

22. British Embassy, "Summary for October 19–November 1, 1954," *FO 371*/Persia 1954/34-104805; British Embassy, "Report on Executions," *FO 371*/Persia 1954/34-104571; American Embassy, "Government's Anti-Tudeh Campaign (1954)," *Declassified Documents* (Microfiche Collection)/ 1975/309—Document A.

23. British Embassy, "Notes on Political Parties (August 16, 1957)," *FO 371*/Persia 1957/34-127075.

24. Nuraldin Kianuri, *Khaterat* (Memoirs) (Tehran: 1992), 287–88.

25. Ali Ansari, *The Politics of Nationalism in Modern Iran* (New York: Cambridge University Press, 2012), 164.

26. Habib Ladjevardi, "Interview with Desmond Harvey," *The Iranian Oral History Project* (Cambridge: Harvard University Press, 1993).

27. Alam, *Shah and I*, 318.

28. Editorial, "Fifty Years of Treason," *Khabarnameh* (Newsletter), no. 66 (April 1976), 1–5.

29. Henry Kissinger, *White House Years* (Boston: Little, Brown, 1979), 1261.

30. Marvin Zonis, *Majestic Failure: The Fall of the Shah* (Chicago: University of Chicago Press, 1991), 268.

31. Abbas Qarabaghi, *Haqaqeh darbareh Bahran-e Iran* (The Truth About the Iranian Crisis) (Paris: 1983). For ghosts of 1953 haunting the events of 1979, see Ervand Abrahamian, "The Crowd in the Iranian Revolution," *Radical History*, no. 105 (Fall 2009), 13–38.

32. British Ambassador, "The New Iranian Cabinet (April 9, 1957), *FO 371*/Persia 1957/34-127074.

33. Ervand Abrahamian, "The Notion of 'Conspiracy Theories' in the Political Culture of Iran (1990)," *Kankash*, no. 7 (Winter 1991), 95–104; Ervand Abrahamian, "The Paranoid Style in Iranian Politics," *Khomeinism: Essays on the Islamic Republic* (Berkeley: University of California Press, 1993), 111–31; Ahmad Ashraf, "Conspiracy Theories," *Encyclopedia Iranica*, vol. 6, Fascicle 2, 138–47; Houchang Chehabi, "The Paranoid Style in Iranian Historiography," in *Iran in the Twentieth Century*, ed. Touraj Atabaki (London: I.B. Tauris, 2009), 155–76; Muhammad Ibrahaim-Fattahi, ed., *Jastarha-ye*

darbareh Toruy-e Tuteh dar Iran (Search for Conspiracy Theories in Iran) (Tehran: 2003).

34. Rasoul Mehraban, *Gushha-ye az Tarekh-e Mo'aser-e Iran* (Glances at Contemporary Iranian History) (Germany: 1982).

35. Hussein Malek, *Dabard-e Prozhehha-ye Siyasi dar Sahneh-e Iran* (The Battles of Political Projects on the Iranian Stage) (n.p.: 1981), 1–122.

36. Mohammad Reza Shah, *Answer to History* (New York: Stein and Day, 1982).

37. Ibid.

38. William Sullivan, *Mission to Iran* (New York: Norton, 1981), 156–57.

39. Ruhullah Khomeini, *Velayat-e Faqeh: Hokumat-e Islami* (Jurists' Guardianship: Islamic Government) (Tehran: 1979), 11–12.

40. Ruhullah Khomeini, *Islamic Unity Against Imperialism: Eight Documents of the Islamic Revolution in Iran* (New York: Islamic Association of Iranian Professions and Merchants in America, 1980), 8.

41. Hojjat al-Islam Ali Khamenei, "Speech," *Ettela'at*, March 5, 1981.

BIBLIOGRAPHY

The Foreign Office documents are available in London at the National Archives (formerly the Public Record Office). The materials for Iran (1951–53) are mostly filled under *FO 371* and *FO 248*. The declassified State Department documents have been published in U.S. Government, *Foreign Relations of the United States, 1951* (Washington, DC: US Government Printing House, 1982), Vol. 5 (Iran); and U.S. Government, *Foreign Relations of the United States, 1952–54* (Washington DC: U.S. Government Printing House, 1989), Vol. 10 (Iran). The archives of the Anglo-Iranian Oil Company are available at the British Petroleum Library at Warwick University in England.

Abrahamian, Ervand. "The 1953 Coup in Iran." *Science & Society* 65, no. 2 (Summer 2001), 182–214.
———. "The Crowd in the Iranian Revolution." *Radical History* 105 (Fall 2009), 13–38.
Acheson, Dean. *Present at the Creation: My Years in the State Department.* New York: Norton, 1969.
Afkhami, Gholam Reza, *The Life and Times of the Shah.* Berkeley: University of California Press, 2009.
Afshar, Iraj, ed. *Khaterat-e Doktor Muhammad Mossadeq* (Memoirs of Dr. Muhammad Mossadeq). London: 1986.
———. *Mossadeq va Masa'el-e Hoquq va Siyasat* (Mossadeq and Questions of Law and Politics) Tehran: 1979.
———. *Taqrerat-e Mossadeq dar Zendan* (Mossadeq's Comments in Prison). Tehran: 1980.
Ahmadi, Hamid. *The Iranian Left Oral History Project.* Berlin: 1985–95.
Alam, Asadollah. *The Shah and I.* New York: St. Martin's Press, 1991.
Amir-Alai, Shams al-Din. *Khaterat-e Man* (My Memoirs). Tehran: 1984.
Amir-Khosrovi, Babak. *Nazar az daroun beh Naqsh-e Hezb-e Tudeh-e Iran* (Internal Look at the Role of the Tudeh Party of Iran) Tehran: 1996.
Ansari, Ali. *The Politics of Nationalism in Modern Iran.* New York: Cambridge University Press, 2012.

259

Ansari, Sadeq. *Az Zendegi-ye Man* (From My Life). Los Angeles: Nashr-e Ketab, 1996.

Arsanjani, Hassan. *Yaddashtha-ye Siyasi: Siyeh-e Tir* (Political Memoirs: 30th Tir). Tehran: 1956.

Ashraf, Ahmad. *Toure-ye Tuteh dar Iran* (Conspiracy Theory in Iran). Tehran: 1993.

Avery, Peter. *Modern Iran.* London: Ernest Benn, 1965.

Azabi, Hussein, ed., *Yadnameh-e Mohandes Hassebi* (Memoirs of Engineer Hassebi). Tehran: 1991.

Azimi, Fakhreddin. *Iran: The Crisis of Democracy 1941–53.* New York: St. Martin's Press, 1989.

Balfour, James. *Recent Happenings in Persia.* London: Blackwood, 1922.

Bamberg, James. *A History of the British Petroleum Company.* Cambridge: Cambridge University Press, 1994.

Bayandour, Darioush. *Iran and the CIA: The Fall of Mossadeq Revisited.* New York: Palgrave, 2010.

Bellaigue, Christopher de. *In the Rose Garden of the Martyrs.* New York: HarperCollins, 2004.

Bill, James. *The Eagle and the Lion: The Tragedy of American-Iranian Relations.* New Haven: Yale University Press, 1988.

Bill, James, and William Roger Louis, eds. *Musaddiq, Iranian Nationalism, and Oil.* Austin: Texas University Press, 1988.

Bozorgmehr, Esfandiar. *Karavan-e Omr* (Life's Caravan). London: 1993.

Bozorgmehr, Jalil. *Muhammad Mossadeq dar Dadgah-e Nezami* (Muhammad Mossadeq in Military Court). 2 vols. Tehran: 1984.

Bullard, Reader. *Letters from Tehran.* London: I.B. Tauris, 1991.

Cable, James. *Intervention at Abadan: Plan Buccaneer.* New York: St. Martin's Press, 1991.

Cottam, Richard. *Nationalism in Iran.* Pittsburgh: University of Pittsburgh Press, 1964.

Curzon, George. *Persia and the Persian Question.* 2 vols. London: Longmans, 1892.

Dahnavi, Muhammad. *Mujma'ahyi az Maktabahat, Sokhanraniha va Paymanha-ye Ayatollah Kashani* (Ayatollah Kashani's Collected Writings, Speeches, and Messages). 3 vols. Tehran: 1982.

Diba, Farhad. *Mohammad Mossadegh: A Political Biography.* London: Croom Helm, 1986.

Dorman, William, and Mansour Farhang. *The U.S. Press and Iran.* Berkeley: University of California Press, 1987.

Dorril, Stephen. *MI6: Inside the Covert World of Her Majesty's Secret Intelligence Service.* New York: Free Press, 2000.

Elm, Mostafa. *Oil, Power, and Principle: Iran's Oil Nationalization and Its Aftermath.* Syracuse, NY: Syracuse University Press, 1992.

Elwell-Sutton, L.P. *Persian Oil: A Study in Power Politics.* London: Lawrence & Whishart, 1955.

Falle, Sam. *My Lucky Life*. London: The Book Guild, 1986.

Fardoust, Hussein. *Khaterat* (Memoirs). Tehran: 1988.

Farmanfarmaian, Manucher. *Blood and Oil*. New York: Random House, 1997.

Fateh, Mostafa. *Panjah Sal-e Naft* (Fifty Years of Oil). Tehran: 1979.

Ferrier, R.W. *The History of the British Petroleum Company*. Cambridge: Cambridge University Press, 1982.

Gasiorowski, Mark. "The 1953 Coup d'État in Iran." *International Journal of Middle East Studies* 19, no. 3 (August 1987), 261–86.

Gasiorowski, Mark, and Malcolm Byrne, eds. *Mohammad Mosaddeq and the 1953 Coup in Iran*. Syracuse, NY: Syracuse University Press, 2004.

Goode, James. *The United States and Iran: In the Shadow of Mussadiq*. New York: St. Martin's Press, 1997.

Harkness, Gladys and Richard. "The Mysterious Doings of the CIA." *Saturday Evening Post*. October 30–November 13, 1954.

Heiss, Mary Ann. *Empire and Nationhood*. New York: Columbia University Press, 1997.

Hejazi, Masoud. *Davare-ye Khaterat* (Judgments of Memory). Tehran: 1996.

Hurewitz, J.C. *Middle East Politics: The Military Dimension*. New York: Praeger, 1969.

Issawi, Charles. *Oil, the Middle East, and the World*. New York: Library Press, 1972.

Javansher, F.M. *Tajrabeh-e Best-u-Hasht-e Mordad* (The Experience of August 19). Tehran: 1980.

Katouzian, Homa. *Musaddiq and the Struggle for Power in Iran*. London: I.B. Tauris, 1999.

Katouzian, Homa, ed. *Musaddiq's Memoirs*. London: Jebhe Publications, 1988.

Key-Ostovan, Hussein. *Siyasat-e Muvazeneh-e Manfi dar Majles-e Chahardahum*. (The Policy of Negative Equilibrium in the Fourteenth Majles). Tehran: 1949.

Khomeini, Ruhullah. *Velayat-e Faqeh: Hokumat-e Islami* (Jurists' Guardianship: Islamic Government). Tehran: 1979.

Khosrowpanah, Muhammad-Hussein. *Sazman-e Afsaran-e Hezb-e Tudeh-e Iran* (The Military Organization of the Tudeh Party of Iran). Tehran: 1998.

Kianuri, Nuraldin. *Khaterat* (Memoirs). Tehran: 1992.

Kinzer, Stephen. *All the King's Men: The Hidden Story of the CIA's Coup in Iran*. New York: Wiley, 2003.

Ladjevardi, Habib. *The Iranian Oral History Project*. Cambridge: Harvard University Press, 1993.

Lenczowski, George, ed. *Iran Under the Pahlavis*. Stanford: Hoover Institution, 1978.

Love, Kennett. "The American Role in the Pahlavi Restoration." Princeton University: Unpublished Paper, 1960.

Lusani, Abul-Fazel. *Tala-ye Siyah ya Bala-ye Iran* (Black Gold or Iran's Calamity). Tehran: 1978.

Lytle, Mark Hamilton. *The Origins of the Iranian-American Alliance.* New York: Holmes, 1987.

Mahdavi, Abdul-Reza Houshang. *Sarnevesht-e Yaran-e Doktor Mossadeq* (The Fate of Dr. Mossadeq's Colleagues). Tehran: 1984.

Mahmud, Mahmud. *Tarekh-e Ravabat-e Siyasat-e Ingles dar Qaran-e Nouzdahum-e Meladi* (History of Anglo-Iranian Relations in the Nineteenth Century). 8 vols. Tehran: 1949–54.

Majd, Mohammad. *The Great Famine and Genocide in Persia, 1917–1919.* Lanham, MD: University Press of America, 1984.

Malek, Hussein. *Darbard-e Prozhehha-ye Siyasi dar Sahneh-e Iran* (The Battles of Political Projects on the Iranian Stage). n.p.: 1981.

Marigold, Stella. "The Streets of Tehran," *The Reporter.* November 10, 1953.

Marsh, Steve. "The United States, Iran and Operation 'Ajax.' " *Middle Eastern Studies* 39, no. 3 (July 2003), 1–38.

Matin-Daftari, Hedayat. *Doktor Hussein Fatemi: Neveshtehha-ye Makhfegah va Zendan* (Dr. Hussein Fatemi: Writings from Underground and Prison). London: 2005.

Matin-Daftari, Hedayat, ed., *Vezeh-e Mossadeq* (Special Issue on Mossadeq), *Azadi* 2, nos. 26–27 (Summer–Autumn 2001).

Matin-Daftari, Hedayat, and Ali Matin-Daftari, eds. *Majmuheh-e Asnad-e Ahmad Matin-Daftari* (Collected Documents from Ahmad Matin-Daftari). London: 1987.

Mavahad, Muhmmad Ali. *Doktor Mossadeq va Nahzat-e Melli Iran* (Dr. Mossadeq and the Iranian National Movement). 2 vols. Tehran: 1991.

McGhee, George. *Envoy to the Middle World.* New York: Harper & Row, 1983.

Mehraban, Rasoul. *Barres-ye Mukhtasar-e Ahzab-e Burzhuazi-ye Melli-e Iran* (A Short Look at Iran's Bourgeois National Parties). Tehran: 1980.

———. *Gushha-ye az Tarekh-e Mo'aser-e Iran* (Glances at Contemporary Iranian History). Germany: 1982.

Milani, Abbas. *The Shah.* New York: Palgrave Macmillan, 2011.

Military Governor of Tehran. *Ketab-e Siyah darbareh-e Sazman-e Afsaran-e Tudeh* (Black Book on the Tudeh Officers' Organization). Tehran: 1956.

Mokhtari, Fariborz. "Iran's 1953 Coup Revisited." *Middle East Journal,* 62, no. 3 (Summer 2008), 461–88.

Mottahedeh, Roy. *The Mantle of the Prophet.* New York: Simon & Schuster, 1985.

Muhammadi, Muhammad-Jafar. *Raz-e Pirouzi-ye Kudeta-ye Best-u-Hasht-e Mordad* (Secret of the Success of the August 19 Coup). Tehran: 2006.

National Movement of Iran. *Notqha va Maktubat-e Doktor Mossadeq* (Dr. Mossadeq's Speeches and Teachings). 5 vols. Berkeley: 1969–71.

Nejati, Ghulam-Reza. *Jonbesh-e Mellishudan-e Naft va Kudeta-e Best-u-Hasht-e Mordad* (The Movement to Nationalize Oil and the Coup of August 19). Tehran: 1986.

———. *Mossadeq: Salha-e Mobarezeh* (Mossadeq: Years of Struggle). Tehran: 1999.

Nicolson, Harold. *Curzon: The Last Phase.* London: Constable, 1934.

Pahlavi, Farah. *An Enduring Love: My Life with the Shah.* New York: Hyperion, 2004.

Pahlavi, Mohammad Reza Shah. *Answer to History.* New York: Stein & Day, 1982.

Qarabaghi, Abbas. *Haqaqeh darbareh Bahran-e Iran* (The Truth About the Iranian Crisis). Paris: 1983.

Rahnema, Ali. *Niruha-ye Mazhabi* (Religious Forces). Tehran: 1985.

Richard, Philippe. "The Identities of the Iranian Zurkhanah." *Iranian Studies* 35 (2002), 313–34.

Roosevelt, Kermit. *Countercoup: The Struggle for the Control of Iran.* New York: McGraw Hill, 1979.

Rubin, Barry. *Paved with Good Intentions: The American Experience in Iran.* New York: Oxford University Press, 1980.

Ruehsen, Moyara. "Operation 'Ajax' Revisited: Iran 1953." *Middle Eastern Studies* 29, no. 3 (July 1993), 467–86.

Sahabi, Ezatollah ed., *Mossadeq, Dowlat-e Melli va Kudeta* (Mossadeq, the National Government, and the Coup). Tehran: 2001.

Safai, Ibrahim. *Rahbaran-e Mashrutiyat* (Leaders of the Constitution). Tehran: 1965.

Safari, Muhammad-Ali. *Qalam va Siyasat* (Pen and Politics). Tehran: 1992.

Sami'i, Shirin. *Dar Khalvat-e Mossadeq* (Mossadeq in Private). Tehran: 1989.

Sampson, Anthony. *The Seven Sisters: The Great Oil Companies and the World They Make.* New York: Viking, 1975.

Sanjabi, Karem. *Omidha va Na Omidiha* (Hopes and Despairs). London: Jebhe Publications, 1989.

Sarrashteh, Hassan. *Khaterat-e Man* (My Memoirs). Tehran: 1988.

Sarshar, Homa. *Sha'aban Jafari.* Beverly Hills: Naab Publishers, 2002.

Sassani, Khan-Malek. *Dast-e Panhan-e Siyasat-e Ingles dar Iran* (The Hidden English Hand in Iran). Tehran: 1952.

Savory, Roger. "The Principle of Homeostasis Considered in Relation to Political Events in Iran," *International Journal of Middle East Studies* 3, no. 3 (July 1972), 282–302.

Seifzadeh, Hamid. *Hafez-e Tarekh-e Afshartous Kebud?* (Who Kept the Secret of Afshartous?). Tehran: 1994.

Shayegan, Ahmad, ed. *Sayyed Ali Shayegan.* 2 vols. Tehran: 2004.

Shefteh, Nasrallah. *Zendeginameh va Mobarezat-e Siyasi-ye Doktor Sayyed Hussein Fatemi* (The Life and Political Struggles of Dr. Sayyed Hussein Fatemi). Tehran: 1985.

Skrine, Clarmont. *World War in Iran.* London: Constable, 1962.

Varaqa, Masallah. *Chand-u-Chun Variyzi-ye Dowlat-e Mossadeq* (Sketches on the Downfall of Mossadeq's Government). Tehran: 2007.

Varjaved, Parvez, ed. *Yadnameh-e Doktor Ghulam-Hussein Sadiqi* (Memoirs of Dr. Ghulam-Hussein Sadiqi). Tehran: 1992.

Walden, Jerrold. *International Petroleum Cartel in Iran.* Cambridge: Confederation of Iranian Students, 1963.

Walters, Vernon. *Silent Missions.* New York: Doubleday, 1978.

Wilber, Donald. *Adventures in the Middle East.* Princeton: Darwin Press, 1986.

—————. *Regime Change in Iran: Overthrow of Premier Mossadeq of Iran, November 1952–August 1953.* London: Russell Press, 2006.

Woodhouse, Christopher. *Something Ventured.* London: Granada, 1982.

Wynn, Antony. *Persia in the Great Game.* London: Murray, 2003.

Yergin, Daniel. *The Prize: The Epic Quest for Oil, Money, and Power.* New York: Simon & Schuster, 1991.

Zabih, Sepehr. *The Mossadegh Era.* Chicago: Lake View Press, 1982.

Zibayi, Ali. *Kommunism dar Iran* (Communism in Iran). Tehran: 1955.

Zonis, Marvin. *Majestic Failure: The Fall of the Shah.* Chicago: University of Chicago Press, 1991.

INDEX

Celebrating Independent Publishing

Thank you for reading this book published by The New Press. The New Press is a nonprofit, public interest publisher. New Press books and authors play a crucial role in sparking conversations about the key political and social issues of our day.

We hope you enjoyed this book and that you will stay in touch with The New Press. Here are a few ways to stay up to date with our books, events, and the issues we cover:

- Sign up at www.thenewpress.com/subscribe to receive updates on New Press authors and issues and to be notified about local events
- Like us on Facebook: www.facebook.com/newpress books
- Follow us on Twitter: www.twitter.com/thenewpress

Please consider buying New Press books for yourself; for friends and family; or to donate to schools, libraries, community centers, prison libraries, and other organizations involved with the issues our authors write about.

The New Press is a 501(c)(3) nonprofit organization. You can also support our work with a tax-deductible gift by visiting www.thenewpress.com/donate.

www.ingramcontent.com/pod-product-compliance
Lightning Source LLC
Jackson TN
JSHW020015141224
75386JS00025B/536

9781620970867